H. J. SHALEV

GETTING
USED TO
SUCCESS

A Practical Guide
Based on a Proven Formula
For Management, Business & Career

This book is lovingly and respectfully dedicated:

To my wife, Osnat, for believing in me, for supporting me unconditionally throughout our journey, and for your patience with my whims.

To my children, Shelly and Daniel, for the inspiration and motivation you instilled in me, and for the countless opportunities to apply the principles of this book within your company.

To my father, Benjamin of blessed memory, who was my first coach, teaching me that anything is possible.

To my mother, Sarah, for teaching me what worthy service is and for instilling in me my love of people.

Getting Used to Success: Develop an Invincible Mindset, Bolster Self-Confidence and Build Winning Habits

H. J. Shalev

Contact:

Tel: +972-54-4877725
Email: info@hagaishalev.com
Website: https://www.hagaishalev.com/en
Blog: https://www.hagaishalev.com/en/blog
Author: H.J. Shalev
Graphic design: Daniel Shalev, Noa Moses, H.J. Shalev
Hebrew Editing: Limor David, Sigal Ziv
English Translation: Tamar Milshtein
Originally Printed in Israel, 2015
ISBN: 9781983354366

H. J. SHALEV

GETTING
USED TO
SUCCESS

DEVELOP AN INVINCIBLE MINDSET, BOLSTER SELF-CONFIDENCE AND BUILD WINNING HABITS

A Practical Guide

Contents

ABOUT THE AUTHOR

Hagai Joshua Shalev is an expert in mental changes that generate more money, an author, workshop instructor, and lecturer in the field of entrepreneurship, management, and personal development. Since 2006, H.J. has **led many managers and business owners to success, accumulating over 10,000 hours of coaching and business consultancy experience.**

H.J. works with business owners and managers who are open to the idea that their habits, beliefs, and emotions determine their level of success more than anything else. **H.J. assists them in changing their thought patterns and their personal/business conduct** in order to enable them to thrive, grow, earn more, and live a better life.

In addition to his B.A. in economics and accounting and being a licensed CPA, H.J. has participated in dozens of business and coaching courses, studied many personal development and consciousness-expanding methods and is constantly learning and developing new methods for success. H.J. lives, breaths, and applies his own teachings every day, and has **personally experienced everything he teaches and guides.** Being a rational and practical CPA, he kept asking himself, "How can I take all the wonderful things I have learned about awareness and effectively translate them into practical results in business, career, and life?" He has researched the subject from every possible angle and developed a unique methodology – which you will learn and apply with the help of this book.

◆

In this book, H.J. integrates the knowledge and experience he has acquired since 1983—both personal and professional—in order to provide you with the **effective and implementable methodology he has developed so you can reap business success.**

♦ ♦

One fine day in November 2005, H.J. faced the biggest challenge of his life with great trepidation: he decided to leave a great job with a generous salary as CFO of a high-tech company without any other work or income alternative. H.J. did that because he disliked his job and didn't see any other alternative to making a significant career change.

This was the beginning of the biggest transformation of his life, during which he went **from being a numbers person to a people person.**

Since making that decision, the personal and professional journey H.J. has undergone has exposed him to the realm of transformation, leading him to develop a unique methodology: the **CO-OP Formula**. This formula, which this book explains, generates a transformation in one's state of being, leading to practical business results.

H.J. can be approached for personal coaching, workshops, and lectures for executives and business owners, in the areas of business changes, career changes, management, and business and personal success.

◆ ◆ ◆

"If you want to build a ship, don't drum up people to collect wood and don't assign them tasks and work, but rather teach them to long for the endless immensity of the sea."

—Antoine de Saint-Exupery

INTRODUCTION
Why should you read this book?

One fine day in November 2005, at the age of 45, I faced the hardest challenge in my life; "my cheese had been moved," and I decided to resign from my job as a CFO without any other work alternative. I grew tired of my job without knowing what alternative career to pursue. What type of career would help me fulfill my life's purpose? What career would I love doing, which would utilize my skills and abilities, be achievable, and maintain the high income level I was used to? So I found myself facing **a career crisis** and a process of change that threatened the financial security of all four members of the family, with no foreseeable solution.

The personal and professional transformation I have undergone, as described in the first chapter of the book, serves as an outline for the entire book. Such a transformation is a dream sought by many who compromise their lives and the amount of money they want to—and can—make due to one circumstance or another. This is an inspirational and practical guidebook written for those many people on how to apply their business potential and achieve the results they have always dreamed of.

These are the people in whose company I evolved, whom I meet daily in my line of work, and from whom I derive my inspiration. I believe with all my heart that they have the power to bring about change in themselves, their business, their lives, and the world at large.

◆

Modern life presents us with the challenge of change over and over. The world around us is constantly evolving at an ever increasing pace. But against this backdrop, we, humans, are averse to change. Change brings about uncertainty and is interpreted by the instincts of the "human operating system" as danger, as a threat to survival.

Thus, most humans try to **avoid change at any cost**, which results in crises characteristic of the second decade of the 21st century—crises in relationships, careers, and businesses.

This is where I found myself.

It was the first time I was ever forced to cope with change, and not just any change—**a major transformation that entailed a change of career, a change of status from employee to self-employed, to building a new business from the ground up and undergoing accelerated personal development that left me an entirely different person.** From a numbers person, I became a people person. And all this while trying to maintain the income level of a CFO in a high-tech company, who earned over $100,000 USD a year with all the fringe benefits, but who was now become self-employed.

This book is not an autobiography, but was born out of my own personal transformation, slowly coming to life during and alongside that transformation. Everything I have experienced firsthand in thirty-two years of career—in business, management, entrepreneurship, and coaching; dozens of courses and thousands of hours of personal development; working with about a thousand people on paths of change through more than ten thousand hours of coaching and counseling—is brought forth to you, the reader, as **a practical guide to changing your career or business.**

As a rational, practical accountant who has also dealt extensively with personal development, I have noticed a major hitch in most awareness theories: they are highly theoretical and abstract. I have met many aware people—extremely aware, even. Unfortunately, the majority were poor, since most theories of awareness lack the bridge that connects them to the business world, so that one cannot translate high awareness into financial and professional success. The question I asked myself, then, was, **"How can I take all the amazing things I have learned from these personal development doctrines and translate them into practical business results?"** I searched for the answer for years; I contemplated, researched, and eventually found it! I developed a unique methodology called the **"CO-OP Formula"** that helps take any thought pattern or habit which doesn't serve us and replace it with a profitable habit that can be implemented into pragmatic results in order to achieve sustainable business success.

Using my skills, I developed a formula that **integrates** the "human operating system" with practical career and business results.

And this is what the book is about. **The book guides you, step by step, on a path of learning and implementing the methodology in your life in general, and in your management, career, or business needs in particular.** All this comes from my unique **integration** between realism and awareness, spirit and matter, and doing and being, emphasizing the **ability to balance and connect** these pairs, which is rather rare in our world, yet is served to you in the pages of this book.

The book is intended for any entrepreneurs, executives, or business owners who are open to the idea that the business or enterprise they are running is a mirror image of themselves, such that the **smallest change in themselves will have a considerable**

effect on their enterprise. Executives and business owners who do not live up to their earning potential; those who **know they can earn a lot more money, but don't know how**; those who understand it requires far more than effective business planning and result-oriented actions to succeed; those who acknowledge that the human factor, or as I call it, the "human operating system," is what determines, above all, the difference between failure and prosperity. The **difference between failure and success is not just talent.** This book guides those executives and business owners who are open to transform themselves to success in their business and management practices by undergoing a process of transformation in which they replace bad habits with good habits, thus making more money. They are getting used to succeeding as well as profiting.

The change depicted in the book is a **mental, "being" one**—a change in thoughts, beliefs, feelings, and habits; a change that leads to better, more effective, more successful actions.

On that note, I would like to congratulate you. The fact that you are holding this book in your hands means that you are aware of the need to change your conduct to produce better results. As you will see later in the book, your ability to remain open and committed to changes is a major factor in the formula for success, and you have already taken a meaningful step in the right direction. I commend you for that and for your willingness to learn new things in order to improve your life!

To make the most out of this book, I recommend you not only read and study its contents, but also **implement its directives**, for I believe that change is **gradual and is best achieved by taking small, consistent steps.**

Once you read the book and begin to implement its teachings, you will understand the DNA of change, how to cope with change, and how to create change in yourself in order to achieve practical results in your business, career, management, and your life in general.

It isn't hard to implement. **With openness, self-discipline, and self-commitment, you can advance steadily towards the results you aspire to.**

If I could do it, so can you!

Finally, before we get started, I want you to know that you are welcome to approach me with any questions you might have regarding your personal development and your success in management, business, or career, and certainly with regards to the contents of this book. Feel free to use the contact information listed in the opening and closing of the book.

GETTING USED TO SUCCESS

WHY AM I RATIONAL AND PRACTICAL, YET STILL NOT SUCCESSFUL ENOUGH?

PART I

GETTING USED
TO CHANGE

CHAPTER ONE:
A Conscious Transformation from Employed to Self-Employed

"Be the change you wish to see in the world."
—Gandhi

Any Business Goal is Possible

If you feel like you are in your comfort zone, trapped under a glass ceiling you wish to break through, this book in general—and this chapter in particular—are meant for you.

"Any business goal is possible." This is my motto when working with people. "Moreover," I declare, "If I could change, so can you." This is the message that will run through this entire book. You see, most people don't fulfill their potential, making do with mediocrity and dissatisfaction. I believe there is another way.

I believe in **courage, initiative, determination, grit, and choice as the shortlist of elements for success in business.** To illustrate that, the book begins with a personal story of how, during a mid-life career crisis, I applied these components in order to create real change in my life; a change that has brought equilibrium to my life and transformed it to the utmost degree. Indeed, I moved from breakdown to breakthrough. So before we dive into the details and the full prescription described later in the book, I am certain you will take away a great deal from my personal story and be able to apply it to your life in terms of how to bring about real and sustainable change, so you can yield the business results you have always wanted.

If I could do it, so can you!

From "cents" to "sense"

I was recently being interviewed for a radio show when the interviewer turned my attention to the initials of my name, which, depending on their order, make up the words **"cents"** or **"sense"** in Hebrew, my native language.

These two combinations of my name initials sum up the journey I have undergone in my professional career of 32 years. The first 22 years were all about **cents**, no doubt. In my work as a CPA and a CFO, I mainly used my cognitive skills and financial abilities. During those years, my emotional intelligence was not fully developed, and my mathematical, logical orientation governed my life.

That changed in 2005, when I embarked on a journey of extensive personal development that enabled me to hone my non-cognitive skills, focusing on all aspects: emotional, spiritual, and awareness-related, thus becoming a man who could more meaningfully **sense** himself and his surroundings.

My personal transformation from a numbers person to a people person is the backbone of this book, since it has allowed me to learn how to cope with change; a change I have implemented in my work and turned into the method this book teaches.

I bring my personal story to you for two important reasons:

Firstly, in order to give you, the reader, the inspiration and conviction that you, too, can undergo change; to help you understand that we, as humans, have the ability to handle change successfully; and to help show that, when you understand the DNA of change, it becomes a lot less frightening than it seems at first.

Secondly, from a personal development standpoint, and as someone starting a brand new business in a field that was entirely new to me, my transformational journey is a dream sought by many. Thus, it is highly likely that you will be able to apply your reading of it to your own life.

One last bit of semantics involving my name: my last name, "Shalev," means "calm" in Hebrew, but I was hardly ever calm during most of my life. I was like a car that only ran on its left two wheels, which are logic and pragmatism (left brain traits). Those two wheels carried me far, but were also responsible for my mid-life career crisis. In recent years I have added the two right wheels into the equation: creativity, seeing the full picture, and intuition (right brain traits). I have also become truly "calm" and my "vehicle" is balanced today and runs a lot better as a result. The full "vehicle model" metaphor in the book is further explored in chapter five.

This is the essence of the transformation I have undergone, which entailed a mental, internal transformation alongside a career, business change. This change upgraded my life and thanks to it, I am a much happier, more self-fulfilled man today.

Dilemmas

It all peaked in 2005, but it began in 2003.

At the age of 43, I began to feel jaded about my work as a CFO. My job had become dull and I felt a strong desire for change and renewal. Simply put, my life was off-kilter.

Up until then, in my twenty years of work I had run a fairly dynamic and interesting professional life: I would change my workplace every three years on average, mostly moving between different high-tech companies, both public and private, which entailed a dynamic, challenging work environment and a lot of work with overseas entities. As part of working for the RAD Group, I participated in their subsidiary's NASDAQ IPO back in 1991, experienced a merger with a major American corporation in 1995, and managed about 30 employees. Still, the moment had arrived when "my cheese was moved" and change came knocking on my door.

Looking into the future, I realized I had anywhere between 25 and 30 years of work ahead of me, and I asked myself, "Is this what I want the rest of my career to look like?" The obvious answer was, "No, not at all."

"Alright, I'll change my profession," I told myself. But what profession would I switch to and how? How would I be able to secure the high salary I enjoyed, which my family's livelihood was dependent on? Would I continue as an employee or become self-employed? And if I chose to work for myself, how would I make it happen?

As you can see, I was facing a tough dilemma and I could not come up with any good solutions. I began to study the market. I spoke to people who I knew and examined comparable jobs I could fill. I soon realized that in my forties, I was no longer a hot commodity in the labor market in general and in high-tech fields in particular. I decided it was too risky to remain an employee at that stage of my life while looking for something new—I did not want my success to be dependent on an employer when my natural aging would not support future opportunities.

Someone once compared a middle-aged employee to an aircraft with one engine. When that engine fails, the employee doesn't even have a parachute and must perform an emergency landing!

And so, **I decided I would become self-employed**, and no longer work in the same field I had worked in as an employee, looking for a role in a field not directly related to finances.

But what was I going to do exactly? And, as a newly self-employed person, how would I reach an income level that could replace the salary I was making—six figures a year with a company vehicle and all the fringe benefits that came with an executive position—to be able to maintain my family's lifestyle? I had no clue. At that point, **fear began to paralyze me**, and it took me two more years of walking the same path, further losing my sense of equilibrium, as the difficulty of facing each new day kept mounting.

The Decision

In 2005, I had reached the end of my rope.

I had just started a new job as a CFO in October, after a seven-month job hunt. For the first time in my life, I started a job that I never liked from the get go. The company was at a low point and a venture capital fund had invested in it in order to revive the company and direct it toward an IPO. I was the last executive to be hired to complete a brand new management staff, including the CEO.

Then, one evening in November 2005, only seven weeks after I had started working for that company, in a heated board meeting in which I revealed some unpleasant data regarding the company's financial state, the investors decided to pull out.

I knew right away I was not going to stay with the company; it had no future without its investors. Those were extremely difficult days, when the last of my hope that I might be able to stay on the known, familiar path faded. I knew the CFO chapter in my life was over for good.

I continued to work for the company through February 2006, while constantly searching for alternatives. No being an employee and no working in finances, remember? So what, then?

At the end of 2005, I joined a multi-level marketing company because I liked the business model of hierarchal passive income. I had a lot of hope for it, but that, too, turned sour in April 2006, when I realized that my integrity was preventing me from selling multi-level marketing to my friends and family, knowing that they were 90% likely to abandon it and never thank me for it. But multi-level marketing exposed me for the first time to the world of personal development, which I found fascinating. This is when the first seeds of change began to propagate in me, and for that I am grateful to this day.

At the same time, I kept meeting with people I knew, examining options such as importing various products, opening a business, or joining an existing business as a partner, but nothing appealed to me. Nothing excited me, and picking something purely for income's sake would have put me right back where I started, in a state of imbalance.

The Crisis

The only support I got in those days was from my wife, Osnat, who understood my distress and agreed to sacrifice our savings so I could have the time to make the change. But our savings dwindled with no solid career solution on the horizon, and it was during those days of emotional and professional crisis that I realized I needed help. Not only was I clueless as to how I was going to bring home more than $100,000 USD a year to support my family, I had no idea what I even wanted to do in my next career! I asked around for help, and people recommended coaching. It was the first time I had heard of coaching, but I had hit a dead end. So, without having any idea what it meant, I sought coaching, and I was hooked! I saw great potential in the field and decided I wanted to be coached regarding my next professional steps, but also that I wanted to acquire the skills of a coach myself. I had not yet decided to pursue a career in coaching, but I was very much drawn to this world and realized that coaching skills would help me in any future occupation I might choose. It gave me the hope to move from breakdown to breakthrough.

The Choice

In May 2006, I started my first coaching course with Tal Ronen and Eran Olenik. I chose them because they offered both training in how to become coaches as well as a framework I could be coached in as part of the course. I caught two birds with one stone—a framework that enabled me to define and implement my next career as well as a chance to hone coaching skills as tools for life and business.

It was love at first sight!

By the end of the first week, I had made my decision: I wanted to be a coach, and one of the best, too! My good friend Noa Ben Arie helped me make the decision by repeating how much coaching was a perfect "fit" for me. Coaching also resonated with three things I used to love:

The first was being a swimming coach during my teenage years and into my twenties, which I loved doing.

The second was knowing for years that I wanted to be a lecturer or speaker at the kind of courses and workshops I had attended with such enthusiasm. As a big fan of seminars and workshops, I always wanted to be on the other side of the podium, as the lecturer or the speaker.

The third thing was that during my years as an executive, I always recruited better employees than myself, and spent a great deal of time mentoring and training them. It was the most gratifying aspect of my work. Whereas most executives would complain about a good employee or manager that left them after finally learning the job, I never complained and was always happy to welcome a newcomer and train him from the ground up. Even back then, in 2006, it was clear I was pretty good at it, since the managers I trained all reached highly lucrative positions in their fields.

Only later, in 2010, did I get a full glimpse of my capabilities. I attended a major conference in which the CFO of the Strauss Corporation[1], the talented Shachar Florence, was present. I had plucked him out of the accounting firm he was working for back in 1995 and hired him under my guidance as my controller. We worked together until 1997, when he replaced me as CFO after I left for another company. Thirteen years later, at that conference, Shachar pointed to me and told everyone present: "You see him? I owe him 90% of what I know."

I was shocked! Shachar was obviously exaggerating the facts,

---

1 The largest food products manufacturer in Israel.

for in those thirteen years since we had last worked together, he'd taken on a few more positions as CFO, served as a CEO for a mediocre tech company, and, of course, was serving as the CFO of Strauss, one of the largest corporations in Israel. Yet Shachar's statement was symbolic, and showed that he attributed the profound success he had experienced to our work together.

The Realization
Back to the coaching course.

From there on, the "what" was clear, and I worked diligently on the "how." How was I to make my career as a coach not only a success in terms of self-fulfillment and enjoyment, but also in terms of financial profit, such that it would properly support my family as my work had when I was a CFO?

First off, I knew I needed broad, ample knowledge. As such, I have never stopped studying since my first coaching course in 2006. The realms of personal development and awareness fascinated me. Over the years, I have participated in about twenty different courses, including courses on Buddhism and Kabbalah, a few training seminars for coaches, an instructors' course (with the scope of a Masters curriculum), a year-long *Course in Miracles*, NLP, Channeling, Theta healing, *Brahma Kumaris*, the *Relationsheep* methodology, ACE Level 1 course, and more, all of which took up thousands of hours.

In addition, I invested countless hours in self-study through the internet, including audio, video, webinars, newsletters, and more from both free and paid programs. I find it interesting that the majority of my knowledge today comes from self-study. My father used to say, "You spend your entire life learning, only to die ignorant." At least I can relate to the first part of the statement.

Finally, I came to understand that the success of my business depended first and foremost on myself. "Okay," you might say, "What's new about that?" I will explain: what I mean by that is my **personal** rather than my professional conduct; the way in which I think and feel, and how my *operating system* functions. Here, I am pointing to the "being," the mental and emotional aspects. In order for my "vehicle" to run smooth and fast, I must align all four wheels, maintain a strong, reliable body, and tune up the engine. This is not necessarily about **how to do things**, but about **who I am—the person at the heart of the business,** and how to guide and control my beliefs, habits, and emotions in order to support an optimal fulfillment of my business.

To that end, despite the lack of sufficient income sources in the first years following the transformation, I adhered to a strict regimen of personal training and counseling with some fifteen therapists and personal coaches in order to become a man who could achieve the results he desired.

Secondly, I realized that working with people was the best way to acquire professional skills and build my reputation. Therefore, as early as the summer of 2006, I engaged in private work with clients; at first sporadically and free of charge, but growing over time in both volume and profit.

Thirdly, I was searching for shortcuts. I thought to myself, "Why start from scratch? After all, it takes time to establish a successful business and build a reputation, so it's better to join an existing business and together create a whole that is greater than the sum of its parts."

I have always been a team player, and this was the opportune moment to demonstrate it, along with my management skills. So I spent the first three years as a coach (2007-2009) in a series of three different partnerships. None of them succeed sufficiently, each for its own reasons. The last one, in which I partnered up with my good friend Rachi Wertheimer, showed the most promise business-wise, yet I felt frustrated, because I could not truly bring my professional capabilities into play and spent most of the time in my colleague's shadow.

Giving Up Something Good for Something Better

This is when I reached another critical turning point in my career. Something in me was waiting to awaken, and it was time to leave something good for something better. So, in late 2009, I parted ways with Rachi. I was working with three different therapists at the same time, each one helping me open up a different blockage in my existence.

Then, in 2010, the floodgates finally opened, and abundance came pouring into my life. I began working with the Colmobil Group[2], which provided me with a lot of work and served as my main client. At the same time, I launched my first website, where I began to write a blog and made the strategic decision to base my marketing on the internet. As an economist, I realized the medium was going to flourish, and getting an early foothold in it would create marketing assets that would drive clientele to come looking for me instead of me looking for them. In 2010, I also developed the details of my methodology, the "CO-OP Formula," the subject matter of this book. Since then, I have been steadily increasing my profit from year to year.

---

2 The largest motor-vehicle distributor in Israel.

If I Could Do It, So Can You!

The transformation I have undergone has, without a doubt, changed my professional and personal life entirely. I am a completely different person today, fulfilling my life's purpose, loving my work, constantly growing and developing, and the sky is the limit! **Balance** is the key word. One can sum up my transformation by changing the acronym from **"CPA"** to **"CPR."** I have been revived and resuscitated!

My life's purpose is to help executives and other business owners do what has become possible for me—to show them that change is not a threat but, rather, an opportunity—that everything is changeable if one desires, and that they and only they are the source of the results they produce. I urge them not to compromise on these results, and remind them that even if they are down, they can still shift from breakdown to breakthrough.

This is what the remainder of the book explores. I am convinced that if you take the directives laid out in this book to heart and perform them as written, you will experience a professional breakthrough and financial prosperity. This conviction is rooted in my own personal experiences as well as those of many clients I have mentored to achieve the same since 2006.

In summary, here are some of the main factors that carried me through those years, so I could achieve balance in my life and get to where I am today:

1. Connection to my life's purpose and an inspiring vision that motivated me.

2. Investment in mental and business infrastructure while applying long-term thinking and planning—approaching life as a marathon rather than a sprint.

3. Determination and grit—not giving up, especially not on myself, and not listening to the truly good people who tried to talk me out of my new found path. My motto was, "Having self-expectations is a must; other people's expectations are merely rust."

4. Ongoing personal development and learning; I never stopped sharpening my mental and cognitive skills.

5. Focusing on offering value to my clients rather than making money. Money will always be the outcome of great, relevant value given to someone in need of it.

6. Even the greatest problem has a solution; I always searched for the solution instead of wallowing in the problem.

7. Taking calculated risks while always moving out of my comfort zone.

8. I kept searching for opportunities and worked to realize them.

9. Staying thorough, systematic, and pragmatic.

10. Healthy body, healthy mind—eating healthily and exercising.

11. Honesty, integrity and credibility.

12. "Always under-promise and over-deliver" – I learned that from Robin Sharma.

13. I gave to others and volunteered to help those who are underprivileged.

14. I surrounded myself with empowering people.

Now let us continue paving the road to your success with the next chapters, where I will share with you my insights and practical tools for self-transformation so you can achieve the results you have always wanted.

If I Could Do It, So Can You!

CHAPTER TWO:
Why Change is Inevitable

"It is not the strongest of the species that survives, nor the most intelligent that survives. It is the one that is most adaptable to change."

—Charles Darwin

Our ancestors spent their entire lives in one workplace, and there was an unwritten agreement between employees and employers that gave them certainty and financial security. Reality has changed, and nowadays, no one has that kind of financial security. Businesses shut down left and right, and recurring recessions cause major unemployment. If you find yourself anxious about your future employment situation, you are not alone. This is true both for employees and the self-employed, especially as they grow older. Therefore, we need to be open and willing, today more than ever, to cope with change[3].

Nature is constantly undergoing change. Even a stone on a

---

3 Throughout the book, I usually use the word "change," though the most accurate term for the content presented in the book is "transformation." I am choosing to do so for the sake of simplicity, since the word transformation may be unclear to some people. The dictionary defines transformation as "a change of form." Indeed, in any change I address, the humans' essence remains the same. What changes is our **form**—our thoughts, words, actions, feelings, beliefs, and so on. Therefore, I invite you to interpret the word "change" appearing throughout the book as "transformation."

desert hilltop slowly changes and wears out as the wind and rain toss it about. Nature's living organisms and plants exist in only two states: either growth and development, or deterioration and death—both of which exemplify change.

Humans are part of nature; thus, change is inherent in them, too. It may manifest as growth and prosperity, or stagnation and standstill, which quickly turn into decline and decay. Moreover, the speed of change in the world is constantly increasing. One need only examine where humanity was 100 years ago, or even 30 years ago, to understand that dramatic changes are now taking place in every aspect of our lives, a lot more and a lot faster than in the thousands of years before. For example, the amount of knowledge in the world in the last few decades doubles itself about every two years, which completely changes the issue of acquiring education. Trying to succeed by merely memorizing information is doomed to fail. Instead, it is vital to change the educational approach to one that allows access to relevant information.

Within this ever-shifting melting pot are we humans—creatures who are naturally averse to change. Change introduces uncertainty into our lives, uncertainty that is perceived by the human *operating system*[4] as danger or even threat to our very survival.

---

4 By using the term "human operating system," as with computers, I mean that which exists at the core of our existence and activates us as humans. To keep it simple, I shall first address the brain and the heart, which are two important intelligence centers linked to each other. In a more abstract sense, I also mean our thoughts, habits, feelings and beliefs. While all these have a crucial effect on our actions and accomplishments, there is still more hidden than is known to scientists, doctors, and researchers alike, and even more so to ordinary people. Just as the coding lines of a computer's operating system are foreign to the

Hence, most people resist change and try to avoid it like the plague. Many of us hold on to the familiar for dear life until we have no choice. And then, when the change is "forced" upon us, it is dramatic, intense, with a strong emotional effect, causing crises in career, business, or relationships. Consider the growing rate of divorce to understand just how intense the winds of change are today.

All of this is amplified and multiplied when we discuss business in general, and small businesses in particular. Here, we're dealing with the lifeline of the business, its very existence and survival, its ability to handle competition and the sometimes paralyzing fear of wondering, "How will I generate clients this month? How will I be able to make ends meet?"

Therefore, owners of small businesses do not have the luxury of resting on their laurels, believing that what was will continue to be. Such an approach is doomed to failure, and they must change.

So change is inevitable. "Change or die," said IBM, years ago. Instead of resisting change, let us examine how we can make it work to our benefit and to the benefit and prosperity of our businesses.

In this chapter, we shall define the foundations of change and understand the correct approach to change that brings success.

---

standard user, so is the structure and function of the "human operating system" a mystery to most humans. Later on in the book, we will illuminate in greater detail how this "human operating system" works, and most of all, how we can change it in order to achieve better results.

Tom's change

Tom (alias), a wood craftsman in his late 30s, approached me in a dire state. His business had deteriorated over the last few years to the point of taking losses and risking shutdown. What had previously worked for Tom was no longer cutting it. His clients, who came through word of mouth, stopped coming, and those who did show up at the small woodshop were not prepared to pay him the sums of money they had paid in the past. Tom knew he had to change his thinking and business conduct, but he didn't know how to do it.

Through the process described in this book, I helped Tom change his business and personal beliefs and habits. Here are the main things Tom changed:

√ His approach to marketing and sales, from "I don't like to market myself," to "Marketing and sales are a legitimate part of my business."

√ Getting rid of procrastination

√ Reinforcing self-confidence

√ Developing a more assertive and less naïve approach to finding suppliers and clients

√ Bidding farewell to perfectionism

√ Acquiring marketing and sales tools

√ Developing a healthy relationship with money

Following these changes and more, Tom's revenues more than doubled and he finally began to fulfill his business potential and earn the sums of money he had wanted. Throughout the book, you will learn and see how Tom implemented these changes.

"People are not rational. Not only are they not rational, you can actually anticipate in what irrational way they will make decisions..."—Prof. Daniel Kahneman, Nobel Laureate in Economic Sciences, 2002

Our world operates according to rules. Most of us don't know all the rules and may sometimes err in adopting an erroneous rule. One such false rule is the paradigm[5] claiming that we, humans, are rational. Much has been said about success and how to succeed. Piles of books have been written about theories, methods and techniques to succeed. Apparently, if you wish to break through and succeed, you need to read those certain guidebooks, implement their instructions, and reap success.

But it's more complex than it seems at the start, probably a lot more so. If it were that simple, many more people in the world would have succeeded, and studies would not be indicating that 80% of Americans are unhappy, with 40% of them truly depressed. It seems to require a lot more than just a scientific, rational approach and implementing the rules as written. While those rules are surely very important and vital to success, there is something else missing in this "success formula."

Ever since infanthood, we are told: "Think, study, work, do, act, make an effort." Most people who take these directives at face value and try to live by them discover that they usually don't work out or yield the desired results. For instance, **how many diligent, tireless people do you know who don't live up to their potential or earn the amount of money they want and**

---

5 A paradigm is a concept, approach, thought, or behavioral pattern and subjective belief which we adhere to completely, believing it to be a fact and an absolute truth when it is not. We shall discuss paradigms in further detail in chapter 13.

could earn? Although taking action is no doubt important, we see time and time again how fine, hardworking people are jamming, running on empty, failing to achieve what they want.

Why is that so? **Why do so many decent, talented people work and labor so hard and yield only mediocre results?**

The answer is that one should also take into account the "human factor," or as I call it, **the human operating system**: how we as humans operate, what motivates us or blocks us, how our emotional makeup works, the workings of our beliefs, habits, thoughts and more. **Here in this complexity our true challenge lies, as managers and business owners who wish to prosper and succeed.**

Later on in this chapter, we will further examine how all these have an impact on our ability to succeed.

"People are not rational," Professor Kahneman tells us, though most of us believe we are, since that is how we were raised and taught. It's not that we don't possess a rational part, but that we are not sufficiently aware of the great impact the rest of our components have on our *human operating system* and our ability to yield results and meet our goals.

Here is an example of the price of irrationality, or better yet, the lack of awareness of it: a 2009 OECD study found that the rate of people who reported negative experiences and depression in countries like France, the U.S.A, Turkey, and Israel was about 30%. Even if the figures have changed somewhat since, that change is negligible. What is important to understand is that the percentage of people reporting negative experiences and depression is on the rise, and sadly the U.S. is not doing well on that front. Simply consider the amount of antidepressants people consume today to realize the severity of this phenomenon.

Such depression debilitates people in their daily life, in coping with challenges, in their conduct, and in the results they produce. Now it begins to make sense why it isn't enough to be rational. Naturally, the question is how to battle that, which we will soon address.

"Our mistakes are ingrained in us but are not experienced as such."—Prof. Dan Ariely in his book, *Predictably Irrational* This statement is critical to understanding the question of how the *human operating system* works. The answer in one word: humans work on autopilot. Our lives are the result of the upbringing we experience and the culture we absorb—from our parents, nursery, school, army, workplace, college, university, the media, etc. All of them have "programmed" us through beliefs, thoughts, habits and emotions we have accumulated over the years, all of which manifest in our actions as well as in the results we achieve.

Millions of years of evolution have also left their mark on our automatic pilot mode. As risk-hating creatures, we prefer to avoid pain than gain pleasure. Fears and concern have a survival advantage: it's better to be afraid for no reason than to be devoured by a tiger; it's better to give up the opportunity to hunt a mammoth if there is a likely risk of severe injury; and it's best not to be the leading hunter but remain in the safe environment of the protective pack.

Thus, we have been programmed for years to err on the side of caution and conservatism, such that today we use those same survival lenses when viewing non-existential or insignificant "risks," such as speaking to an audience, feeling self-conscious, failing in some area, or getting fired. All of these are a few degrees less serious than being devoured by a tiger, yet the modern world at large would respond to such scenarios with nearly the same level of anxiety.

In essence, we are using an outdated software for a modern system.

All these components of the *human operating system* are within us but invisible to us, acting automatically rather than rationally, which may be harmful or even destructive at times, yet we aren't aware of it at all. For most of us, this system is like a black box whose components and operation are foreign to us.

Hence, one of my prominent conclusions from working with about a thousand people since 2006 is that **the biggest challenge humans face is a mental one.** Not just what to do and how to act, but first how to manage and channel our thoughts, feelings, beliefs, and habits in an effective, beneficial way. This is where change comes in, since these faculties are usually not working in an optimal way that promotes success. Not because we are not talented and smart, but because no one taught us how to manage these faculties and navigate ourselves towards fulfillment and success!

Only when we succeed in coping with the mental challenge, step out of the automatic pilot and change, are we able to act with a *positive EYE*[6], properly implement the familiar rules of success, achieve our goals, and prosper.

---

6 EYE stands for **E**fficiency, **Y**ield, and **E**xpediency. This term will occur throughout the book.

Upgrading the Human Operating System

Here is a nice metaphor that illustrates the *automatic programming* principle very well:

As newborns, we are like a brand new computer bought in a store; we have a state-of-the-art operating system with no glitches or viruses, everything is running smoothly—simply perfect. In addition, the computer has no applications or data, a clean slate. When we observe children ages 1 to 3, it's easy to notice their boundless energy, daring, learning ability, and how quick they are to catch on to patterns.

But right about then, the new computer is loaded with applications and data, mostly from parents and educators. At the same time, bugs show up, as well as clashes between applications, blue screen crashes, and viruses and other technological pathogens. And so this *operating system*, which worked so perfectly when we were children, begins to falter and malfunction.

As a result, when we reach adulthood, our *operating system*— like an old computer—is no longer working optimally. It slows down, freezes, blinks with error messages, requires ongoing maintenance, and sometimes even crashes and needs to be restarted. In order to allow the "computer" to regain its old capacity, its **operating system must be upgraded**.

Metaphorically speaking, this is the work I do with my clients and this is what is required of us—to upgrade our *human operating system*; to download updates, block security loopholes, clean up viruses, fix bugs, remove applications we no longer need and install new ones, erase old data that takes up memory, and so on and so forth.

Thus far, the analogy to computers is perfect, yet there is a catch. When dealing with humans, one cannot simply throw away the computer for a new one; therefore, the most drastic step we can take when all else fails is to **reformat the hard drive**.

So the answer to optimum functioning lies in fixing the *operating system*, which only few of us do. Imagine the following absurdity: our faltering computer ceases to function properly and does not produce the desired output, and we blame the screen for it and swap it—or even worse, take a marker and try to draw the desired output on the screen. Humans act similarly in their real lives. **People have a tendency to treat the symptom rather than the cause**, and this is a grave mistake. Throughout the book, we shall visit a few examples of this approach.

◆

In reality, the required actions focus on performing a **conscious mental change** designed to restart our *human operating system*; to revive, rebuild, refresh, and restore its power, that same ability to maximize our human potential, as we did as children.

How do we do that? We shall find out in the next chapters.

Robin Sharma once said, *"Adults are nothing more than deteriorated children."* This is an excellent statement with which to sum up this subchapter.

From Logic to Awareness

The transition from pure logic to logic integrated with awareness was something I experienced during my own self-transformation. Up until 2006, I was only logical. My mind consisted of only one switch: makes sense/doesn't make sense. Everything started and ended with the question of whether it was logical or not. I outright rejected any ideas of awareness, intuition, and mysticism. What else could you expect from a geek who worked as a CPA for 22 years?

But things didn't work the way I wanted them to. I had a successful career as a CFO, but deep inside I wanted much more. I didn't see myself serving in finance management positions forever. I wanted to become a CEO, manage a bigger group of people, contribute more to the organizations I was working for, innovate, create, be more influential among people and organizations.

But this didn't happen; I couldn't break through the glass ceiling. I never even noticed the glass at that time. My outdated *operating system* was holding me back, but I didn't realize it and couldn't understand why I wasn't getting ahead.

That is how my midlife career crisis came about, which led me to despise my profession and seek change, as I described in chapter one.

◆

The transformation I have since undergone has been, first and foremost, mental, and more specifically has been rooted in abandoning my worship of logic and opening up to awareness.

Aside from logic, I added other components to my *human operating system*: I learned to open up and access more of my feelings and intuition, the unconscious mind and human spirit within me; I have tapped into my human power, my ability to transform and initiate change, the possibilities of choice and the way in which

I create my reality; I have learned to accept reality and let go of my need to control it fully; I have developed emotional intelligence and learned to better implement the rules of success.

I have discovered my multidimensionality as a person, shifting from pure logic to a far greater awareness. What happened as a result—changing careers, taking on a new occupation and starting an independent business from scratch in midlife—became a lot more attainable and doable. When one discovers his multidimensionality, new possibilities open up to him all of a sudden. All at once, reality seems different and life changes. Suddenly, his ability to achieve results and reach the goal he desires takes a quantum leap.

Incidentally, I later heard about a study in which they asked the managers of the 500 top companies in the world based on Fortune Magazine's rating (the Fortune 500) about the main factor in their success. Back then, I was amazed to hear that the most common answer was intuition. Today, it seems obvious to me.

Not Relying On My Brain Alone

My shift from logic to awareness didn't happen overnight. When I started coaching people in the summer of 2006, I was still purely rational. Equipped with old paradigms, I took the coaching skills I had just learned—especially the concrete ones such as business planning—and began to implement them. First on myself, in the business I had just established, and at the same time on the clients I slowly gathered.

As a diligent, studious man, I was sure of my success. And once more, something didn't work. My own personal results, as well as those of my first clients, were delayed. Among my first clients was

John (alias name), a hair stylist who owned a hair salon. John wasn't a businessman, but an expert at his craft who wanted to translate his professional abilities into more money in his bank account. My challenge was to help John turn his occupation into a business. In keeping with my approach at the time, I worked with John enthusiastically on a business-minded approach and basic business tools such as business planning. To my surprise, and although John was hardworking and diligent, this approach didn't work. John achieved some results, but they were too limited to create a significant difference in his business.

I didn't understand why. What were the causes for John's lack of success? How could he be hardworking and diligent, yet maintain an unsuccessful business?

This is when I began to get to the bottom of it. Back then, I was constantly in a coaching framework, as part of the coaching courses I took, and so I began to get feedback from my coaches whose key words included, "Let go, accept, flow, trust." At first, I didn't understand what they meant. It slowly dawned on me that I was only operating on logic and ignoring all the other components in my *human operating system*. So I began to acknowledge more and more the importance of the "being" factors at the core of my actions; how my perception and programming over the past 46 years of my life were sabotaging my actions. I realized there was incongruity between the programming of my unconscious mind and my wishes as they reflected in my conscious mind[7].

At the same time, I began to gradually change the focus of my coaching method from one that mainly relied on goals and indices

---

7 I shall discuss the conscious and unconscious minds in greater detail in Chapter Six.

to a method that heavily integrated "being," mental, and behavioral coaching.

Why Am I Hardworking and Diligent Yet Still Unsuccessful?

Right from my first days self-employed, I was aware of the harsh odds facing a new business, most of which shut down within three years. I was shocked! Imagine a person who invests all their time and money to open a business, pouring heart and soul into it, only to learn that they will most likely have to close their business and all of that hard work will be for nothing. On a personal level, I was alarmed. I couldn't fathom the possibility of my business failing. What would I do then? What field would I work in? How would I earn a living? Would I have to go back to being an employee? Those were the questions that occupied my mind in those days.

I began to study the matter more closely. I researched further and found the following facts: **first**, studies show that **people utilize on average only 7-15% of their potential.** This might explain why most entrepreneurs and business owners don't earn the amount of money they could, and so their businesses don't survive. In fact, each and every one of them truly believes they can make it; most entrepreneurs do share the desire and vision to succeed, which are vital for thriving entrepreneurship. And still, in spite of that, most new businesses close within 3 years.

Second, small business owners are influenced by the stress accompanying a new business venture; they are terrified of failure. Thus, even if they are hardworking and diligent, something in their actions goes wrong, because it's hard to succeed from a weak emotional state.

In one sentence: **they lack the knowledge and habits that**

cultivate fulfillment, satisfaction, abundance, and a happy life!

As a small business owner myself, I had to seek new knowledge and habits in order to fulfill my vision for my second career. Later on, whatever I had tried firsthand that worked, I used in my coaching with my clients.

Human Being

Let us further explore the meaning of "knowledge and habits." We will start by a process of elimination: I do not mean rational knowledge and habits, practical guides that teach you how to open a business, what to do and how to perform the basic business functions such as operations, marketing and sales, management, etc. Naturally, all of these are important and welcome knowledge for every manager and business owner, but they are only the tip of the iceberg, the first and most obvious route any manager or business owner will turn to in order to succeed. Volumes upon volumes have been written on the topic, and so it is not the focus of this book.

In professional language, we call these the **Doing** elements. Before we continue, I shall mention the source of this highly logical approach: it is rooted in the way we are brought up from infancy, to operate from a proactive[8], diligent, practical, rational

---

8 "Proactivity" is a term coined by Stephen R. Covey in his book, *The 7 Habits of Highly Effective People*, a bestseller used in organizational behavior today. The term means taking initiative and responsibility in order to be ahead of the game in acting and influencing a situation. Proactive behavior includes taking actions ahead of future situations, instead of waiting for those situations to occur and only then respond-

approach. Again, there is nothing bad about it, but, while an essential requirement, *Doing* is not enough to succeed.

Doing <u>alone</u>, as vital as it may be, is not enough to prosper and achieve goals.

Why is that so? Because we, humans, are not **Human Doings** but **Human Beings**. English refers to us in this manner for a reason. Our foundation is **Being:** Who are we? What are our beliefs? What motivates us? What is our life's purpose? What is the source of our habits? How do we control our emotions? How do we think? To sum it up: how does our *human operating system* work? Furthermore, **how do we change the automatic way in which it operates in order to thrive and succeed?**

In this regard, more is hidden than is known; science has yet to decipher the existing laws of this matter, and therefore, while this book is being written, most rational people still opt to ignore the elements of **Being**[9]. Not because it isn't important, but because they are strangers to it, and have no idea how to use it for their benefit.

◆

No one teaches us about the **Being** part! To me, this is the biggest failure of the traditional upbringing we absorb throughout our life

---

ing to them (reactivity, which is the opposite of proactivity).

9 The reduced, narrow meaning of this term in the book is the human infrastructure and the myriad of abstract elements in the human entity. *Being* includes thoughts, feelings, beliefs, and habits. The term also encompasses less defined elements like the human spirit, the human psyche, awareness, etc. One can also define *Being* by a process of elimination: it is everything that is not *Doing*. The full meaning of the term *Being* will gradually become clear throughout the book.

from various educational frameworks—our parents, preschool, school, college, university, and workplaces. Our culture in general is one of **Doing** rather than **Being**.

Let us further illuminate the importance of **Being** in fulfillment and success.

The Right Order of Fulfillment

In chapter twelve, we shall more closely examine the *Being* model, which explains the right order of fulfillment according to the formula **Being → Doing → Having**. Here, I shall outline this principle in its most basic level, which I call *"The Fulfillment Pyramid."* It is illustrated in diagram 2-1:

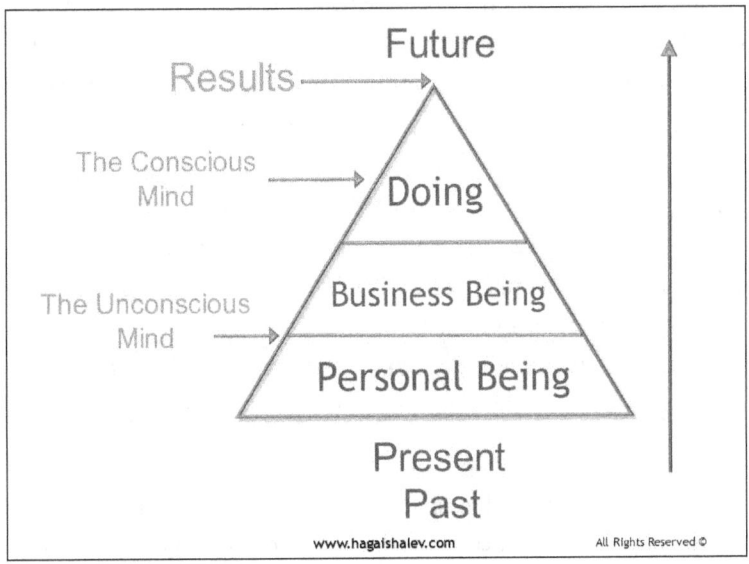

Diagram 2-1 – The Fulfillment Pyramid

Let's review from the bottom up: we all have a past from which the present is derived, and we march towards the future and the results we wish to yield. That is to say, the direction of our movement follows the arrow upward, literally and figuratively. The way up passes through the **Fulfillment Pyramid**. In looking at the pyramid, we start at the top: It is obvious that in order to achieve results, we must do certain things and take action—**Doing**. The problem is, acting according to our upbringing, we rush there first, which is akin to erecting the last floors of a building without first laying the foundations and the lower level floors. This results in the building collapsing; the same goes for building our businesses, our careers, or any other initiative if we start with the **Doing** and ignore the other steps.

It is the same when we approach consultants who only teach us how to **do**. For example, if I am a business owner who dislikes selling (as I was when I first became self-employed), no matter how many sales techniques I have learned, as long as I haven't changed this limiting belief about sales that sits at the bottom of my being[10], my sales efforts will not be effective enough.

As we shall see in chapter six, this is because what determined 95% of my results was the limiting belief that lay at the background of my unconscious mind—not the actions was I taking using my conscious mind. Irrational, remember? So disinterest, fear, and aversion to sales will negatively affect my intonation and body language. These will unconsciously transfer to my potential

---

10 Here are numerous limiting beliefs regarding marketing and sales which I have recently encountered when working with clients: "I don't like to sell, I don't know how to sell, I want to be the professional in my business and prefer someone else to market and sell for me, I'm afraid to hear 'no' from a client, sales people are sly and unreliable, you need to convince in order to sell and I'm not good at that," and so on and so forth...

client and sabotage the sales techniques I have learned so well, because what we actually say only accounts for about 7% of our effect on others; the rest is determined by intonation and body language, which mostly manifest unconsciously.

Similarly, if I dislike my occupation as an employee, no matter how much I strive, my results at work will be inferior and my boss will notice that, and I may even get fired—again, a similar situation to mine at the end of my days as an employee. Likewise, if I am up for consideration for a job, my lack of passion for that occupation will be unconsciously registered by the interviewer and minimize my chances of getting hired.

Treating the Cause, Not the Symptom

So what is the solution? The **Fulfillment Pyramid** teaches us that the "first floors" are our **Being**. In order for our **Doing** to have a positive **EYE** and yield results, we must first tend to the foundation of our "building," and only then handle the rafters.

I chose to divide **Being** into two stages:

First, the **Personal Being**: Who am I as a person? What are my values? What are my basic paradigms? What do I like to do? What are my core beliefs? What is the level of my emotional intelligence? What are my **TTT**[11] (see diagram 2-2)?

---

11 Thoughts, Terms and Tasks. These three "T's" create a fourth T, which is The Reality of our life. Their order is important, because every fulfillment begins with Thoughts, continues with the Terms we impose on ourselves, and ends with our Tasks, with the meaning of things we do; the result is The Reality we create for ourselves.

For example, am I a procrastinator? Disorganized? Perfectionist? Do I have low self-confidence or get easily upset? All these are habits (in the broad sense of the word)[12] that don't serve me, making success very difficult if not impossible to attain.

Now, what is my **Business Being**?

It's how I think, express myself, and act as a business owner or employee. What is my vision? Am I emotionally committed to that vision and to my goals? Am I free of mental inhibitions about being the salesman of my business? What is my approach to time management? To managing employees? To managing business tasks? To money? What is the true occupation I love doing?

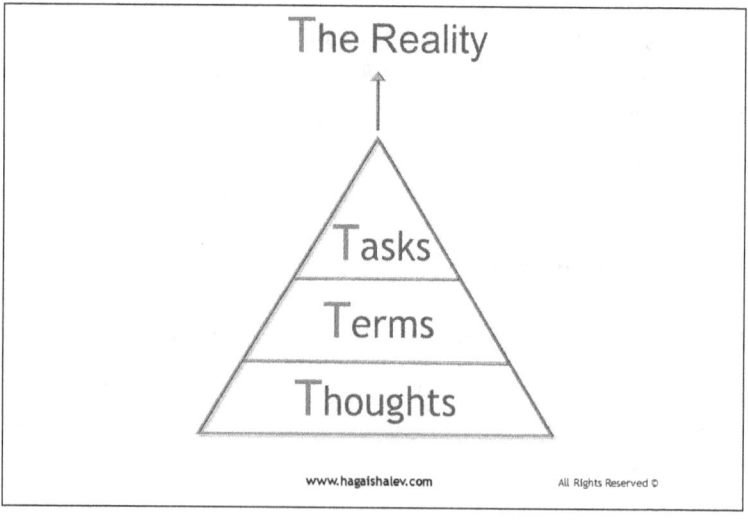

Diagram 2-2 – The TTT Model – 3 T's that create a forth T

---

12 Throughout the book, I will use the word "habits" in a very broad sense, to mean all of our thoughts, beliefs, feelings and actions. They are the components in the *human operating system* that serve as part of our **Being**.

What is the Source of Change?

All of these are important questions most people cannot even answer, let alone change their conduct to accommodate. But before you lose hope, shut the book, and give up your transformation in light of this great challenge, here is a calming thought: every person faces challenges in his life, yet we all have opportunities to grow and develop during the course of our existence, along with the ability to make changes in our lives. Since 2006, I have taken about 20 different self-help courses and underwent dozens of training sessions while undergoing personal *doing* and *being* work with about 15 different instructors and coaches, mostly working on my mental side, enabling me to reach the level of success I enjoy today.

As a result, I am not the same person I was in 2005, because **I have changed nearly every aspect of my personality**: from a judgmental, skeptical and angry person, I have become optimistic, positive and calm. My last name, which means "calm" in Hebrew, finally fits me! These changes have led me to a position today in which I can pass along all the knowledge and information I have accumulated to you, and so **allow you a shortcut into your own personal development and transformation.** All that I have learned, I first tested on myself, and only that which worked for me has made it into the melting pot from which this book was born.

In fact, it is actually the informal knowledge that I have acquired through thousands of hours of reading, watching, and listening to books, lectures, webinars, and recorded programs that has helped me most to develop the methodology outlined in this book. Naturally, my 22 years as a hired executive in the business world laid the foundation of knowledge and experience that has helped me to achieve and succeed. However, if it were not for the **Being transformation** I have undergone, I would not be standing here today and my potential would not have been fulfilled.

More about this transformation will be detailed later in the book, but for now, I will say this: my personal challenge was, and to some degree still is, to depart from strictly rational thinking, learn to accept reality, learn to live with uncertainty, let go of the need to control, and trust my abilities and the laws of the universe.

I wholeheartedly believe that we are all meant for greatness, and that for each one of us success is still possible. To reach it, we must understand the **right order of the *Fulfillment Pyramid***, identify the weak points in our ***Business and Personal Being***, and change them so that they become a strong foundation for our ***Doing***, acting and fulfilling ourselves as the foundation of our new being, with a *positive **EYE***. From here on, success becomes much more attainable.

Therefore, my strongest recommendation is: resist the temptation engrained in us from infancy to first *Do*. Work on the *Being* first—your existential foundation as a human, as well as a manager and a businessperson. Only then can you go back to the execution—the *Doing*—and succeed big time!

◆

In this chapter, we touched upon the foundations of change. Later on, we shall become familiar with my entire methodology for creating an active change, the *"CO-OP Formula,"* while learning and working on the non-trivial connection between ***Being*** and ***Doing***.

In the next chapter, we will review a few practical applications of change, before delving into the depths of transformation in later chapters.

I shall close with words by the Belgian author Charles Dubois: *"The important thing is this: To be able at any moment to sacrifice what we are for what we could become."*

CHAPTER THREE:
The Three Key Principles of Success
(Which Most People Are Not Familiar With)

"When you change the way you look at things, the things you look at change."

—Wayne Dyer

This book is a practical guide. As such, let's familiarize ourselves with the three key principles of the *human operating system*, which will open up a window of opportunity for you to immediately begin changing habits that no longer serve you. Starting in chapter seven, we will delve into the **"CO-OP Formula"** which will teach you, step by step, how to make changes in your *human operating system*.

There are **three key principles** most people aren't familiar with which critically affect success. I witness their effect on my life and my clients' lives daily. Most people are unaware of how these principles work, due to the *program* most of us live by, and so are unable to use them in a way that can lead to success.

In this chapter, we will learn how to identify these three key principles, so you can begin to implement them in your life.

Here is a brief summary of these principles:

1. *The Focus Principle*—what you focus on expands, while the rest diminishes or may remain non-existent.

2. *The Positive Approach* Principle—a positive approach helps us succeed in life, while a negative approach hinders success.

3. *The "Above the Line"* Principle—positive feelings are energizing and motivate us to act with a *positive EYE*[13], which yields success.

Let's delve into these principles so you can familiarize yourself with them and learn how to apply them in your life.

The Conscious and Unconscious[14] Mind

Our conscious mind, which we use to perform daily cognitive functions in our life, can only handle one thing at a time. That is to say, unlike what most of us assume, people cannot multi-task unless some tasks are performed automatically, out of habit, by the unconscious mind[15].

For example: you must have experienced driving home while immersed in deep thoughts or on a phone call, and suddenly arrived at your destination without remembering the journey. You obviously noticed your route, yet you cannot recall it. Why? Because the unconscious mind was the one driving your car (an automatic habit). Your conscious mind was occupied with

---

13 **EYE** – Efficiency, Yield, and Expediency.

14 The more prevalent term is the "subconscious mind." I prefer to use the term "unconscious mind," because "sub" has a hint of inferiority, which is not at all the case with the unconscious mind. On the contrary, the unconscious mind is a million times stronger than the conscious mind.

15 I shall go into more detail about the conscious and unconscious mind in chapter six.

one task, and thus was unable to take on anything else—i.e., "noticing" the route.

Here is another example: when you meet a stranger, and you exchange names, have you noticed sometime later that you really didn't get his name? Your ears heard it, but your conscious mind didn't register it because it was preoccupied with something else—perhaps with your shyness when meeting a stranger, perhaps with his appearance, or even just with your daily worries[16]. Moreover, sometimes this happens with more than just one word, not just a person's name but with an entire statement. Your thoughts wander, occupying your conscious mind, which in turn cannot absorb your partner's words. This, among many other examples, teaches us that our conscious mind can only absorb and handle one thing at a time. By the way, unlike common belief, this holds true for women as much as men. Their supposed predisposition towards multitasking is only demonstrated if, simultaneous to activating their conscious mind (like talking on the phone), they are engaged in another daily chore, which is an automatic habit performed by their unconscious mind. Perhaps women are more flexible in how their conscious mind quickly shifts from one matter to another, but this is a different topic which is irrelevant to our discussion.

That Which You Focus On is Where You Advance

Hence, the question of what your conscious mind is occupied with at every moment is critical, because this is what fills up your consciousness and holds your attention while other things, as

---

16 Here is a small tip on how to remember a new person's name: focus on the person in front of you, remove any other thought, and listen carefully to the person talking, listen to his name, and then repeat his name to yourself three times.

important as they may be, are pushed aside and neglected.

This is the first key principle concerning the *human operating system*, which I call the *focus principle*. This principle simply states the following: **what you focus on fills up your world and "grows," whereas everything else in your world may become "non-existent" at times when it is out of your focus.**

Before we talk further about the *focus principle* and its significance, let's examine a few more instances of it in our life: we say that a pregnant woman is more likely to notice other pregnant women around her; or if you buy a certain car model, you tend to see a lot of identical cars around you.

Here is a personal story that perfectly illustrates the *focus principle*:

Once, my daughter called me at ten at night asking me to buy her a toothbrush. She had just returned from a scout camp and was heading out to another camp the following day, and had lost her toothbrush on the way. I was on my way home when she called, having finished my regular workout at the gym (the same one I have been going to twice a week since 1999). I immediately started thinking of my route home and where I could find an open drugstore to pick up a toothbrush. My conclusion was that I would have to divert from my usual shortcut home, but I told myself, "Pay attention, you might still find an open store at this hour."

A few seconds later, I took a right turn at a corner I had been to about a thousand times before. As usual, I looked to the left to check for oncoming traffic, only to discover that, right across from me, Friends Drugstore was open and ready to let me in. Up to that moment, and though my eyes had glanced at it a thousand times, I never saw the drugstore. Of course, it was always there, but up until then my consciousness never sought it because I didn't need a drugstore at that hour before, and so I never noticed it until that night.

Happy as can be, I bought the toothbrush for my daughter and realized, for the billionth time, how powerful the **focus principle** is. I am certain you can find numerous examples of how you have applied this principle in your life.

◆

Here is the main point:
Most people are not aware of the *focus principle*. Therefore, they don't use it to their advantage, by focusing on the important things in life. Instead, their focus is automatic and many times spitefully directed towards their difficulties and problems, thus magnifying them, capturing their consciousness and preventing them from seeing the opportunities and possibilities available to them.

The Three Filters that Distort Reality

Notice how many bits of information your senses absorb every second. Stop reading for a moment and turn your attention to your senses, one after another: What do you register? What do you hear? What do you see? What do you smell? What do you feel? What tastes are in your mouth? Notice the abundance of information. Our senses absorb thousands of pieces of information every second. Most are absorbed by our unconscious mind, while our conscious mind absorbs only about ten bits of information per second. What information bits does it absorb? That's right, it absorbs whatever bits of information we are focusing on at the moment.

In fact, the *human operating system* is designed in such a way as to constantly omit information absorbed by our senses. Why? Because if all this information were to enter our conscious mind, we would be overwhelmed by it and unable to function; therefore, we were born and shaped by evolution or the Creator in such a way that **only what we focus on penetrates and fills our consciousness, while all the rest is "non-existent."** One can view the *focus principle* as a distortion of objective, factual reality—a **filter** that screens reality and enables only a portion of it to penetrate our consciousness.

Furthermore, there are **two additional filters** that distort objective reality as it is perceived by our subjective consciousness:

The **second filter** is the limitation of our senses. Our senses don't absorb all the details of our familiar reality. For example, we only see a small portion of the light wave spectrum and only hear some sound frequencies. Among the waves our senses cannot decipher are ultraviolet, X-ray, and Gamma waves, and the sound frequencies shared by dogs, whales, and other animals. Our sense of smell is also limited in comparison to animals. In fact, if we examine sense by sense, we will realize that we don't register nearly all of the world's objective reality, but only a very small part of it. Hence, **there is a reality out there which we do not sense.**

The **third filter** proves the following: we tend to absorb things that are congruent with our world view, and skip things that are incongruent with our world view. These are essentially our paradigms through which we perceive the world. We see it many times in evaluating others. The way in which we perceive them dictates how we interpret their actions. For example, if your paradigm tells you that a person is successful, you will notice his actions as "proof" that will reinforce this paradigm. On the other hand, someone else may view him as unsuccessful, and he too, will be able to find "proof" of it using relevant "facts" that prove that person's lack of success.

This filter is similar to the *focus principle*, but is also different in that it not only speaks about the technical aspect of focusing, but also on a deeper aspect of consciousness related to our belief systems and outlooks.

Another example of the third filter is our self-esteem: people with low self-esteem tend to view themselves as incapable of taking self-realized actions, such as opening a business. However, people with high self-esteem are more inclined to view themselves as capable of taking those same actions.

Henry Ford said of this: "Whether you think that you can, or that you can't, you are usually right."

"We don't see things as they are, we see them as we are"
—Anais Nin

As humans, we have different outlooks; each one of us wears a different "pair of glasses" through which he sees the world differently from others; the "glasses" through which we perceive the world determine our experience of reality.

The question is, what type of "glasses" do we walk out into the world with every day, how were they shaped, and how can we redesign them to serve us better and lead us to success and prosperity? More about that later in this chapter.

The three filters I have mentioned here distort objective reality as it penetrates our subjective consciousness. We don't see the world for what it is; we see it for what we are. To me, this is one of the most fascinating ideas: **different people view the same things differently**, thus giving different meanings to the same facts. One will say, "The market is plunging, it's time to sell," while another might say, "It's a rare opportunity, buy now." What seems a crisis to one person is an opportunity for another. One may see a breakdown while another sees a breakthrough. Imagine if all people viewed and interpreted reality the same way—the world would be a very boring place to live in, wouldn't it? This is one of the world's marvels: **everyone possesses all three filters, yet each person uses them differently, seeing a different reality**; a subjective interpretation of an objective reality.

In Psalms 115, verses 5-6, it is written: *"Eyes have they, but they see not; they have ears, but they hear not."* Indeed, we all see and hear, but it doesn't mean that this is what our consciousness absorbs, because these three filters screen, distort, and warp our experience of reality.

The Magic Word—Attitude

The Second Key Principle that affects our ability to succeed involves our **attitude** towards life. The same "glasses" we mentioned in the last subchapter—are they rose-colored or black? Are we positive and optimistic regarding the circumstances[17] of our lives, or negative and pessimistic?

---

17 One of the definitions of "circumstance" is a set of conditions connected to an event or an action. We interpret the word throughout this book as mostly negative events that happen to us outside of our direct control. For example: weather conditions, natural disasters, governmental decisions, macroeconomic events, etc.; but also what my boss told me to do, what happened to me on the way to work, diseases of various sorts, an angry client that messed up my schedule, and so on.

One of the most amazing works written about humans' attitude is *The Magic Word—Attitude*[18] by Earl Nightingale, one of the personal development pioneers in the U.S. from the 1950s and 1960s.

To sum up Nightingale's message in one sentence: a positive attitude to life is a key factor in our ability to succeed.

Following are a few quotes from Nightingale's statements: *"No matter what people do, wherever you find people doing an outstanding job and getting outstanding results, you'll find people with a good attitude...*

Successful people come in all sizes, shapes, ages, and colors and they have widely varying degrees of intelligence and education. But they have one thing in common: They expect more good out of life than bad. They expect success more often than failure. And they do succeed...

A great attitude does much more than turn on the lights in our worlds; it seems to magically connect us to all sorts of serendipitous opportunities that were somehow absent before the change. Maybe that's what people mean when they say we're lucky. Suddenly, we do find ourselves getting the so-called "breaks."

When you begin to develop a better attitude, you should realize that you've already placed yourself among the top 5 percent of the people—among the most successful people on earth..."

---

18 This is the first of 12 best-selling audiotapes known as *Lead the Field* and issued by Nightingale in 1987.

LOT: Location, Operation, Time

It's easy to see where Nightingale comes from in the decisive approach he presents. We like to work and spend time with positive people. Since we live among other humans and are dependent on those around us in daily life, it's natural that a positive person's interpersonal communication, attitude towards others, and his ability to give will encourage others to accept him, cooperate with him, and even give back to him. This is the essence of the factors leading to a positive person's success.

Moreover, Dr. David Hamilton[19], a chemist who studies the mind's influence on the physical body in general and on illnesses in particular, describes the results of a study on his website, finding that optimistic people live about seven years more than pessimistic ones. If they do live longer, chances are that optimistic people are probably healthier, have more energy and power, and thus are in a better position to reap success in their lives.

◆

Here is another example of how a positive attitude affects our success, this time using the million-dollar question, "What make certain people seem luckier than others?" Richard Wiseman, a psychologist from the University of Hertfordshire in the United Kingdom, author of the book, *The Luck Factor*, wrote an article about luck published in the U.K. in 2003:

---

19 See http://drdavidhamilton.com. I have been a subscriber on his blog for a few years now, and I have learned a great deal from him about the mind-body connection.

"...Over the years, I interviewed and worked with 400 volunteers, women and men, who defined themselves as 'lucky or 'unlucky.' The findings have clearly revealed that **the behavior patterns and thoughts of unlucky people are responsible for much of their fortune.**

Take the case of chance opportunities. Lucky people consistently encounter such opportunities, whereas unlucky people do not. I carried out a simple experiment where I gave volunteers a newspaper and asked them to look through it and tell me how many photographs were inside. On average, the unlucky people took about two minutes to count the photographs, whereas the lucky people took just seconds. Why? Because the second page of the newspaper contained the message: **"Stop counting. There are 43 photographs in this newspaper."** *This message took up half of the page and was written in type that was more than 2 inches high. It was staring everyone straight in the face, but the unlucky people tended to miss it and the lucky people tended to spot it.*

Personality tests revealed that unlucky people are generally much tenser than lucky people, and research has shown that **tension and anxiety disrupts people's ability to notice the unexpected.** *The same goes for luck – unlucky people miss chance opportunities because they are too focused on looking for something else. They go to parties, intent on finding their perfect partner and so miss opportunities to make good friends. They look through newspapers determined to find certain types of job advertisements and as a result miss other types of jobs. Whereas lucky people are more relaxed and open, and therefore see what is there rather than just what they are looking for!*

In order to examine if it's possible to increase the amount of good luck that people encounter in their lives, I created a "luck school" that taught people to think and behave as if they were lucky, based on the principles my researches yielded. The results were dramatic: **80% of people were now happier, more satisfied with their lives and, perhaps most important of all, luckier!** *Take Carolyn, for example. After graduating from "luck school", she has passed her driving test after three years of trying, was no longer accident-prone and became more confident."*

◆

I fully identify with these statements, since I have experienced them in my own life. For about 25 years, despite my comprehensive financial expertise as a CPA and my profound understanding of investments and finances, I never looked after my own interests—I didn't make even a single investment in order to increase my future personal capital. Conservatism and caution prevented me from taking advantage of many opportunities that came my way, but I simply didn't notice. After undergoing my mental transformation, things changed. I suddenly saw an abundance of investment opportunities. And it was right when I was still struggling to turn my new occupation into a successful, prospering business, and money was tight, that I decided to make four successful investments that have increased my capital a great deal. After deciding on these investments, I was able to find the financial resources to execute them.

Hence, due to my change in attitude, I went from being "unlucky" to being "lucky."

So let us say that LOT stands for **L**ocation, **O**peration, and **T**ime. That is, getting lucky is a matter of being in the right location (consciously speaking as well), at the right time and operating correctly (including cognitive decisions, such as positive focus and attitude).

The Parents' Critical Mistake Hinders the Success of their Adult Children

Now, let's connect the dots. We saw that the *focus principle* teaches us that what we focus on expands (as if the rest is "nonexistent"). Furthermore, we saw that a *positive attitude* to life is a key factor for success.

One might ask, **what kind of attitude and focus does the average person demonstrate through his life?** How does he apply these two principles? Does his attitude and focus support his success or not?

From my experience, most people's attitude is not positive enough and their focus tends to remain on daily problems and worries. The outcome is that these worries and problems "increase" and fill up their day (according to the *focus principle*), hindering them from implementing a positive attitude in their lives, hence their ability to succeed is terribly diminished (according to the *positive attitude principle*). Moreover, according to the *focus principle*, he who dwells on negativity cannot see the positive, thus missing at least some of the opportunities and chances he encounters in life.

In other words, the negative focus and attitude most people possess prevents them from living up to their fullest human potential, prospering, and succeeding.

◆

Let's examine these issues in more depth by reviewing an average person's life, from infancy to adulthood, who is educated in the Western world and absorbs the culture we are a part of:

As children, we absorb our first experience of the world from our parents. The latter usually haven't taken any courses on parenthood, and in general raise their children according to what they have learned from their parents. Thus, the principles of raising children are inherited and passed through the generations. Unfortunately, the most critical mistakes are made at such an early, significant stage in those infants and children's upbringing that it affects their entire life.

As parents, we are concerned with our children's well-being, which makes us protective of them. While this attitude is human, reasonable, and well-intended, it results in the average child absorbing from the get go a range of negative expressions, such as, "This is forbidden, you cannot, no, be careful, that's not allowed, it's not nice," and on and on. Moreover, as parents, we are usually unaware of just how negatively influential conversations with our spouses about our children are, how they listen and take in our fights, criticism, cynicism, and other types of negative statements and behaviors.

Children, for their part, lack proper judgment; therefore, everything their parents say is immediately registered by their unconscious mind and interpreted as the ultimate truth. As I will expand on in chapter six, our unconscious mind determines 95% of the results of our actions. The problem is that this mind is usually inaccessible, hence the difficulty in changing habits and beliefs which originate in the unconscious mind. There is one major exception to this rule: the unconscious minds of children 6 years old and under are usually accessible. This is why young children make excellent students and are quick to absorb new things. Those directly enter their unconscious mind, where they are "burnt" and fixed onto their *operating system* for life, for better or worse.

Going back to parenthood and raising infants, it's easy to see the lack of awareness among most parents regarding the effect of their **T**houghts, **T**erms, and **T**asks (**TTT**) on The Reality their children experience. It is their negative *TTT* that usually leaves an unfavorable imprint on the young children, "programming" their unconscious minds as well as their results to favor negativity for the rest of their lives.

In essence, this is one of the reasons for the argument I raised earlier about how most people don't live up to their fullest human potential and settle for an average range of 7-15% of the full potential. In large part, this is because negative focus and attitude are already imprinted in the mind in childhood.

"The pessimist sees difficulty in every opportunity. The optimist sees the opportunity in every difficulty."—Winston Churchill

Even past the age of 6, children's upbringing is mostly poorly balanced between positive and negative, leaning more towards negativity. Most education systems are outdated. There are far too many students per teacher, and so teachers find it difficult to control the classroom and give their full attention to each student. The outcome is that teachers usually give little attention to the quiet, successful students, instead keeping busy handling problematic students who are disruptive and academically challenged. It's clear that here, too, the negative focus promotes a negative attitude and "expands" at the expense of positivity and the ability to succeed.

Moving along to the mature adult, one can see two main environments that shape and influence personality:

The **first** is his work environment. Too many organizations are focused on problem-solving. They give far more negative feedback than positive feedback to their employees. Most managers don't spare too many kind words. The average manager wakes up in the morning and asks himself, "What problems do I need to handle today?" And while it's obvious that a manager needs to solve problems, the secret here is to **measure and balance**. Focusing on the problems only "amplifies" them, filling up a manager's entire day so that he lacks the ability to dedicate time and attention to new opportunities and possibilities. Thus, the latter gets pushed aside rather than promoted, and the business world is mostly focused on the problems. Here, too, **the negative focus inhibits positivity and hinders success.**

The **second** environment is the media we are exposed to and the culture we live in. We are flooded with thousands of messages every day from different screens (some say that we are exposed to some 3,000 advertising messages daily!) and the nature of such messages is highly influential on our unconscious mind as well as our consciousness. Unfortunately, in the current culture of the West, negative messages have higher ratings, therefore the media tends to engage in them more. Thus, every newscast begins with the negative news in our area, most of the newspaper headlines scream out negativity, our culture tends to be overly critical and sometimes even judgmental and cynical, political corruption trickles into governmental institutions and the business world, etc. I shall stop here, since there is really no point in me naming all the forces of negativity in our daily lives.

The Negative Automatic Programming That Prevents Success

The writing on the wall is clear: from infancy to adulthood, there is not enough balance between the positive and negative in our culture and media. Too much focus on the negative only "expands" it, fills up our day, occupies our conscious mind (that can only handle one thing at a time), keeping away the positive, and trickles into the unconscious mind of most people, further programming them for negativity. Above all, **this conduct is automatic and is performed unaware of its destructive implications.**

The inevitable conclusion is that most people do not live up to their potential because their *attitude* is not *positive* enough: they are more focused on the dangers and risks in their lives, on the negative, the fears and possibility of failure, rather than the opportunities and chances, the positive, the potential for success and good in their lives. Lacking a *positive attitude*, success, prosperity, wellbeing, satisfaction, and happiness in their lives as well.

Moreover, as we saw in chapter two when analyzing the need to be open to change, modern culture is not the only factor programming us for negativity. Millions of years of evolution have also programmed us to favor caution, conservatism, fear, and skepticism. All of these are permanent dwellers in our *operating system* today, planted in us as automatic pilot with negative seeds that sabotage success and affluence.

The "Above the Line" Principle—*The Broader General Rule*

Let us now take the focus and attitude principles one step further. So far, we have dealt with two specific cases that illustrate a much broader principle. We shall now move to the more general case, which is the **Third Principle** of success.

Above the line	proactive	presence	happy	praise & empowerment	
internal locus of control	desire	acceptance & letting go	"what, how" questions	high responsibility	
	positive focus	vision	forgiveness	strong commitment	love
high results	effective	awareness	positive attitude	higher self	high integrity
positive emotion	high energy	enthusiasm	good communicator		vibrant

---

poor responsibility	need for control	limiting paradigms	"why?" questions	stuck in the past	
fear	judgmental	Suffering	reactive		
poor integrity	negative focus	victim	needy	blame	weak commitmen
ineffective	poor results	automat	ego	unaware	negative attitude
Below the line	negative emotion	low energy	uncommunicative	tired	

Diagram 3-1 – Above and Below the Line

Let's look at the black line at the center of diagram 3-1. I call it an "emotional separation line." The emotion on it is neutral—neither positive nor negative. We make a distinction between situations that are **above the line** and situations that are **below the line.** *Above the line* are the positive places in which we experience positive emotions, positive energy, and empowerment. *Below the line* are the negative places, where we feel negative emotions, negative energy, fatigue, and lethargy. Every person has experienced these situations at times. In fact, this is one of the most common ways in which the dualism which is so typical of humans comes into play.

Now let's get down to details and further understand these terms (see diagram 3-1)[20] by starting *below the line:* **below the line,** we are immersed in negative feelings; our energy is low; we don't communicate well with ourselves and our surroundings; we're tried, suffering from physical and mental exhaustion; we are not effective in our actions, and our results are poor. *Below the line* we act automatically and our ego is very dominant; here, we are unaware, with a *negative attitude* to life and *focusing on the negative*, as these terms have been used in this chapter. *Below the line*, we are often victims of *circumstances* and of others; here, we "need"—money, relationships, recognition, etc. The "need" is characterized by coming from a place of scarcity; therefore, the connotations are negative and we are *below the line*. Here, there is blame—we blame others or ourselves.

"If you have one foot in the past and one foot in the future, you're pissing on the present"—Malachy McCourt

Below the line, our commitment is weak and our responsibility is poor; we have a very strong need to control our *circumstances*; we crave control of others, of everything that is happening in reality, of the past that wasn't bright, of the weather, and so on. The thing is that we can't always control all these, simply because they are beyond our field of influence[21].

This is a very important trap that a good many fall for, so I will shed more light on it: humans have a strong desire to control everything that happens around them.

----

20 This is not a full list of all the characteristics of these two terms, nor shall I go into detail on each characteristic. I shall discuss the conscious and unconscious minds in greater detail in Chapter Six.

21 In his book, *The 7 Habits of Highly Effective People*, Stephen R. Covey calls it "Circles of Concern & Circles of Influence."

One of my favorite comedy skits is about a soccer team's fans, who demand to once and for all decide on who the players, coaches, results, and weather of the game will be. This may sound absurd, but the real absurdity is that most of us act this way in daily life. Every time we complain, get steamed up, and treat something that is beyond our control as "not okay" (the weather, the way we were brought up, the mistakes we made when we were younger and didn't...etc., etc.), we drop *below the line*, and as we shall soon see, this is a serious blow to our success.

Moreover, the exaggerated need to control reality is an expression of a far broader principle. I shall demonstrate this by describing a short experiment I do with my clients in our first meeting: I ask the client to extend his or her hand towards me while locking the elbow with an open palm. I give no other instructions. Then I open my palm and place it on the client's palm, starting to apply force on it and gradually increasing the pressure. I have done this experiment hundreds of times, and 99% of the time, my client applied opposing force to counter mine, keeping the elbow locked and resisting my pressure. Why? Why resist and exhaust yourself when you could simply bend the elbow, retract your hand, and let me fall forward, as is customary in martial arts?

◆

This simple experiment illustrates one of the most common automatic habits in our society: **we automatically resist nearly everything.** Notice how each time something that concerns you changes in your surrounding (aside from when it is clearly to your advantage), you first and foremost resist. This resistance is so deeply engrained in us that we often don't notice it; it's simply an instinct that we obey automatically. As long as it's applied to things in our direct control, the resistance is reasonable and logical.

However, many times we resist things that are out of our control, where there is no point in resistance. The most absurd example for that is resisting the past. Since we cannot change the past, what is the point of making it "not okay," even if things happened that were not to our liking (with our spouses, our partners, or within ourselves)?

Furthermore, according to the *focus principle*, when we focus on the past we cannot look to the future. Someone once said, *"It's best if we turn our full attention to the future, since this is where we are destined to spend the rest of our lives."* He was right, no doubt. **What is the point of dwelling on a past that is unchangeable, when the present is the only moment in which we can impact our future?**

To sum up, our need for control is manifested in our automatic resistance to *circumstances*. Resisting things that aren't in our direct control, like the past, is a *below the line* characteristic. Notice how this resistance leads to suffering, another *below the line* characteristic.

"Why? Because..."

As kids, we tend to ask a lot of questions about why things happen the way they do. But when those questions become rhetorical and pointless because they are unanswerable, adults usually get confused and don't know what to answer, so they'll simply say, "because." This is another *below the line* characteristic. Note that these are not the same "why" questions as those that attempt to research and find the causes and reasons for certain phenomena. The latter are welcomed and necessary as the basis for scientific research. What I am referring to are different "why" questions, which, unfortunately, are more common in our lives, such as, "Why is this backpack in the middle of the room? Why can't you come home on time? Why is your room untidy? Why am I such an idiot? Why can't I do things the right way for once?"

These "why" questions are admonishing, accusatory, pointless; they focus us on the past, on things we cannot change, and naturally stir up resistance in the person being asked. These are rhetorical questions whose answer is unimportant. According to the *focus principle*, here, too, the focus is on blaming and on the past, and the resistance they produce prevents a solution-oriented, productive dialogue; therefore, they are characterized as *below the line*. We shall soon find out what are the right questions to ask.

◆

Other things that lie *below the line* are: reactivity, which means responding to circumstances automatically; fear, the strongest negative emotion and the mother of all other negative emotions; poor integrity, which stems from a weak mental state and being judgmental towards ourselves and others.

While this is not a full, complete list, it makes the point clear. All these habits and their derivatives are *below the line*.

Above the line—The Better Place to Be
Now let's see what it means to be *above the line*:

Above the line means being emotionally positive, having high energy, being enthusiastic and highly communicative with others and with ourselves; having vigor, energy and power. *Above the line*, our actions are effective, and our results are good; we are aware of ourselves and others; our attitude is positive; our integrity is strong; we are focused on the positive aspects of our lives and work to promote them. *Above the line*, we experience an *internal locus of control* [22], which means that we always have the option to respond to our life's *circumstances*, even if they are harsh. *Internal locus of control* is the opposite of victimhood, which is a *below the line* characteristic, otherwise known as an *external locus of control* [23].

Above the line, we lead rather than being led; we "want" rather than "need." Wanting is great; it is accompanied by positive emotion and positive, enhancing energy. The moment it becomes a "need," it turns into "neediness", which is a *below the line* concept.

In chapter eleven we shall discuss, among other things, vision, which is an *above the line* characteristic. Vision is foundational to a person and his business. It indicates the power behind the owner and his business, his meaning in life, his purpose and the things he loves and is good at. These are all positive characteristics and therefore vision is *above the line*.

---

22 An internal locus of control means I am the cause of the results I achieve in my life. I set the tone with which I run my life, and thus influence the reality I experience. This is the opposite approach to the *automatic program* and victimization, an approach that contains choice, consideration, and effectiveness. Despite the encumbering *circumstances* around me, including those which I don't control, I can always choose how to respond to them. This holds for better or worse. That is to say, it doesn't mean my choices are always correct; if I have erred, I take responsibility for my error, learn from it, draw conclusions, fix it, and move on.

23 External locus of control is exactly the opposite of internal locus of control.

Other characteristics *above the line* are forgiveness (the opposite of blame) and love, which is the strongest positive emotion. It's clear that when we come from love we are positive, everything flows smoothly, and life is beautiful—no doubt *above the line*. *Above the line* our commitment is strong, we are accepting and letting go (the exact opposite of the need to control *below the line*), asking "what and how" questions (which I call questions of opportunity and possibility) instead of "why" questions. I believe there is no bad without good and that "what and how" questions help us find the good in even difficult situations. For example, when *circumstances* aren't to our liking, we ask, what can I do with this? How can I handle it? What have I learned from it? What good is in it? What does it allow me to do? How do I solve this?

My favorite question is, "What good is in it?" because it enables us to quickly change focus and search for (and find) the positive opportunities and possibilities in even negative *circumstances*. Try it; "What is good in it?" works wonderfully.

Helen Keller once said, *"When one door of happiness closes, another opens; but often we look so long at the closed door that we do not see the one which has been opened for us."* The investment story which I mentioned earlier in this chapter is a perfect example of this statement.

Finally, *above the line* we are proactive, present, in the here and now, which is the opposite of being stuck in past frustrations or future worries; *above the line*, we are happy, and therefore are able to empower and praise others as well.

The Full Emotional Spectrum

So far, I have described two oppositional aspects, but in essence I have also drawn an emotional spectrum. On this emotional spectrum, we shall add the red graph on diagram 3-2 – the *Sine Wave*. The sine wave is the most common pattern in nature. Everything in nature follows a sine wave: tidal ebb and flow, day and night, the seasons of the year, life cycles, and more. Even in economics, we see periods of ebb and flow. As they say, c'est la vie!

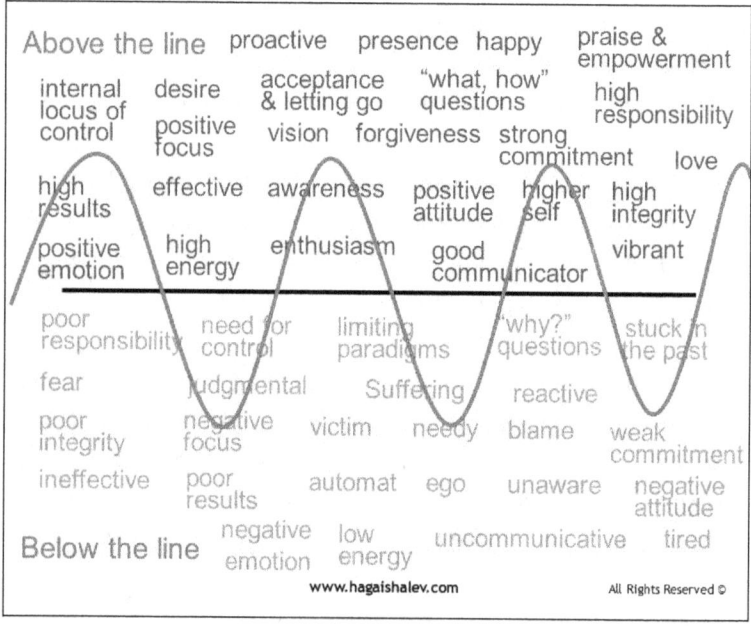

Above the line — proactive — presence — happy — praise & empowerment
internal locus of control — desire — acceptance & letting go — "what, how" questions — high responsibility
positive focus — vision — forgiveness — strong commitment — love
high results — effective — awareness — positive attitude — higher self — high integrity
positive emotion — high energy — enthusiasm — good communicator — vibrant

poor responsibility — need for control — limiting paradigms — "why?" questions — stuck in the past
fear — judgmental — Suffering — reactive
poor integrity — negative focus — victim — needy — blame — weak commitment
ineffective — poor results — automat — ego — unaware — negative attitude
Below the line — negative emotion — low energy — uncommunicative — tired

Diagram 3-2 – The Emotional Spectrum of the Average Person

Humans are like that too: one day we are successful, and the next day we're not. One moment we feel positive—*above the line*—and the next we feel negative—*below the line*. The red line in diagram 3-2 illustrates the emotional fluctuation of an average person. Sometimes they experience hours or days *above the line* and sometimes hours or days *below the line*, fluctuating between these two states with countless in-between states. For the sake of simplicity, we shall name the states *above the line* "positive" and the states *below the line* "negative." Accordingly, a person experiencing these states will either be in a *"positive state"* or in a *"negative state."*

Some people are generally in a negative state, so we shall refer to them as mostly *below the line*. These people usually have a negative response to *circumstances;* they are pessimistic, judgmental, skeptical, accusatory, often possess many limiting paradigms, are victims, are being led, are focused on what is not working in their lives, etc. The red line of people in a negative state is lower than that of the average person presented in diagram 3-2—see diagram 3-3.

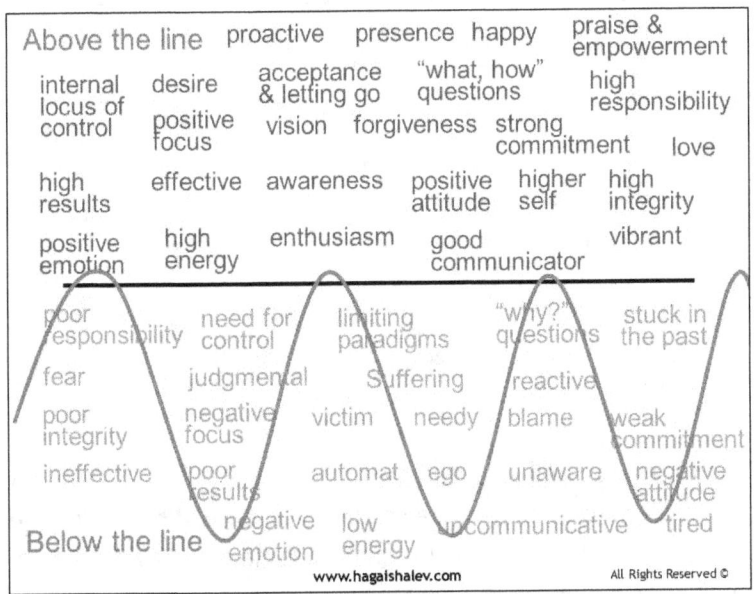

Diagram 3-3 – The Emotional Spectrum of a Person in a Negative State

In contrast, there are also people in a predominantly positive state, as illustrated in diagram 3-4. We shall refer to them as mostly *above the line*. These people usually feel positive, have high energy, communicate well with others, have a positive attitude and focus, tend to forgive quickly, etc. They possess most of the characteristics that are *above the line*. The red line of people in a positive state is higher than that of the average person presented in diagram 3-2—see diagram 3-4.

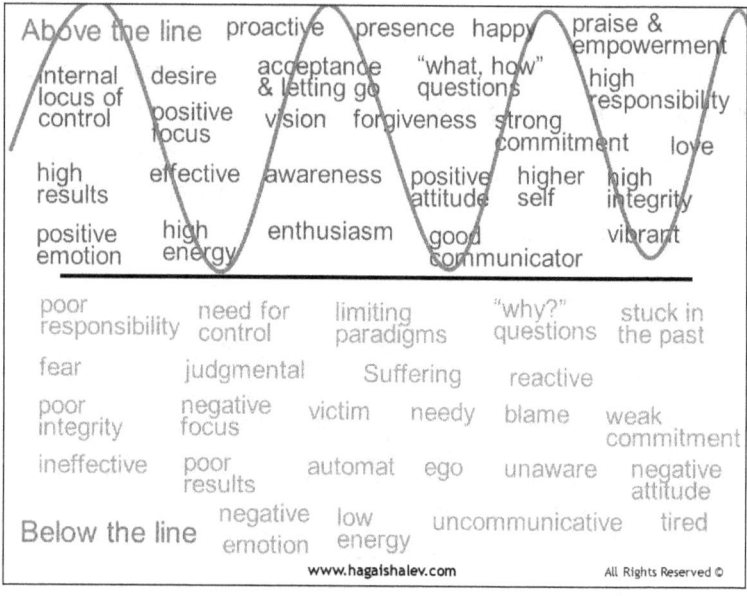

Diagram 3-4 – The Emotional Spectrum of a Person in a Positive State

Where Does All This Lead?

After understanding the characteristics of the **Third Key Principle** presented in this chapter (which most people are unaware of), we shall discuss how all this relates to success.

First, it's important to understand that the emotional sine wave (the red graph) of every person is not fixed but changeable. It's true that initial placement on the emotional spectrum is determined according to each person's personality, his upbringing, his surroundings, and the culture he lives in; however, every person can raise or lower the wave to be either *above the line* or *below the live* using his *TTT*.

Does that sound strange to you? I can relate. The paradigm we live in, based on our upbringing and culture, has taught us that our personality is fixed and unchangeable. Aside from the discouraging determinism of this paradigm—for if it's really true, we are the victims of our personalities—this paradigm is factually incorrect.

Here are two examples of why:

The **first** one is myself. In many ways, I am not the same person I was on the eve of my change in 2005. As I described in chapter one, from a judgmental, skeptical, and negative person, I have become an accepting, optimistic, and positive one; and if you don't believe me, you can ask my wife Osnat! That is, I managed to raise my wave and it is now way *above the line*. Like any person, I naturally have my ups and downs, but even my downs are a little *above the line*, or only slightly below it.

The **second** example is the research conducted by Dr. Bruce H. Lipton, an American biologist and scientist who researches the effect of our thoughts on our cells. His 2004 book, *The Biology of Belief*, outlines the essence of his theory. In a nutshell, Dr. Lipton discovered in his research that our beliefs affect our perception, which, in turn, affects our innate genetic code! Yes, this is no mistake: by changing our belief system, we can change the function of our genes! And if this holds true for our genes, why wouldn't we be able to change our behavioral and mental habits? Meaning, if you have habits and qualities that drag you *below the line*, you can change them and raise yourself *above the line*! This is the pure science of today, not some trendy spiritual method.

When I first heard about Dr. Lipton's research back in 2006, I sighed in relief, because if the common belief were true—that we inherit our parents' genes without being able to influence the way they function—where would our freedom of choice be? How would that correlate with humans' amazing aptitude for transformation as has been proven for generations?

How Does All of This Relate to Success?

This is where we draw the **second conclusion** from the *above and below the line* model, as illustrated in diagram 3-5:

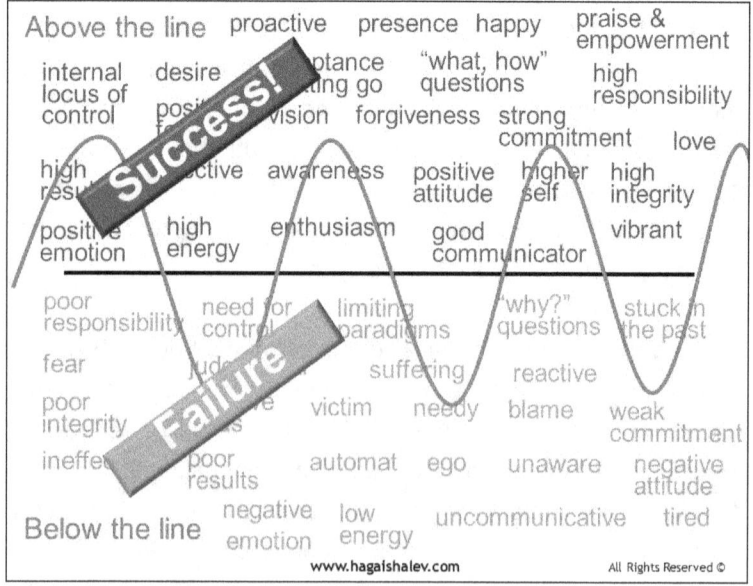

Diagram 3-5 – The Connection between the Emotional Spectrum and Success

There is a direct connection between where we are in relation to the line—above or below—and success and failure. It's apparent that people who are particularly negative, mostly *below the line*, are in a spot that makes it tough to succeed. We mentioned focus and attitude earlier as specific elements that affect success. Well, *below the line* there far more factors than just a negative attitude and focusing on the negative that prevent success and lead to failure. Here, we don't have the energy, communication skills, influence, or relationships required in order to succeed, to name a few.

On the other hand, being *above the line* is proven to ensure success. Here, our attitude and focus are positive, and we're proactive, show initiative, communicate well, experience more love, vigor, and enthusiasm, are effective in our work, have high awareness, etc. It's quite obvious how all these promote and bring about success.

So from now on, remember that in order to succeed, you need to aspire to live *above the line*; you must raise your emotional sine wave so that you find more *above the line* characteristics in your life to help you succeed. **The more you reach *above the line*, the more successful you will be in your life in general and in your business or career in particular.** In other words, I am referring to *change*; change your *TTT* in order to act with a *positive EYE* to create a better reality.

◆

I have already mentioned that change for the better, *above the line*, is attainable, and you are clearer now on why this book deals so thoroughly with change, encouraging you to open up to it: **because change paves the road to fulfillment and success.** It's as simple as that!

In this chapter, we discussed three key principles for success: the *focus principle*, the *attitude principle* and the *above the line principle*. We reviewed and learned the "automatic path" each principle represents—a path we automatically follow but which rarely serves us—and how choosing to consciously implement each principle will pave a road to success.

These are preliminary *tools* I am giving you in chapter three for immediate implementation. If you take each principle as is and implement it in your life, you will be able to bring about positive change right now and experience more success in your private life in general, as well as your business or management position in particular.

The question that's probably nagging you now is:

How do I do that? How do I overpower the automatic pilot and choose to implement these principles in reality, methodically and persistently over time?

This is the essence and objective of this book: to present to you the unique methodology I have developed to inspire an effective, result-producing change—*"The CO-OP Formula"*—and to guide you on how to apply it in your life so as to raise you *above the line* to reap success.

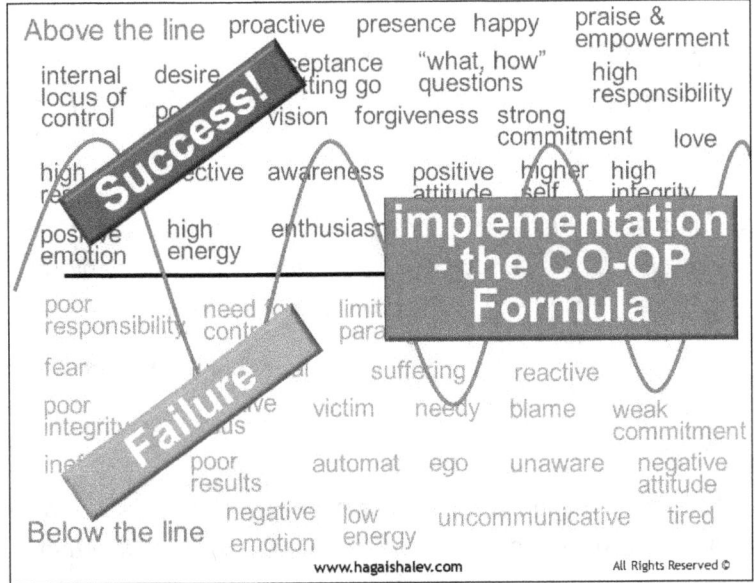

Diagram 3-6 – How to Rise Above the Line?

We will begin to discuss the *CO-OP Formula* in chapter seven; until then, let's deepen our understanding of the essence of transformation and create the foundation needed in order to implement the *CO-OP Formula* in a *positive EYE* and in the best, most successful way.

CHAPTER FOUR:
Why do most Attempts to Change Fail, and What are the Principles for Successful Transformation?

"The reasonable man adapts himself to the world; the unreasonable one persists in trying to adapt the world to himself. Therefore, all progress depends on the unreasonable man."

—George Bernard Shaw

In the previous chapters, you have seen why change is essential and received preliminary tools to perform a positive change that yields results. If you are like most people, you're probably experiencing butterflies in your stomach right now. The *program* is trying to maintain "autopilot" mode at any cost, so as to avoid transitioning into a "manual" mode that is more aware and has a *positive EYE*. Moreover, your *human operating system* is automatically resisting the change. It perceives change as a real threat, as real as any threat to your survival; it produces doubt and fears, a transformation-sabotaging chemistry, and in doing so hinders the process of transformation. This is where most changes fail; people give up and go back to the comforting, known, and familiar *program*.

But not you!

You are here with me in this book, and in this chapter you will learn five principles that will enable you to successfully undergo your process of transformation. By applying these principles, you will be able to overcome your built-in resistance to change, successfully cope with the mental challenge entailed by transformation, and begin to pursue it in your own life.

I shall present the five principles using five diagrams, since a picture is worth a thousand words.

From Anticipated Future to Desired Future

The process of undergoing transformation in general, and a breakthrough[24] in particular, is illustrated in diagram 4-1:

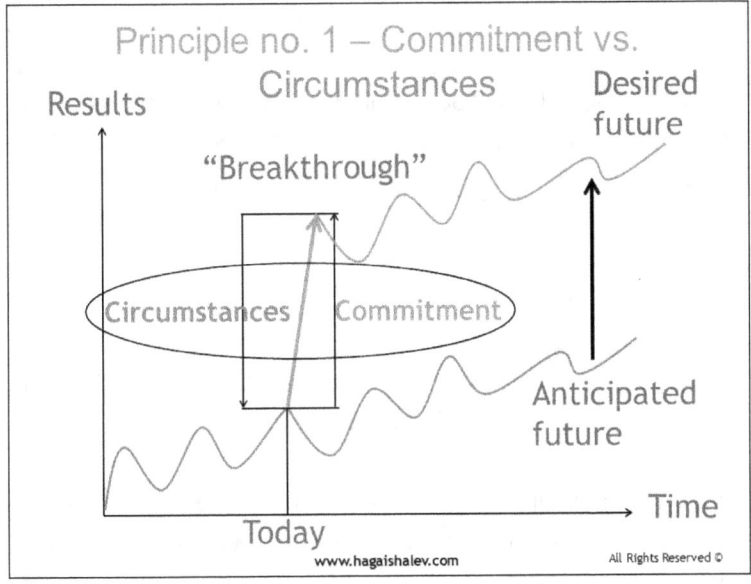

Diagram 4-1 – Principle number 1 for undergoing a successful transformation process

---

24 "Breakthrough" is a type of transformation. It describes an ambitious, dramatic leap in results in a relatively short time period, while declaring such intention **in advance**. I strongly believe that a breakthrough transformation is the best way to set goals and achieve them. I shall expand on this term in chapter 11.

Let's focus only on the red line for a moment. The line in the sine wave increases, showing people's standard progression along the time axis. It has two main characteristics:

First: it has ups and downs, expressing the fluctuations we usually find in human action. As I mentioned before, everything in nature moves according to the sine pattern: day and night, seasons of the year, ebb and flow, life cycles, etc. So do we humans, experience emotional, mental, and physical fluctuations, all according to this pattern.

Second: the red line is on a rise from left to right, showing us how people constantly progress and improve over time thanks to their accumulated knowledge and greater experience. As a rule, one can say that people in general and businesses in particular usually achieve better results as they move further along the time axis.

However, the red line doesn't reflect a change in our daily routine. It assumes "business as usual," therefore reflecting our "anticipated future" on its right end—that is, where we are expected to arrive if we continue our current conduct.

Those wishing for a higher level of results in the future are required to change their thinking and conduct in order to depart from the *automatic programing* and reach their desired futures. The top portion of the diagram reflects this change: It shows that during a "breakthrough" transformation, the red line hikes up according to the black right arrow and turns into a green line. This was accomplished due to a sharp, dramatic hike in results during a relatively short time period, as is reflected in the green arrow pointing upward. Suddenly, the green graph points to a new area of opportunities that leads us to our "desired future," with a higher level of results at any given point in the future. It is clear that such a transformation enables us to reach a future that wasn't attainable before the transformation.

The Wondrous Lift Force

Let's examine the major forces applied in such a transformation. The two thin black arrows in diagram 4-1 reflect these forces: The thin arrow pointing upward is the **Lift Force**. This force relies on our **commitment**, which motivates us to reach a breakthrough. This force is what helps us find the power and emotional strength to make a change. Churchill once said, "The price of greatness is responsibility." Indeed, taking responsibility for our lives and committing to change is a strong, powerful catalyst for making that change.

◆

I would like to take a moment to ponder the word "responsibility." In Western culture, and especially in businesses, when we ask, "Who is responsible for so and so?" we immediately become alert and the automatic question, "Who is to blame?" comes up, because the common interpretation for "responsibility" is blame. Who is responsible = who can be blamed. This, unfortunately, is one of the biggest, most blatant examples of injustice in the interpretation of a word. In fact, the word "responsibility" has nothing to do whatsoever with blame. On the contrary, one of Oxford dictionary's definitions of the word "responsibility" (relevant to our discussion) is "a moral obligation to behave correctly towards or in respect of."

This means that responsibility enables us to maintain a moral or social principle. Furthermore, "responsibility" is a compound made up of the words "response" and "ability;" that is, the **ability to choose a response.** I really like the following quote by Dr. Deepak Chopra, which beautifully sums up the proper definition of the word "responsibility": "Responsibility means not blaming anyone or anything for your situation, including yourself. Having accepted this circumstance, this event, this problem, responsibility then means the **ability to have a creative response** to the situation as it is now."

◆

Going back to commitment: everyone has experienced incidents in their lives where "failure was not an option;" situations where you found great strength to achieve extraordinary results. The parents among us will certainly be able to remember such situations among the things we have done for our children.

The change I underwent in 2005 was one such situation. I so desperately **did not** want to return to the wasteland of being a hired employee; I did not want to face myself or the world and admit that I had given up, or even worse, failed. So much so that I discovered incredible emotional strength that pushed me to cope with changing careers, overcoming the challenges that lay before me, and breaking through to a new road in both my personal and professional life. Furthermore, after working with nearly a thousand clients, I can easily check off **commitment** as one of the key factors to success. Ever since I started on my new path in 2006, I have made sure to measure my clients' success rates. It's a simple index—how many of them have reached their goals and declared that the coaching process was successful? Well, the overall success rate of my clients is about 70%. "Great," I told myself, "And what about the remaining 30%? What is preventing the remaining 30% from succeeding? What is missing there?"

Over the years, I have discovered that there is one main answer to it: **the remaining 30% lacked commitment.** They lacked the willingness to cope with the challenges ahead and lacked the willingness to do whatever it takes to reach a breakthrough in their lives. This is the main reason why their process of transformation did not yield the anticipated outcome.

◆

So from now on, remember that commitment is an essential ingredient in undergoing any transformation or fulfillment, let alone in experiencing a breakthrough. There are no better words than those of Abraham Lincoln to end this subchapter: "Commitment is what transforms a promise into reality. It is the words that speak boldly of your intentions. And the actions which speak louder than the words. It is making the time when there is none. Coming through time after time after time, year after year after year. Commitment is the stuff character is made of; the power to change the face of things. It is the daily triumph of integrity over skepticism."

The Force that Intercepts Commitment

Still, in making a change there is an **Intercepting Force** that inhibits change and keeps us in the status quo. This intercepting force is what I call *circumstances*. *Circumstances* intercept *commitment* and the intention for change; all those stories and excuses we tell ourselves about why we do not make a change. Here are a few examples:

"I'm too young/old."
"It's not the right time."
"I don't have enough money."

"I don't have enough time."

"My boss doesn't allow me."

"It's impossible."

"Tomorrow/next month/next year will be more suitable."

"You can't do business in this country."

"When the economy is slow you have to be more cautious."

And so on and so forth...

All of these are really inner voices[25] in our *operating system* that resist change. They come up automatically, the outcome of evolutionary survival roots, and express an unconscious, *below the line* emotional reaction. I have seen people come up with *circumstances* that intercept their *commitment* to change so many times, when I know (and they do too) that choosing to let *circumstances* take over is wrong.

Any process of transformation pits our *commitment* against our *circumstances*. In the conflict between the two, only when the *commitment* is stronger than the *circumstances* does the lift force overpower the intercepting force and allow the transformation to take place. The challenge of those undergoing the transformation, then, is to strengthen their *commitment* and weaken their *circumstances* so that the increasing *commitment* can forge ahead to carry out the transformation and lead to a breakthrough.

When I work with clients on making changes, and *commitment* overrides *circumstances*, extraordinary things happen and the clients achieve incredible results. This observation may be

---

25 In my work, I use an excellent tool that helps manage these negative inner voices; I call it "the ego and the higher self." I will review this tool for you in chapter 13.

simplistic, yet it is precise, clear, and powerfully effective. I invite you to use it when undergoing your own transformation.

Before we sum up the first principle for undergoing transformation, here is a brief note: the leap between the red graph and the green graph may seem as if it's happening all at once in the diagram, but it is not so simple. In fact, as with most changes in nature, even a sudden breakthrough is an evolutionary transformation that takes place gradually over time, step by step.

◆

There is no better quote than George Bernard Shaw's to close this subchapter:

"People are always blaming their circumstances for what they are. I don't believe in circumstances. The people who get on in this world are the people who get up and look for the circumstances they want, and if they can't find them, make them."

So Cozy It Gets Prosy and You Want to Mosey

Diagram 4-2 reflects the second principle of undergoing a successful process of transformation: **in order to undergo successful transformation, you must move out of your comfort zone.** The comfort zone is where we spend our daily routine. Here, all is familiar, known, safe and cozy. Seemingly a great place to be! But routine eventually wears you down; the comfort zone becomes boring; the psyche in the comfort zone yearns for change, growth, and development.

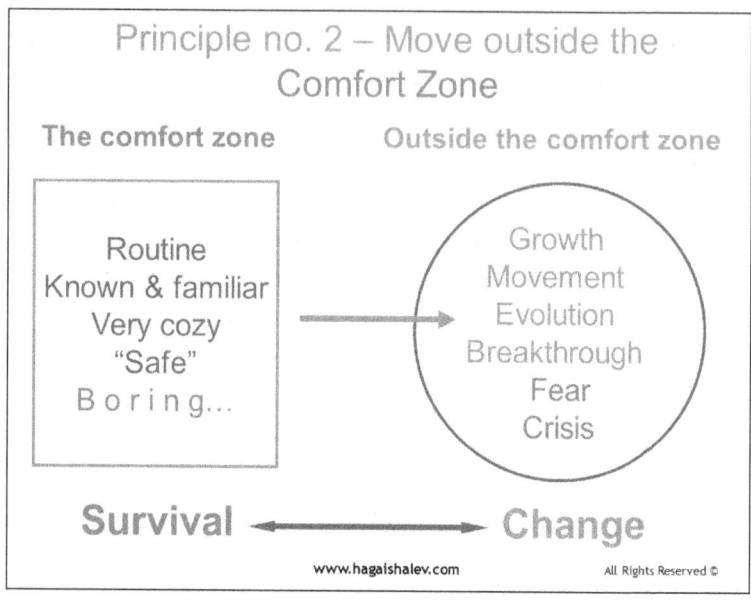

Diagram 4-2–Principle number 2 for undergoing a successful transformation process

On the one hand, our tendency to remain in the comfort zone is founded on a strong, primal survival instinct. From our days as prehistoric man living in forest clearings, we knew we were safe there. We knew that every venture outside the clearing exposed us to enemies, natural disasters, predators, and danger. Therefore, we didn't leave the clearing very often, and when we did it was usually in a group. Thus, although the "forest clearing" has changed quite a bit, and the "dangers" lurking outside it are no longer that existential, the *automatic program* and the evolutionary roots still rule us and control us for the most part. They spread doubt and fear, tempting us to remain in the warm and cozy boundaries of our comfort zone.

On the other hand, as we discussed at length in chapter two, transformation is nature's way, and we as humans are part of nature. Therefore, the **drive for change** is embedded in us and is reflected in every aspect of our modern world. Change leaves its mark on every area of our life, increasingly affecting us as time progresses; simply look back at where we were a hundred years ago if you want an example of the accelerated system of changes humankind has since undergone.

There is, then, an ongoing conflict within people between the tendency and desire to remain in their comfort zones, and the drive for change. They cannot coexist, and so we must choose between them, which is no easy decision to make; for unaware people, it is nearly impossible, as their default is usually to stick to their *automatic program* and stay in their comfort zone.

Incidentally, the comfort zone is considered a safe place, when in fact its sense of safety is an illusion. As we discussed in chapter two, when the world around us changes, we cannot remain stagnant, and fixation on the comfort zone guarantees a disruption in our routine and the potential for crisis. If we consider an employee, for example, his comfort zone is his current workplace. At first glance, he seems to have employment security and can sleep soundly. However, in our ever-changing modern world, this security is an illusion. Macroeconomic changes, market fluctuations, frequent changes in trends, and bad management often lead businesses down a slippery slope and cause major layoffs. Similarly, even mega corporations such as Kodak, Nokia, Microsoft, and others fire employees as part of their default response when their business activity drops. More often than not, an employee in his forties or older who has been laid off finds it hard to get rehired. At times, he has to reinvent himself if he wants to make a decent living working in a field that fits his skills and desires. The sense of security in the comfort zone, then, is mostly an illusion.

In summation, in order to undergo change and adapt ourselves to the ever-changing environment, we must overcome the survival instinct that is blocking us and be willing to leave our comfort zone. We must think, feel, and do things differently than we would within the comfort zone. We need to connect to our true power, overcome doubt and fear, be daring, and confront challenges and crises. Although a crisis may happen within the comfort zone, its resolution will always be found outside the comfort zone.

I shall close this subchapter with a rhetorical question by Robin Sharma:

"The place where your greatest fears live is also the place where your greatest growth lies. Why would you ever run away from that?"

What Don't We Know That We Don't Know?

"We are all wise, all elders, all learned in Torah."
From The Passover Haggadah

In the realm of personal development, the following distinction is made between three worlds of knowledge[26]:

1. What we know.

2. What we know we don't know.

3. What we don't know that we don't know.

---

26 For the sake of simplicity, I shall use the following abbreviations later in the chapter: K for what we know, DK for what we know we don't know, and DK DK for what we don't know we don't know. There are a few versions to this knowledge model; I chose the one that is most relevant to us.

This distinction has immense significance in terms of our ability to change, as we shall see, and constitutes the **third principle element of undergoing a successful process of transformation.**

What we know (K) fills up our being and daily life. This is where our focus lies, this is the work world we know, and this is where our paradigms and our comfort zone lie. When we base our TTT on what we already know, we create time and time again the same known and familiar reality. Hence, it's clear that our current world of knowledge, as big as it may be, doesn't create change.

Even the areas we know we don't know (DK) present a relatively small potential for change, one which we would call a *first order change.* Firstly, most people avoid acquiring new, meaningful knowledge after they have completed their formal and college education, thus essentially remaining within the boundaries of their existing knowledge (K). Secondly, those who do expand their knowledge and study frequently still remain within the limitations of the known and defined, evolving into a largely predictable, limited reality. This argument does not in any way diminish the importance of learning, which is always desirable and laudable, but only sets the stage for a greater degree of transformation—a *second order change*, as we shall see below. Learning something new we don't know (DK) is an expression of a normal process of growth and development in our culture; however, this process usually doesn't express humans' full growth potential. This is because the portion we don't know usually represents only a segment of that unknown knowledge—that which we know we don't know (DK). For example, I am not familiar with medicine, nuclear physics or a hundred other disciplines, and while I am aware of this, if my heart so desires I can study these disciplines while undergoing a rather apparent and defined change.

"To know what you know and what you do not know...that is true knowledge"—Confucius

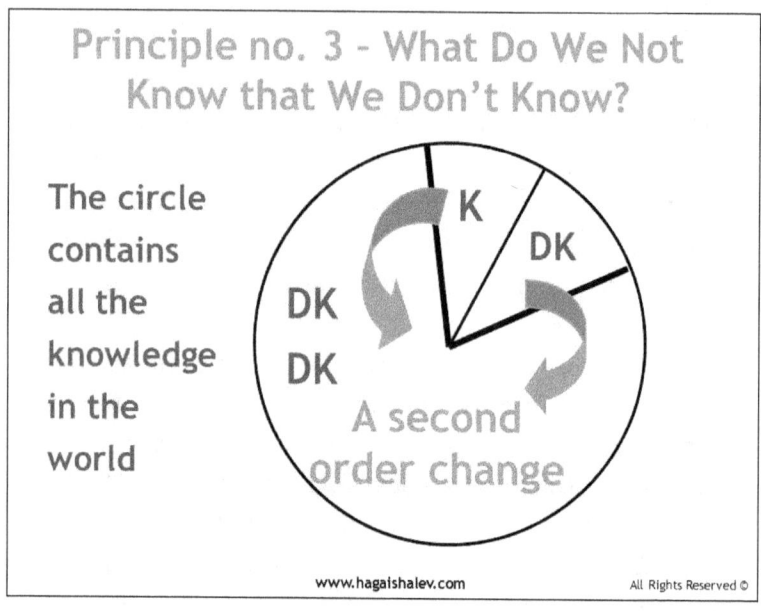

Diagram 4-3—Principle number 3 for undergoing a successful transformation process

As diagram 4-3 illustrates, the true potential for change lies in the third area of knowledge, that which we don't know that we don't know (DK DK). Notice that the first two segments (K, DK) cover only a small area of the entire world of knowledge. There is a vast amount of knowledge which we don't know, and which we are unaware of not knowing (DK DK). Sounds complicated? Read it a few times over and think about how many times you discovered (usually by chance) something new you didn't even know existed. Remember how you were suddenly faced with new, unexpected opportunities, so that the intensity of the change was stronger and more significant in your life than a *first rate change*.

This was the case with me when I happened upon the area of personal development in 2005. Suddenly, I found a whole wide world close to my heart that I didn't even know existed, one which deals with how humans act, think, and are motivated or inhibited; what affects their relationships with others, their attitudes, their ability to overcome hardship and challenges, their ability to change, their self-confidence and self-belief, and finally, their ability to achieve results!

The discovery and study of the field of personal development enabled me to make a breakthrough in my career and move from a hired CFO to a self-employed business coach, develop my methodology, and ultimately write this book. It is no doubt a *second order change*.

This is also how great breakthroughs in human history came to be: how Archimedes unintentionally discovered density while in the tub, how Fleming discovered Penicillin, or how the apple fell on Newton's head under the tree, which led to the discovery of gravitational force. These coincidences led to unexpected discoveries that arose from the third area of knowledge: what we don't know that we don't know (DK DK). That is to say, by being open and committed to departing from defined areas of knowledge, we can discover new worlds we didn't know even existed. This in itself enables us to break the boundaries of our life's paradigms and discover new realms that are the essence of any substantial *second order change*. It is worth noting that this approach is challenging for most people, who prefer certainty, but it is precisely through letting go of certainty and adopting a "not knowing" approach, and sometimes even embracing chaos, that true discoveries are made and opportunities for incredible transformation present themselves.

Therefore, in order to make a *second order change*, and a *breakthrough* in particular, you should come from a place not knowing, of letting go and even chaos, and only then seek the worlds of knowledge unknown to you and which you are unaware of not knowing.

Integrating Doing and Being

"Success comes before work only in the dictionary," said Vidal Sassoon. Indeed, our society respects and values entrepreneurship and proactiveness. We acknowledge people who have done everything by themselves, who have excelled in their work and made great achievements. However, **hard work is not the only ingredient in success.** Think for a moment; do you know diligent business owners who didn't succeed? Or the opposite—business owners who didn't work hard but did succeed? I am sure you know some of both. This shows that there is another factor, aside from *Doing*, that is crucial to making a change and getting on the road to success.

This factor is *Being*.

It's not **what** business owners and managers alone do that will determine their success, but **how** will they do it. What is their emotional state while *Doing*? Are they frustrated, fearful and anxious? What are the habits that lie at the core of their *Doing*? Do they possess habits that impede them, such as procrastination and perfectionism? What are the limiting beliefs at their very core, which sabotage their logic, diligence, and hard work? For example, do they wholeheartedly believe in their ability to sell their products with adequate success?

We discussed this at length in the *Fulfillment Pyramid* model in chapter two, emphasizing the importance of **Being** in fulfillment and success. In this chapter, we will emphasize the integration of **Being** and **Doing** as the basis for any successful change.

A successful process of transformation is illustrated in diagram 4-4:

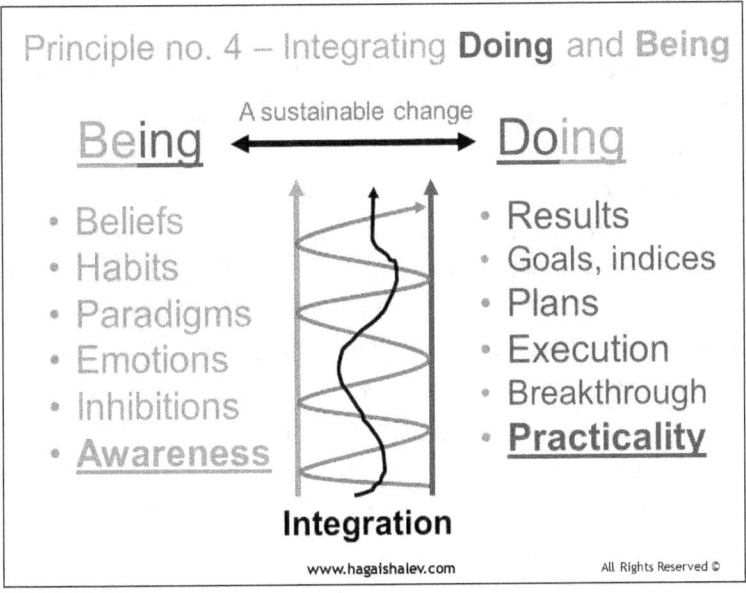

Diagram 4-4—Integration of Being and Doing

On the one hand, while undergoing a process of transformation, we aspire to **logical, practical Doing,** reflected on the right side of the diagram: goal-setting, assigning performance indices, planning and then executing the plan. There is no argument regarding the importance of these things. On the other hand, focusing on the right side of the diagram alone usually will not lead us to our destination. Why? Because we all agree that humans are complex creatures; we have beliefs, habits, paradigms, fears, and other dire straits that impede our success. These inhibitions are reflected on the left side of the diagram, which expresses out

mental side. Ignoring them usually causes delays our advance along the right axis, wasting energy and achieving poor results; "running on empty," as they say.

The Solution: Integrating the Doing Components and the Being Components.

The red line in diagram 4-4 illustrates how to apply this principle to change with a *positive EYE*: staying true to practical needs, we will start on the right side of the diagram, with actual *Doing—* **practicality**. However, the moment we get stuck, we will move left to the **Awareness** side to pinpoint and uproot the impeding factor so we can cheerfully return to the right, practical side, advancing on the road of *Doing* towards the results. Nevertheless, the day is near when we might experience inhibition and impediment again. This is when we return to *Being* on the left in order to release the next mental block before continuing with our plan on the right practical side. And on we go, back and forth, until we reach fulfillment at the top of the right blue arrow. The red line reflects the integration between *Doing* and *Being*, meaning that only an integration between the *Doing* side and the *Being* side can enable a sustainable change that will lead us to the fulfillment of our goals and of our human potential. In chapter two, we presented *Being* as a stage prior to *Doing* in the *Fulfillment Pyramid* model. Here we present them as two **parallel** components. Why is it different? Well, the *Fulfillment Pyramid* is the more precise model. Nonetheless, my experience has taught me that when we proceed to implement the change on a practical level, the best way is the **integrative way**.

I shall further explain this: as human beings brought up on the foundations of *Doing*, it is important for us to show achievements as soon as possible. These achievements, located on the right side of the diagram, constitute the fuel that motivates the **Doing** process. Besides, it's more effective to handle the **Being** components of the *operating system* in succession and, when between one component and the other, we can experience the meaning of each component in reality through our results, shown on the right side of the diagram.

Therefore, as said, the integrative model of **Doing** and **Being** presented here is the recommended way to implementing a constant, sustainable change.

The uniqueness of this book is illustrated in the zigzagging line between the axes—the one that connects them. This is where the **balance** between the *Doing* and *Being* is achieved, where the not-so-obvious integration between the two extremes on the human map is attained. The unique methodology of the **CO-OP Formula** will show us the way to connect them starting in chapter seven.

What could be more fitting than to close this subchapter with words by the poet and philosopher, Goethe: "Before you can do *something* you must *first be something.*"

When You Are in the Zone, You Express Your Full Tone

"You cannot teach a man anything, you can only help him find it within himself"

—Galileo Galilei

The expression "to be in the zone" used by the NBA league describes the player's state of being when everything is going his way: he shoots precisely, passes the ball expertly, reads his opponent's moves like a book, and in general takes the game upon himself and leads his team to victory. I am certain you have experienced situations in your life where everything went smoothly—you were at your best, in your *zone*, and achieved amazing results. I have experienced these moments when giving a great speech at a lecture or in private coaching sessions, not knowing where these words came from, as if the entire universe spoke through me and helped me express myself to the best of my ability.

To me, the goal of any process of transformation is to identify and become familiar with your *zone*, the place where you fulfill your life's purpose, and stay there **permanently.** This is where the challenge begins, because most of us don't know what our life's purpose is or where the heck our *zone* is.

Diagram 4-5—Principle number 5 in undergoing a successful transformation process

Diagram 4-5 Illustrates That:

We begin our adult life at a certain point on the white spiral, close to the sides of the square. Then we begin to search for our *zone*, the white spot in the middle. This is where we connect to the core of our existence, where we live out life's purpose, utilize all of our skills and abilities, love what we do, fulfill our aspirations, are highly driven and enthusiastic—where everything is going our way and we are happy. The good news is that throughout the course of our lives, we come close to the *zone*, as illustrated by the white spiral in the diagram, and some of us even find it at a relatively young age. These are people who know what their life's purpose is and work diligently and vigorously to achieve it. Yet, many others spend their whole life searching for their *zone*.

Hence, knowing your personal *zone* is an important principle in your ability to bring about a successful change. A person who don't know what his *zone* is may spend time, energy, and a lot of money searching his way through life, going on a rough journey with limited achievements.

On the other hand, a person who knows his *zone* is connected to a vision, a purpose, values, dreams, and his true desire. All these create an excellent foundation on which to build a successful, effective change. For instance, when I discovered my *zone* in 2006—helping business owners fulfill their business potential—I was filled with desire, courage, and the faith that anything is possible, and these fueled my process of transformation and self-actualization.

The conclusion is that in order to undergo a successful transformation, you should first open up to discover the true place within that brings you fulfillment, satisfaction, and happiness, and then persistently aim to reach it.

◆

To sum up this chapter, a successful process of transformation should rely on the following five principles:

1. Be open and committed to the transformation process and don't let *circumstances* make decisions for you.

2. Move out of your *comfort zone*, give up the survival strategy, and take risks.

3. Be open and willing to go to unknown places which you don't know you don't know, and be open and curious so you can identify them.

4. Integrate **Doing** with **Being**.

5. Define your **Zone** and actively aim for it.

The words of French author Marcel Proust brilliantly express the main message of this chapter: "The real voyage of discovery consists not in seeking new landscapes, but in having new eyes."

These five principles teach you and illustrate what it's like to view your reality through new eyes—by being more aware, abandoning the *autopilot*, and paving a path of change, with a *positive EYE*, towards fulfillment and success. If you apply these five principles, you will create a fertile ground for change in which your seeds of transformation will be planted successfully and your tree of life shall flourish and thrive.

◆

In the following chapter, I shall examine the process of transformation via one of my favorite metaphors: the vehicle model. With this metaphor, I shall sum up everything that we have learned so far, as well as use it to demonstrate the rest of our journey of change in the chapters thereafter.

CHAPTER FIVE:
From Two Wheels to Four Wheels

"Rescue" = "Secure"

Many times in life, specific events are harbingers announcing deeper processes to follow. In this chapter, I wish to share with you a life-changing event I experienced, using it as an example that will enable you to successfully undergo your own transformation. This is to save you from having to experience your own life-changing event, which may be traumatic at times.

Such was the event I experienced on May 18th, 2005. That day, I barely survived a road accident with my red Piaggio Vespa at a major highway interchange, and was rushed to the hospital in an ambulance. I had a right shoulder separation at the AC joint and had to undergo surgery and shoulder rehabilitation in the months that followed.

It was a life-changing event for me.

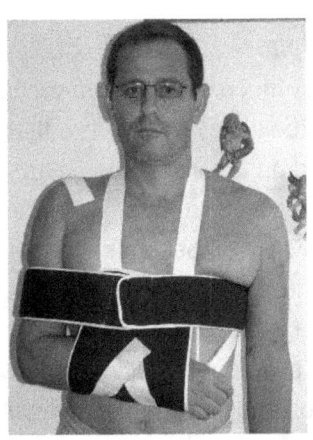

After 22 years, I gave up the Vespa and **switched from driving two wheels to driving four** wheels—a car. Later that year, I also gave up my profession of 22 years as a CPA and CFO. These identical numbers indicate that these two events were not coincidental. That accident foreshadowed the change that was upon me: on the day of my accident, I was on my way to a job interview for a CFO position in another company and in the same field I had worked in and gotten bored with. In retrospect, it is ironic that the accident actually "curbed" me from repeating the same mistake.

This was a major wakeup call for me, a clue I failed to see at the time of the accident. Furthermore, the physical switch from two wheels to four wheels has a corresponding aspect in the realm of consciousness, as you shall see later on in the chapter.

Since the accident, I have learned that anything is possible, both in speedy physical rehabilitation as well as making career and life changes and in fulfilling my purpose. Very often, great changes begin with transformative events, such as that accident in 2005, a negative event which ultimately paved the way to enhancing my life!

The Vehicle Metaphor

I like metaphors very much. They are an excellent tool to help you to think outside the box; they are the few that hold the many and enable us to expand our perspectives so as to better understand life's situations. Moreover, metaphors are memorable, and so serve us well in conveying messages effectively. I have employed several metaphors in previous chapters. In chapter two, I introduced the computer metaphor, from which I borrowed the term *Operating System* I so frequently use. In chapter one, I mentioned the vehicle metaphor, and first noted my transition from two to four wheels. Further along this chapter, I will elaborate on the vehicle metaphor in order to illustrate and clarify a comprehensive transformation process. The metaphor will cover both the components of change we have already discussed earlier, as well as those we will discuss in the following chapters.

A Brand New Car

We all know the feeling of a brand new car. That excitement when you receive and experience something completely new, still wrapped in the manufacturer's plastic. All the senses come into play here, including the fresh scent in the car and its shiny color, which illicit in us a strong, positive emotional reaction. So are we, humans, the moment after we're born: everything is new and fresh, all the systems are tuned and sharp, everything runs like clockwork, simply perfect! That new baby smell is intoxicating, our potential is full, set and ready, well prepared to travel through the vicissitudes of life. All the filters are clean, not a speck of dust, clear water, pure oil, pollution-free carburetor, and an engine roaring a harmonious, clear note. As kids, we are invincible, anything is within our reach! Our "driver," our awareness, or what we sometimes call the human spirit or soul, are new and untrained in driving, but are curious and enthusiastic, and concentrate more on challenges and learning than on difficulties and fears.

But then the vehicle begins to drive long distances. Slowly but surely, all of its systems begin to experience wear and tear. It needs service, tune-up, cleaning, repairs and other forms of maintenance in order to preserve its driving and transport capacities. The systems that were once so sharp and effective when new begin to screech and shift out of balance. The vehicle gets old, consumes more fuel, emits more smoke, eats more oil, gets banged around, scratched up, loses color, and sometimes even gets into accidents.

So do the kids growing up; they begin to travel on the paths of life, experiencing landscapes and sights, some magnificent and some less so. Their home and other living environments leave impressions on them, trials and tribulations; they fill up with paradigms, limiting beliefs, negative emotions, and habits which do not always serve them.

The infinite potential they had when they unwrapped the plastic is ragged and repressed. Life's trials hit them again and again, eating away at their perfection and purity. The wear and tear increases, causing the vehicle to lose its performance. All these put a spoke in their wheels.

I have already mentioned in chapter three how limited parenting styles among most parents harm their children's ability to fulfill their potential. In the vehicle model, this was the environmental influences that hindered the vehicle's performance. Yes, in many ways this is inevitable, since everything in nature has a life cycle along which it withers and dies. However, does our "vehicle" receive the "optimal" service throughout its lifetime, which will slow down its depreciation and extend its life despite its natural aging? I'm afraid the answer here is "no." Most car owners neglect their vehicles, skimping on maintenance and quality parts, thus accelerating the vehicle's depreciation and reducing its performance.

Would You Pass the Driving Test Today?

You're probably familiar with the expression used for experienced drivers: "With that driving style you'd never pass a driving test today!" How many of us drivers remember the meaning of all the traffic signs? How many of us maintain safe distance, a crucial rule that prevents the number of road accidents? This is to show that as drivers of a vehicle, we tend to forget rules and cut corners on the road. The same goes for our conduct in life.

Moreover, most people don't "drive their vehicle" with all four wheels. Similar to how I used to "drive my vehicle" using only the two left wheels of rationality and practicality, other people use their "strong wheels" and tend to neglect the others. Naturally, their ability to maneuver and advance are limited, if not absent entirely; but it's usually hard to notice that from the driver's seat. Just like the driver who sometimes doesn't notice that his car is running out of gas, getting overheated, or even has a flat tire! He simply doesn't "sense" the vehicle or dashboard.

The same applies to our journey through life. We have a conscious mind and an unconscious mind, but most of us only know how to use the conscious mind, thus not fulfilling the entire gamut of our vehicle's capabilities[27]. Another, even more common distinction, is that which differentiates between the right brain and the left brain. The left brain governs the properties of rationality, realism, intelligence (consider—intellectualism), logic, attention to detail, and the *Doing*. This was my strong brain before my transformation— the two left wheels my vehicle operated with. And while these are good, strong wheels that carried me far up the ladder of my career and fulfillment, they required constant maneuvering, hard work, even expertise, only allowing me to partially fulfill my potential. In contrast, every vehicle also has two right wheels, analogous to our right brain. This brain governs all the emotions, awareness, creativity, big picture thinking, intuition, and the *Being*. In retro-

---

27 I shall expand more about the unconscious mind in chapter six, but I must mention here that the unconscious mind includes, among other things, our beliefs, habits, and memories.

spect, only when my professional path had reached a dead-end on the *Doing* side and I added the two right wheels, i.e., the *Being* side, did I realize how much my driving had been limited.

As said, most of us don't use all of our vehicle's wheels; that is to say, we fail to integrate all parts of our brain, and so the quality, range, and speed of our journey are compromised. This is also considered a "violation of driving rules"—the rules of nature, since nature aspires to optimize resources and combine all of nature's available resources at any given time.

And so an accident is sometimes needed, both figuratively and physically (as I have experienced) in order to create change, improve one's limited function, and fulfill one's human potential to its fullest. It is a wakeup call or life-altering experience that shuffles all the cards and promotes change. Unfortunately, instead of checking on the car in time for an overall tune-up, most people wait for a crisis, an accident, and sometimes a total loss before they realize that they need to make a change in their lives, as I have experienced firsthand. The good news is that if we put the cost aside for a moment, there is always an alternative that upgrades both the vehicle and the driving experience, even if it means buying a new car sometimes. The same goes for any changes in life.

Expanding the Metaphor – Vehicle Breakdown Versus Life's Challenges

Let's delve into other meanings in our vehicle metaphor by examining the parallels of a vehicle or driver breakdown in real life. The following table draws a comparison between the two. The point of this comparison is to illuminate and illustrate our automatic conduct. Through this comparison, we first and foremost become aware of our vehicle's automatic steering as a precursor to learning how to release this *autopilot* function in the next chapters by making choices with a *positive EYE*:

	The allegory – the vehicle or driver breakdown or roadblocks:	The moral of the story – Life's challenges
1	We are tempted by the comfort of modern driving accessories, such as automatic transmission and cruise control, and sometimes "fall asleep on duty" while driving and are not alert enough to respond to changing road conditions.	We live on autopilot mode, dwelling in our comfort zone and unaware of our need or ability to change with the changing *circumstances* around us.
2	We use the wrong fuel or diluted fuel offered to us in gas stations.	The "fuel" in our life is our thoughts (More about it in chapter ten.) We tend to get stuck in loops of negative thoughts that encumber our conduct in life.
3	The vehicle's steering wheel isn't calibrated and pulls the vehicle off the road.	People tend to get side tracked from the goals and plans they set for themselves, and are not persistent or determined enough; sometimes they go astray.
4	The road conditions are tough.	Life's *circumstances* are challenging.
5	Worn out or deflated tires lead to a waste of fuel, delay our arrival, and cause a hazard of slipping.	Ineffective human conduct, wasted energy, delayed achievement of goals, inability to resist temptations, diversion from goals.
6	There is no spare tire, or it's not inflated, or the jack/lug wrench is defective—all these pose a risk of getting stranded.	People get stranded in life because they didn't plan ahead—they don't have enough alternatives to cope with unexpected hiccups in life, they have no financial reserves.

7	Careless driving diverts attention from the road and leads to accidents: using cell phones, speeding, drunk driving, and disobeying driving rules.	Poor habits, *circumstances*, and events around us distract us from focusing on our life's purpose. Hence, we don't use our full capability, our results suffer, and crises sometimes occur.
8	Drivers who look in the rear view mirror too often are delayed in their progression.	People who spend too much time and focus looking back into the past. This keeps them stuck in the past and *below the line*, preventing them from focusing on the future and the objectives ahead.
9	When driving at night, the headlights only shine about 50 meters ahead and the rest of the road is dark. Still, the drivers rely on road signs, maps and GPS to reach their destination.	Coping with the uncertainty of the future: we usually don't see the entire path to our goals. Therefore, we must trust the predetermined route while focusing on the nearest visible milestones.
10	With physical fatigue there is a risk of falling asleep while driving.	Physical and mental fatigue drags us *below the line*, hinders our sharpness and vitality when performing tasks, and delays the achievement of goals.
11	Other car malfunctions: out of tune engine, engine burning oil, water leakage, pollution, and more.	Negative emotions drag us *below the line*, depleting our energy and our ability to succeed and prosper.
12	Malfunctions in the transmission gear, the vehicle gets stuck on low gear, or the gears don't shift smoothly.	Difficulty moving on to the next stage in life; blockage!

We can see that there are many similarities between us and our vehicle. The comparison table above mirrors and sharpens your daily conduct and opens up the possibility of expanding your awareness to your *automatic* functions so that you can make changes to them.

Don't Judge a Book by Its Cover

Are you familiar with the bumper sticker: "Old hag, but ahead of you!" Well, some vehicles look old and beaten up, but they last for years, are super reliable, and are cheap to maintain. Those vehicles are in high demand in the used car market and are said to have a good resale value. This is because what sets the price of a vehicle is not necessarily its look, but its functionality: the manufacturer, durability, cost of maintenance, and, of course, its performance and engine quality.

Similarly, people's physical appearance doesn't necessarily indicate their success. It's not the car model, the house, or the clothing brand that necessarily indicate success or lack of. Take Warren Buffet for example: he is considered the best investor in the world, but drives a fairly modest car—a 2009 Cadillac. Like the vehicle, it is the inner qualities of our *human operating system* that determine our success, i.e., our "engine": our emotional intelligence, our ability to remain *above the line*, our *TTT*, our ability to act with a *positive EYE*, to possess qualities such as perseverance, grit and determination, courage, good communication with others, and other characteristics which I examine and analyze for you in this book.

Furthermore, the driving quality and our ability to reach our destination depends both on the driver and on his ability to maintain his vehicle—physically, mechanically, and by choosing the proper route. We know that a well-kept vehicle is worth more and is in higher demand in the automobile market. The driver is analogous to you, the reader; how much do you care for your "vehicle" and maintain it? Just how much do you look after your *operating system* and maintain your body? Health, fitness, weight, nutrition—all of these are important aspects that will enable you to reach far over time. On the mental side, how much do you take responsibility for your life and conduct yourself with *inner focus* in order to succeed? Here, too, the vehicle analogy gives a broad perspective and refines the awareness.

Instead of automatically following habits that may sabotage success, let's drive our "vehicles" with awareness and care, thoughtfully choosing both the destinations and the most effective navigation to reach them.

From Balancing Numbers to Balancing People

Unlike me, you don't have to be involved in an accident in order to move from two wheels to four wheels. This book will help you make the transition in the smoothest way possible. As someone who drives on four wheels today thanks to my transformation, I can attest that my experience of cruising through life is enhanced and heightened immensely. Making the change is a double challenge: **First**, identifying your missing wheels and adding them on; mine mostly entailed focusing on the following skills I was lacking: intuition, emotional intelligence, creativity, awareness, letting go and accepting reality, the ability to contain people and situations, and cognitive flexibility. **Second**, it is important to connect and balance all wheels to create harmony, cohesion, and synchronicity between all the components of *the human operating system*. Finally, we should check for and fix any flat tires or other wrenches in the gears.

A balanced, amply fueled, properly serviced and aligned vehicle, with sufficient air in the tires according to the manufacturer's instructions, whose driver is alert, focused on the road and abiding all traffic laws, will reach its destination safely and faster. We, too, will be able to better fulfill our human potential if we can integrate our left and right brains and the conscious with the unconscious; if we use our **TIRE**—Thoughts, Ideas, Routines, Emotions—wisely, and combine them with our rational skills, which I call **GIFT**— Goals, Indices, Function and Tactics.

Clients approach me when something in their "vehicle" is not functioning—whether one or more wheels are missing, they have a flat tire, or have spokes in their wheels. My job is to identify the malfunctions, help them fix the flat tires, **join** all four wheels, see that they are **balanced,** and remove any spokes so that they can drive their vehicle to their destination and reach their goals.

The key word is **balance.** Just like all the wheels in the vehicle must be synchronized and aligned, so all the components in our life must work harmoniously to drive our "vehicle" to success. This applies to synchronicity between the four human dimensions: physical, emotional, spiritual, and mental. Of all four dimensions, we tend to place more importance on the physical dimension, i.e., the *Doing*, while the other three—which mostly constitute the *Being*—are pushed aside, mainly due to lack of awareness and knowledge of how to harness them for our success.

In the vehicle metaphor, stability depends on the chassis. This is the body that connects all four wheels together. The chassis is analogous to the connection between all of our qualities, characteristics, skills, and dimensions. My goal in this book is to serve as the *balancer*—not of the balance sheet as a former CPA, but between the *operating system*'s components; between the four wheels of the human body, and between *Doing* and *Being*. Here, too, it's nice to see the connection between my first career and my second career—**from balancing numbers to balancing "wheels,"** i.e., balancing people on their road to success. Today, I am naturally more balanced between the practical and the mental, the rational and the spiritual; I am fulfilling my potential, more confident, emotionally stronger, calmer and more peaceful. Hence, my "vehicle" also is balanced and drives much better. Most importantly, life is so much better and happier. After all, isn't that our life's purpose?

This is my unique perspective and tidings served to you in this book: **creating a balance and integration between all four wheels, and most of all, between *Doing* and *Being*.** This integration is one of the greatest challenges on the road to success.

From chapter seven on, you will learn, experiment, and apply the **CO-OP Formula** that serves as the chassis in your "human vehicle." The formula will help you connect all four wheels so that your vehicle, too, will reach its destination successfully.

◆

I shall close this chapter with the famous quote coined by Henry Ford, the captain of the automobile industry: *"If everyone is moving forward together, then success takes care of itself."*

CHAPTER SIX:
The Silent Partner That Determines Your Results

"Nurture your minds with great thoughts, for you will never go any higher than you think."

—Benjamin Disraeli

In the previous chapters, we dealt with the essence of change and the conditions required to cultivate it. In this chapter, I will begin to entertain the question of how to create change and the springboard to help carry it out. You will be introduced to your silent partner, **the source of most blocks in your life.** You will learn how your brain works, which part of your brain most affects your potential results, and why changes must first take place in this part. Eventually you will learn how to tackle that part of your brain so as to impart the changes that will enable you to reach your desired goals.

The Brain's Brain

Most of us associate the word "brain" with the control center governing all processes in the body. We all know that the brain is essentially the "boss." It sends commands that enable us to lift our hand when we decide to, push the brakes when we sense danger on the road, as well as performing some more complex processes relating to our imagination—like imagining what would happen if we forgot our spouse's birthday.

But what if the brain itself had a control center—a brain's brain?

What if that control center were hidden, working behind the scenes, and inaccessible to us? This chapter discusses the mystery of the brain's function, and how it affects the habits and choices we make in our lives. It is worth noting that scientific research on the brain is relatively young and has gained momentum only since the end of the 20th Century, with the development of innovative imaging systems such as the CT (Computed Tomography Scan, or, in the case of CAT, Computerized Axial Tomography) and the MRI (Magnetic Resonance Imaging). Therefore, we are inundated with new discoveries about the brain, which sometimes invalidate old paradigms that had been accepted up until now.

How are the Brain and Facebook Related?

The common assumption is that there is a connection between the brain's size and its ability to function. Expressions such as, "a brain the size of a pea," or "narrow-minded," etc., indicate a limitation in the cognitive abilities with direct correlation to the brain's **size**. Nowadays, this assumption is considered wrong: research and analyses examining countless brains, among which were those belonging to famous geniuses (Einstein, for example), show that the size doesn't matter! What does matter is the number of synapses—the links between the nerve cells, i.e., neurons, in the brain. The number of neurons in the brain is about a hundred billion (10^{11}), and each neuron has about 1,000 synapses connecting it to other neurons by way of electric currents. A quick bit of math shows that we have approximately 10^{14} synapses in the average human brain. This is no doubt an immense network inside approximately 1.5 kilograms of "grey cells," all in an area the size of a fist.

If we compare the number of neurons to the number of Facebook members, the synapse are the social connections between these members. That is, the brain has a "social network" between all its cells, which links an enormous amount of "friends" in order to transmit an unfathomable amount of content. All of which are stored in a rather small "box" weighing less than 3.5 lbs. Amazing, isn't it? By the way, due to this network's elaborate activity, our brain consumes 20% of the oxygen we breathe, 30% of the water we drink, and 40% of the nutrients we extract from our food. Indeed, this little tike must be constantly fed and catered to in order to work for us.

Clearing a Path through the Jungle

The links between neurons are of great importance. **The higher the number of synapses between neurons, the better and faster their communication is**. Every time you learn something new, you create a new synapse between the neurons in your brain. If you practice or repeat what you've learned, you're reinforcing the new connection created, causing it to gradually become permanent. There are many ways to easily illustrate this point: just recall how hard it was for you to learn a new subject in math, and how simple it became after you solved many problems that enhanced your comprehension of that math. Each problem improves access to the brain cells processing the information, and creates more links between the neurons responsible for learning that topic. This is how we acquire any new habit, like learning to play a new musical instrument or keeping a regular fitness routine.

This is analogous to making your way through dense jungle vegetation. At first, it takes a lot of effort to cut through, but gradually, bit by bit, you pave a route and make headway step by step. The more times you go down that path, the more accessible it becomes, until the entire way is paved and you can easily run along it. Similarly, any habit is really a "pathway" in our brain. Each time we access it, it's naturally more convenient to walk through the familiar path than to pave a new one.

But reality changes frequently and many of the pathways in our brain, which once led to pure spring wells for drinking and bathing, are now contaminated. The power of habit leads us again and again down that familiar road to those turbid waters, causing us to often give up the challenge entailed by paving a new route to the living waters, which have simply wandered to a different place in our jungle through the power of change.

Thus, we can say that learning anything new, or acquiring a new habit, is like clearing a path through the jungle. It's hard at first, but the moment we've cleared the way and created synapses that link between the neurons, it becomes easy and pleasurable to walk along it.

There is nothing quite like sports to illustrate this point. As a youth, I was very active in many sports. When I was 18, I even won third place in the Israeli national Judo championship for 136 lbs (yes, I once weighed that little). In my twenties, I still practiced here and there, but in my thirties, when my kids were born, I stopped practicing altogether. The turning point came in 1999, when I was 39 years old. A friend introduced me to an excellent fitness program, run by one of the best, most unique trainers in Israel. It was love at first sight! Despite the difficulty of sticking with an intensive physical practice late at night (9 p.m.), I felt like I was slowly clearing the way through my own jungle until the habit was formed. Almost 16 years since my first practice, I am still motivated to show up to 90% of the practices, twice a week, willingly and joyfully, in spite of—or perhaps because of—the amount of sweat I shed. It has become one of my strongest positive habits, and any deviation from it arouses discomfort. Indeed, after paving a new road, it's very easy and familiar to walk along it!

Forest Rangers at Any Age

One of the most common blocks my coaching clients face is the age factor. "Change careers? At my age?!" they say, and I detect the fear in their voice, the hesitation to embark on a new career journey and face challenges "at their age." They don't know that one of the most amazing, effective qualities of the brain is its ability to develop and grow at any age, known as "brain plasticity." There is no age limit on creating new pathways in the brain and acquiring new skills; the more you invest time and passion in learning and engaging in new activities, the easier the path becomes; you will have paved the way and be able to reap the reward of joy and satisfaction in the process. In that sense, the brain is like a muscle that can be trained and developed even at an advanced age.

This is certainly a challenge—remembering that we can choose to renew, develop, and grow at any stage in our life. Perhaps the most prominent example for this challenge is the late Israeli president, Shimon Peres, who, even in his 90s, served as an excellent president and lead a full life of learning and fulfillment.

Hence, the only wonder is, what influences our ability to pave new pathways in our brain? Is a sharp machete, some determination, grit, and persistence all we need, or is there another hidden, shifty factor that most "path pavers" are not familiar with? More about this in the chapter ahead.

"I really want to, but..."

We have all witnessed our own difficulty sometimes in reaching a goal we set for ourselves; we decide it's really important to us, make an effort, invest time, money, and energy, and then something gets in the way—and suddenly, our initial enthusiasm fizzles, dissolves, making way for fear, doubt, and hesitation. Procrastination takes hold of us and we promise ourselves that tomorrow we'll act with more conviction to fulfill our pledge... and so on, day after day, "tomorrow" becomes "next week," then "next month," and most times, "never." Our initiative dies out. We go back to square one, frustrated and disappointed, convinced that we've tried but that it is "impossible." Sometimes, a traumatic experience may sabotage any future attempt to challenge ourselves again, since we've "already tried and it didn't work."

Anyone who's experienced dieting or any attempt to uproot an ingrained habit, not to mention an addiction, fully understands the gap between decision and execution; "I really want to, but," we usually say. On one hand, we've made a conscious decision: to withdraw, to change, to act; but on the other hand, we find ourselves reaching for that cigarette, that bar of chocolate, or that credit card, as if our hand had a life of its own...

What is going on here?

Above the surface, we see the activity of our **conscious mind**, the "war room" that seemingly runs us. However, this mind is only the tip of the iceberg in the vast cerebral activity constantly taking place in our *Operating System*; those who are familiar with icebergs know that most of the mass resides underwater.

The Phantom of the Opera—the Secret Conductor of our Life's Symphony

So who is truly in charge of our ability to achieve goals, thrive, and succeed? How much control do we have over our own minds? And how do we explain the recurring phenomenon of "I really want to, but?"

Well, there is another slick, mysterious cause standing between us—armed with will power and determination—and the attainment of our goals. **It is the unconscious part of our brain.** If we compare our mind to a computer, the unconscious mind is our super-computer, since this mind is about a million times more powerful than our conscious mind, constituting 83% of the total brain mass—a super-computer indeed!

What is our unconscious mind? Its name gives away its nature: it is the part of our mind whose activity we are unaware of, although it is constantly active and vital to our existence. This "automatic pilot" is in charge of involuntary functions. Here are the main ones:

First, the 24/7 running of our body. The human body is the most intricate system in the world. Think about all the things that happen inside your body at any given moment: the function and interaction of the organs, the breathing, the blood circulation, metabolism, cellular development, immune system, sensory processing, and so on. All of these are automatically run by our unconscious minds, without any human intervention.

Second, our unconscious mind includes all of our life's **memories** down to the smallest detail; everything is stored there. If you've ever happened to hear or see a hypnosis session in which a person is hypnotized and regresses back twenty years, you've witnessed how he can describe in great detail an event that took place many years ago. Our unconscious mind is a well of secrets that doesn't lose the smallest drop; you simply have to know how to retrieve the desired memory from the correct storage area.

Third, the unconscious mind includes all of our **beliefs**, including our self-image; those we have collected over the years—mostly in childhood—about our place in the world, our abilities, relationships with others, etc.

Fourth and last are all of our **habits**, stored and filed away in the unconscious mind. All the "paths" we have cleared in our "jungle" originate from the unconscious mind.

The True Operating System—a Multiprocessing Computer System

One of the more memorable technological developments in the field of computers has been the transition to multi-core processors that can split processes and perform a few tasks simultaneously. This is precisely how our unconscious mind works, able to process enormous amounts of information—about a million commands—at the same time, whereas our conscious mind can only perform one task at a time—one thought, one action. As we saw in chapter three, we can consciously become attentive and focused by making room for only one thought at a time. Indeed, our thoughts rush, creating ever-changing continuums in a matter of moments, but the rule remains the same: only one conscious thought can get our full attention at any given moment, versus a million processes taking place simultaneously in the unconscious mind. Furthermore, the unconscious mind is a real slave driver, active 24/7, even while we sleep, lose consciousness, or are in deep sedation; it never gets tired. Meanwhile, the conscious mind is inactive during sleep and may even falter during waking hours. Lastly, our intuitive abilities are attributed to our unconscious mind, and mystics believe that it is linked to the infinite wisdom of the universe and to other unconscious minds.

If we compare ourselves to a mega corporation, its real manager is the unconscious mind, while our conscious mind is like a baby that cannot even run a department of the company—not because he isn't smart or talented, but because his processing abilities are too limited. This is one of the main reasons why most people only use a fraction of their personal potential; in essence, they are trying to run a major conglomerate with a baby's brain.

Compliments aside, the unconscious mind has quite a few limitations. For example, it works like a tape recorder: it's constantly recording things taking place in us and around us without choosing what to absorb and what not. It doesn't distinguish between right and wrong, but accepts everything as truth, processing and storing the information in its grey cells. It doesn't grasp time, but operates in one mode only, the present, expressing itself in the present through the conscious mind. If you keep saying to yourself: "I'm good, I'm successful," the unconscious accepts it and "believes" it, which is also working to fulfill it in reality through the conscious mind. The problem is that most of us actually think and speak in completely opposite tones; we remind ourselves how "bad, unsuccessful, or unappreciated" we are, as well as other judgmental, negative personal statements. They, too, are accepted by the unconscious as truth, and it "plays back" what we record on it.

Who Wins?

It's easy to see that we are at our best when the conscious and the unconscious are collaborating and operating in unison. Our two processors are then working in synchronicity, where the powerful "silent partner" cultivates, supports, and guides the conscious mind on how to operate in reality. Suddenly, everything "flows," everything "works," and the positive results arrive. This way, our unconscious is working to serve the needs of the conscious mind and everyone is happy.

But what happens when our two minds disagree? What if our conscious mind activates the willpower and says "yes" (yes to dieting, yes to quitting smoking, yes to a better paying job, yes to a change in relationships), but the unconscious mind doesn't cooperate because it was programmed exactly the opposite way? It's clear that they don't have equal strength; **the unconscious mind mostly wins.**

What if you wish to succeed, want to be rich, and are willing to work diligently and persistently for it, but your unconscious mind harbors a contrary, limiting belief that says, "I (you) have no chance of succeeding," or, "I'm (you're) not good enough?" Then in 95% of the cases, this limiting belief will intensify. Thus, despite your conscious willpower and best efforts, most chances are those efforts won't bear fruits.

Indeed, the unconscious overpowers the conscious nearly 95% of the time! This means that 95% of your results are determined by the unconscious mind and only 5% by the conscious mind.

Our operating system works in the following way: the conscious mind serves as the vessel for the unconscious mind. Unconscious beliefs activate the conscious mind to search our environment for patterns matching those beliefs, even if they don't serve us. In essence, the conscious is subjected to unconscious paradigms, so that if our unconscious self-esteem is low, we will tend to find "proofs" for it in our surroundings. These "proofs" will serve as confirmation feedback, therefore continuing to reinforce our low self-esteem. This is another example, this time via our unconscious mind, of the three filters that shape our perception, as reviewed in chapter three.

In these cases, the conflict ends with a long list of excuses created by the conscious mind about why the change we wish to make is impossible, despite its initial desire. This is the point where we give in to *circumstances*, **helplessly facing the inner, controlling-yet-hidden power of the unconscious mind.** Furthermore, our inability to fulfill ourselves and succeed based on our conscious will alone is a frustrating, miserable experience. We are emotionally hurt, dropping *below the line*, and as we've seen in chapter two, our ability to thrive and succeed gets hit once again by the spokes in the wheels of our "vehicle."

And it Only Gets More Complicated...

Since this book deals with transformations, we must do something about this anomaly, so we can change and transform. We must access the unconscious mind and change the code that no longer serves us so that it matches out conscious desires. This way, our two minds will work cohesively to lead us to our destination, to a safe haven, and to success.

But this is where the plot thickens, because **the unconscious is not accessible** by conventional means. Nature has blocked it off. Why? Because we can't let a "baby" take up the seat of CEO in the megacorporation that is us; because our conscious mind can only perform one task at a time, and so how can it give the "super-computer" orders on how to run our body, our memories, beliefs, and habits—so many tasks—simultaneously? You realize it can't do it! Our conscious mind isn't intelligent enough for that, and it can make a lot of mistakes on the way and harm creation's most amazing invention.

Furthermore, if the conscious orders the unconscious to stop the heart from beating, for example, or stop working because it's tired, or any other "silly prank," it may be playing with fire that could burn our entire foundation; it becomes a risk to our survival, and this, nature or the Creator could not allow for.

In the "jungle pathways" metaphor I used earlier in this chapter, the pathways in our brain are actually located in the unconscious mind. In the case at hand, not only do we have no choice but to walk down the old habits'[28] paths in the unconscious mind that no longer serve us, we don't have the proper tools to pave new paths—i.e., the new *habits* we wish to adopt.

I shall end this subchapter with a quote by Charles Noble: "First we make our habits, then our habits make us." Indeed, through the myriad *circumstances* of life, we program our unconscious mind without realizing it, creating in it the *habits* that "play" automatically and determine the results in our life.

Grab a Flashlight, We're Going In

Before I present solutions on how to access the unconscious mind, let's get to know things from a scientific standpoint, using a model that clarifies which part of the brain is dominant in different scenarios. Science explains various brain activities using a brain wave model. Studies of the brain have shown that it functions in a frequency range of 0.1 Hz–100 Hz. This is a very large range which is typically divided into four frequency groups:

The first group is called Beta waves, which function at a range of 14–100 Hz. This is our waking state through most of the day time, as we go about our normal activities—working, driving, doing physical exercise, etc. In this state, our conscious mind is very active and there is **no access** to the unconscious mind.

---

28 To simplify, I will use the word "habits" from now on to include the gamut of components making up the human operating system; not just behavioral habits in the familiar sense of the word, but also habits of thought, beliefs, and emotions.

The second group is called Alpha waves, which function at a range of 8–13.9 Hz. These waves characterize a state of relaxation and ease, where our conscious mind slows down its activity and the pace of our thoughts slows. In this state, access to the unconscious mind begins to open, we enter a slight state of trance29, are more affected by external messages, our learning ability increases, and our intuition expands. These waves are characteristic of pre-sleep and waking up states. Meditation also begins with these waves, where access to our unconscious mind increases creativity and a lot more ideas come up. For example, I often experience revelations when I am showering or in the bathroom. More than once, I've stormed out of the bathroom straight to my office to write down ideas that come up in this state. These are flickering moments of the unconscious transmitted to the conscious mind under Alpha waves.

The third group is called Theta waves, which function at a range of 4–7.9 Hz. The common state in this range is dream sleep, also known as REM (Rapid Eye Movement) sleep. In this dream state, the eyelids flutter even though the eyes are closed, thus lending the name REM. In this state, the conscious mind isn't active; the only activity is in the unconscious mind. Here, our creativity increases along with our learning ability, the unconscious mind is accessible, and the potential for changing our *habits* increases. However, because our conscious mind isn't active during sleep, we naturally cannot utilize this access to our unconscious mind in order to take advantage of these possibilities. Therefore, the challenge is to reach Theta waves in a state of wakefulness, when the conscious mind is active and can give orders to the

---

29 An abnormal state of consciousness, between sleep and wakefulness, similar to a hypnotic state. Characterized by a partial or full detachment from the physical environment.

unconscious mind so it can be transformed. There are various methods for achieving that, the most common of which is Theta Healing.

The fourth group of waves is called Delta, which function at a range of 0.1–3.9 Hz. This frequency characterizes deep, dreamless sleep. In this state, the unconscious mind is even more accessible, increasing the Theta waves' characteristics. You're probably familiar with the phrase, "let's sleep on it." This isn't a mindless phrase; it refers to the unconscious mind's increased processing abilities during deep sleep. This is when it works to handle the issues most important to us, often offering solutions as it "knocks" on the gates of our conscious mind as we rise, or sometimes even in the middle of the night. Have you ever experienced waking up all of a sudden with a new idea to solve a nagging problem? What did you do? If you didn't get up and write it down right away, most likely you'll have forgotten it by morning, so next time, make sure to do it. It's in those moments that your super-computer is providing you with invaluable insights.

The Exceptional Ones

There is one exception to the rule stating that our unconscious mind being inaccessible during waking hours. Although this exception doesn't apply to adults, I shall review it here, because it's important to the parents among us. I have previously stated in earlier chapters that most parents aren't always aware of the effect their upbringing styles have on their children, so that they sometimes disrupt the latter's *operation systems*. Parents' natural concern and constant effort to protect their children causes the latter to hear a lot of "no," which weakens them as adults. I have dealt with this extensively in chapter three when talking about positive focus and attitude. Now, we can further say that children six years old and younger sometimes display brain frequencies that are lower than Beta waves during wakefulness. This is not necessarily caused by anything or anyone, but is a natural state in childhood. That is, up until the age of six, parents and teachers communicating with children have "free access" to their remarkable unconscious world. This is why many children at this age seem a little "flighty" or "dreamy"—they have an open communication channel with the unconscious! If you've ever wondered how all these messages that shape your adulthood made it into your unconscious mind to begin with, the answer is that many of them were assimilated in childhood.

If so, we should pay attention to how we adults approach small children, because what they hear is quickly and deeply assimilated into their unconscious. This is also why children are excellent students and are quick to acquire habits and languages. That's no wonder, since everything is absorbed directly into their unconscious mind and immediately turns into a habit, for better or worse. So, for example, being told "no" too much during childhood may be interpreted as "unable" by the adult that is trying to create a change in his life. This is really the "unconscious voice" of the adult. The unconscious mind is closed and sealed around the age of six. From this moment on, gaining direct access to it will be a lot harder. The adult, unaware of how to change the unconscious, will live with whatever was assimilated in his childhood for the rest of his life.

Hence, **a great deal of the programming that sabotages success in the unconscious mind of the adult stems from negative messages assimilated in his childhood.** Therefore, every adult that comes in contact with children, especially a parent or a teacher, must handle them with utmost care in regard to messages that affect their *TTT*.

So What Can Adults Do to Access Their Unconscious?

By now you realize that the challenge facing anyone who wishes to fulfill his potential, thrive, and succeed lies in harnessing his unconscious mind to benefit his conscious wishes. To do that, he must find a way to access the unconscious mind and program it to promote his goals. The average person, subject to automatic programming during his life, cannot make a meaningful change in his life without reprogramming the unconscious mind. Accessing the unconscious mind is crucial in order to pave new paths and assimilate new and better *habits*. Thus, **every process of transformation must first include a change in the limiting perceptions of the unconscious.** Otherwise, without being able to influence the authentic human *operating system*, a change made on the conscious level alone is doomed to fail.

From time immemorial, great men in the history of mankind have acknowledged this need and developed various methods to bypass the "gatekeeper" creation has placed between the conscious and the unconscious mind.

Here are some methods to access the unconscious mind and embed in it changes with a *positive EYE*:

1. Directing our conscious thoughts to benefit goals that are important to us **before falling asleep and upon awakening.** These are the "twilight" moments when the brainwave frequency fades into alpha and a rare, albeit short, opportunity arises to glimpse into the unconscious. This is the most critical moment to implement a positive focus and attitude. It's not a coincidence that the first directive in Judaism, as well as other religions, is to express gratitude for what you have upon waking up, even before you get out of bed. Instead of the automatic reaction of, "Man, I can't believe it's already morning, I don't feel like getting up, I don't feel like starting the day, I wish I could sleep in," gratitude focuses us on the good things we have in our lives. Nothing should be taken for granted: the fact that we're alive, healthy, have a roof over our head and food to eat, and are surrounded by beloved people, etc. All of these are transmitted to our unconscious minds in this window of opportunity to access it upon waking up. Indeed, morning gratitude is a powerful tool in harnessing the unconscious mind in your favor.

The moments before falling asleep are also a rare opportunity to give instructions to our unconscious minds to work for us during the night in solving problems that may bother us. Posing questions to the unconscious such as, "What is the solution to this matter? How should I handle this matter?" is an excellent tool in directing the unconscious to perform its nightly background work so it may serve us. It's recommended you address the conscious mind directly and ask, "Dear unconscious mind, please solve (blank) for me." Note that in many homes, the standard protocol before bedtime is to watch TV and sometimes even late night news. This is one of the biggest mistakes when using these rare moments of access to the unconscious mind to actually imprint on it the worst news of the day, commercials, and other messages that serve the cable channels instead of serving your success. I suggest you avoid that at all cost!

Famous geniuses in human history used these and other techniques to harness the unconscious mind to better fulfill their potential and achieve their goals. Einstein, Mozart, Edison, and Beethoven are among them. Thus, it's not just a high IQ that contributes to success, but also developing skills to access the unconscious mind and making it work for your benefit. This is something anyone can learn and implement! When examining how to utilize the human potential beyond the average 7-15%, it's easy to see that access to the unconscious mind and programming it to serve our goals is one of the best tools to achieve that.

2. Meditation is one of the most powerful tools to access the unconscious, common to all religions since ancient times. Meditation slows down the brainwave frequency to at least alpha waves, while keeping full alertness so one can access the unconscious through the conscious mind. There are many types of meditations; I practice my daily meditation for about a half an hour every morning while thinking about the goals I wish to achieve and imagining them materializing, and have done so since 2006.

3. Hypnosis. This, too, is an ancient tool that causes the brainwave frequency to slow down, below even alpha. Hypnosis is known more as a method for retrieving memories from the unconscious mind, but is also a quick and elegant way to access the unconscious mind and make changes in it. A slight hypnosis may occur via communication, such as a conversation or watching TV. Paul McKenna, a famous hypnotist, claimed that watching TV is a trans-hypnotic experience: the viewer forgets about his surroundings and immerses himself in watching the screen, so that everything that unfolds on it seems alive and real. Thus, the viewer automatically suspends his judgment of reality and deludes himself into thinking that what is said and done on TV is the ultimate truth. To this extent, there are beliefs that advertisers use the hypnotizing power of TV to influence the unconscious to buy their products. There is also a self-hypnosis technique where the person hypnotizes himself; I have learned Dr. Robert Anthony's self-hypnosis technique and implemented it with considerable success in order to create changes in my unconscious mind.

4. Theta Healing. This method slows down the brain waves to a Theta frequency and enables direct access to the unconscious. This method was developed in the U.S. by Vianna Stibal in 1995, and has quickly spread around the world.

5. NLP. This acronym stands for Neuro-Linguistic Programming. This is another well-known method that is even more common than Theta Healing. This method was developed in the 1970s and is based on the idea that thought and speech are performed in patterns that influence results no less than the content of the thoughts or words themselves. Learning these patterns enables a structured, methodical approach to making changes in people.

6. Relaxation, letting go, and acceptance. As humans, we strive for certainty and maximum control over our lives and future. However, this proactive approach doesn't always prove itself. We may work, strive, invest, research, and still not get to where we want. I mentioned this in chapter two: when we need something and must have it, we fall *below the line*, which is a mental state that hinders success. This is the moment to let go and try a different way, using the unconscious mind. The more we learn to yield control, the more open access we will have to our unconscious mind, gliding into relaxation and sleepiness. Those of you who have pondered a question or a problem for a long time and arrived at a solution only when you dropped on the couch, letting go of the issue in your head or even giving up on finding a solution, surely remember what I'm talking about. It's like the story of Archimedes, who discovered how to calculate the specific weight of substances in the bathtub, of all places, and called out, "Eureka!" Here is my own idiom that illustrates this point: *"What doesn't work by force or mind, works when resigned. Let go, give it up, and it will all line up..."*

Don't Blame Your Willpower

Here is a **summary** of the important points I discussed so far in this chapter:

The unconscious mind is a major, key component in our *operating system*; it is the automatic pilot, the paved pathways, the super-computer. The unconscious enables us to quickly perform a myriad of vital, daily tasks we call *habits* without overloading our conscious mind, which is relatively limited in comparison. This function is beneficial up to the point where it burdens us when the programming of the unconscious mind is contradictory to our conscious wishes. To our surprise, willpower doesn't usually help us here, and the unconscious mind overpowers its conscious counterpart in almost 95% of all cases. Once we understand that, we want to change the unconscious, but find out that it's blocked to changes. Luckily, humanity's masterminds have developed a number of methods to help us access the unconscious mind and reprogram it to help us promote our goals. A number of the common methods were reviewed above.

It's important to emphasize that you cannot introduce change into your life unless you ensure that your unconscious mind is synchronized with your conscious wishes. Since whatever is ingrained in your unconscious mind was mostly embedded there in a random, uncontrolled manner, **it is recommended you implement one of the routine methods I've mentioned above in any process of change. They allow a controlled access into the unconscious, in order to make the necessary changes to bring you closer to your goals.**

However, there is another method for accessing the unconscious and making changes to it. Though it may not be as glamorous or yield as immediate results as others, it is a highly effective method for achieving sustainable, long-lasting results. My methodology, the **CO-OP Formula**, is based on this method. I ask you to be patient for a little longer, because the next chapter will introduce it to you. Indeed, from chapter seven on, you will learn how to create changes in your unconscious mind using the *CO-OP Formula*—an organized and proven methodology for changing *habits*.

I shall end this subchapter with a quote from Napoleon Hill[30]: "Whatever the mind of man can conceive and believe, it can achieve." This quote can be seen as directed towards the unconscious mind: when a person succeeds in thinking up goals, believing in them, and assimilating them into his unconscious, he is harnessing it to his benefit, thus paving his road to success and prosperity.

---

30 Napoleon Hill is considered one of the first researchers of success in the modern age. His famous 1937 book, Think and Grow Rich, is one of the best sellers of all time. Up until Hill's death in 1970, the book had sold about 20 million copies, and many millions thereafter till today. Hill researched the power of habits and self-perception, and the role they played in people's success. His book is a detailed guide to achieving success in life, designed for the ordinary person who wishes to achieve success in all areas of life. The book is based on research Hill conducted over 20 years, examining the causes for success among the world's richest people in the beginning of the 20th Century. Even today, Hill's theory is considered one of the most organized, extensive studies on success and personal development. Many of today's prominent personal development teachers were inspired by Hill's writings.

How Come Other People Always Run Into Bill Gates in the Elevator?

Sometimes we feel like others have better luck than us. They seem like their star shines brighter and opportunities simply come to them. This is one possibility, but there is another, more logical one: if we change the data in our unconscious mind, reprogramming it according to our goals, such opportunities will be our lot, too. Meaning, it isn't about some miracle or sheer luck, but about how our unconscious—the super-computer—draws the conscious mind's attention to what otherwise escapes its limited radar. I mentioned it in chapter three when quoting an article by Richard Wiseman. When we focus on a certain topic and add it to the task list of our unconscious mind, things begin to happen. We "suddenly" meet people who can better guide us towards our goals; in the bookstore, we pick up a book that deals with **exactly** what we need to get moving; we are inspired by billboards, random conversations with friends, and even our own dreams. What is really happening here is that our unconscious mind is kicking in, focusing the lenses through which we view the world on relevant information that only seems to randomly "jump out at us." I see these types of occurrences all the time, both in my life and among my clients. Although I am certain of their existence, I'm not convinced I can rationally explain these phenomena, so I will attempt that at another time.

◆

Here is a vivid, personal example that happened recently: When I last met with a good childhood friend, I told him just before we parted of my plan to sell an apartment I own, which is still under construction but has made a considerable growth in value since I purchased it. I bought it about four year ago strictly with loans, and now had to repay some of them; that's why I wanted to sell it.

My friend told me right away, "Why don't you sell the apartment you live in instead, and allow the apartment under construction to come to full fruition as a completed unit, and this way you can save by not paying capital gains tax for an apartment that isn't livable yet?" At first, my conscious mind automatically resisted: "But I already have a plan and I have begun to execute it, why is he coming with this strange idea all of a sudden?" But moments later, my intuition[31] surfaced in my conscious mind and made it very clear: "There's something to it that's worth looking into." On my way home, I mulled over the idea and by the time I arrived at my doorstep, I realized it entailed a profit of more than a hundred thousand dollars, and that I was going to go for it. Thus, a random conversation with a friend gave birth to a rare opportunity. What were the chances that I would have missed this if I had been less aware and focused? Very high, since up until a few years ago I didn't even notice such opportunities, as I mentioned in chapter three. I am certain that being able to access my unconscious mind and reprogramming it to be courageous and open to new initiatives is what led me to take advantage of this opportunity. My father, Benjamin, of blessed memory, used to say, "Everyone happens upon their luck; some don't stop to grab it, but those who do, materialize it." This is so wise and true!

Intuition aside, some of the credit goes to the *focus principle*

---

31 Some define "intuition" as insights that have no rational explanation. Others define it as information we receive through our connection with a higher, universal awareness. I don't plan on providing one literal explanation for it, but will only assure you that from the moment the goal is assimilated into the unconscious mind, that unconscious becomes our helper in identifying opportunities, meaning our "intuition" works. Do you have to know the source of electricity in order to use it? Of course not. The same goes for intuition.

I discussed in chapter three. If my conscious is focused and searching for new options, I will probably find them. Still, I believe that the main factor in such "luck" is in fact a powerful unconscious mind, alongside which the conscious mind is less significant. I use intuition a lot in my life and especially in my work. What I so easily dismissed up until 9 years ago has become a key, legitimate tool that enables my unconscious mind to successfully navigate my way.

Yes, It All Goes Back to Childhood, Again...

As big fans of *Doing*, most people may jump up at this point and rush to implement one of the techniques I have mentioned for reprogramming the unconscious mind to create the desired changes and harness the "luck goddess" to their benefit. If you are one of them, please stop, because you should first know what language the unconscious mind understands, and how to "speak" to it so that the messages penetrate its gatekeeper in the most effective way to achieve maximum results. Here we go:

"Stop daydreaming and do something with yourself!" What child hasn't heard this from his parents? The hidden assumption is that he who daydreams doesn't do anything to get ahead in life, a "space cadet" of sorts. Our forefathers believed that the right thing for a dreamy child is to engage in practical activity that can be proven on paper or held in the hand—in other words, tangible things. He who stares into space, seeing exhilarating images in his mind's eye, is simply "wasting time." Right?

The answer is no! As you've already seen in this chapter, a daydreaming state is natural among children, due to the slower wavelengths their brains operate in. What enables dreaming is the **imagination**, since it's impossible to daydream without activating the imagination. If so, imagination is more than legitimate among children. It is also a vital tool for children and adults alike to create the reality we want, as you shall soon see.

"Logic will get you from A to B. Imagination will take you everywhere."

This statement was made by someone who could hardly be suspected of being impractical; the man who Time Magazine crowned as the "Man of the 20th Century"—Albert Einstein. He also stated the order of priority between the two: "Imagination is more important than knowledge. Knowledge is limited. Imagination encircles the world." Einstein is definitely worth listening to, since he became famous for knowing how to fulfill his maximal mental potential, both conscious and unconscious, to reach his impressive scientific achievements. Indeed, Einstein had extraordinary skills in more than just physics. He pinpointed the place that encompasses all processes related to change and growth: the imagination. Or, as Walt Disney defined it later on, "If you can dream it, you can do it." Indeed, our imagination is the creative room of the human brain. Everything in the world is born twice: First in someone's fervent mind, and only then in reality. Every great project began as a vague idea, the drawings of the imagination. Only later did the impressions of the imagination become defined concepts—worded, sketched, engineered, and formulated into a plan for execution, where the engine weaving form and matter is enthusiasm and vision. If so, Disney's statement could be rephrased as, "If you want to do something, to accomplish and thrive, you must first dream it!"

The Imagination—the Domain of the Unconscious

Another reason why dreaming and imagination are so vital to fulfillment is that it's **a language our unconscious understands.** Alluring images of the future are conjured up in our imagination in a language our unconscious receives and absorbs the fastest, especially if they are sprinkled with positive emotions. It's exactly the same action Napoleon Hill asks of us in the aforementioned quote—*"conceive and believe"* in order to achieve; that is, using the imagination to assimilate our goals into our unconscious mind. Instead of "playing back" the negative *automatic program* ingrained in the unconscious throughout our life against our will, we can use the imagination to harness our super-computer to help its neighbor, the conscious mind, fulfill that which our soul desires.

I have already mentioned that our *TTT* determines our reality. Here is an example of how much the second T—Terms, as in words—influences reality. Are you familiar with the expression, "Even in my wildest dreams I can't see this happening?" Notice how this statement is guaranteed to block the imagination, avoids using the unconscious' language, and thus hinders fulfillment. Because if a person can't see the things he desires in his wildest dreams, i.e., his imagination, then there's no chance he could see them come to life. As I said, **dreams and imagination are the first stage in any human creation.**

Even our sages acknowledged the significance of imagination as building a vision and a dream for reality. Rabbi Nachman of Breslov said, "You are where your thoughts are. Make sure your thoughts are where you want to be." Our unconscious thoughts are the "pillar of fire" that walks in front of us and paves the way towards our goal. Therefore, we should show them exactly where we aspire to go via the imagination, which is a language they understand. In chapter ten, I shall expand on how to direct our thoughts to create the reality we want.

Let the Imagination Soar, Land in Reality

Tony Robbins, the master life coach, motivational speaker, and business strategist, beautifully illustrates the importance of the imagination in fulfillment by using the following diagram, which he calls the *Success Cycle*:

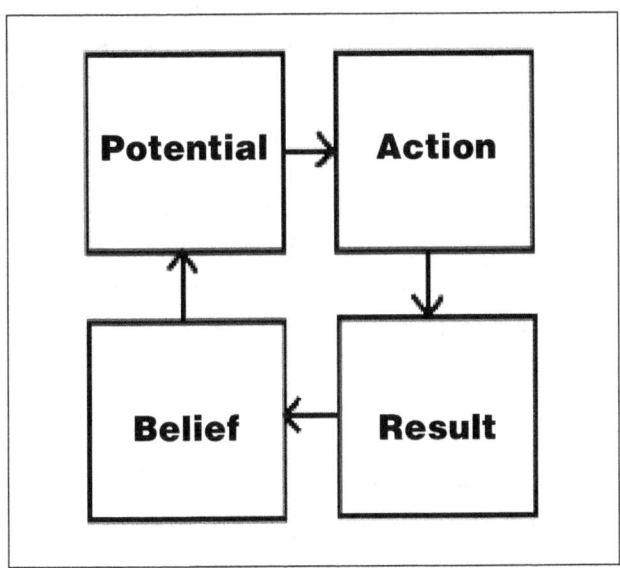

Diagram 6-1 – The Success Cycle by Tony Robbins

It's evident that when the cycle is moving clockwise, a positive momentum is achieved, the cycle feeds itself, and the road to results and steady improvement is paved. **But what part of the cycle should a beginner entrepreneur start from to initiate an impetus for success?** Most people will say that one has to begin with "belief." This is a very logical statement, for a strong belief is vital to fulfillment. However, it's not easy to develop belief; you can't just assume it, since it is abstract and assimilated in our unconscious mind. Therefore, Robbins claims we should actually start from the "results." "How come?" you'll surely say,

"That's the final destination I want to reach, how can I start from the results?" The answer is found in the famous proverb, "Think on the end before you begin." The road to results begins with an idea, with planning, and, most relevant to our discussion, **with imagination**. Robbins says we must start with the results **in our imagination**. Come up with an exciting vision, see the results of its fruition in our imagination, have a full sensory experience of them in our imagination—mainly emotionally—and thus assimilate them into our unconscious mind. That is how belief can develop in the *operating system,* fulfilling our potential, motivating us to act, and leading us to tangible results; and vice versa, as the results reinforce belief, so with each round of the success cycle its power grows. This is how we acknowledge the significance of programming the unconscious to serve our goals, "speaking" its own language—the language of imagination—in order to instill our wishes in it.

The Four Statements I Whisper to My Kids at Bedtime

You have been able to appreciate my passion towards bringing up children in a way that programs their unconscious mind for success; here is an important tip I learned from Robin Sharma:

Sharma recommends reciting empowering statements to children at bedtime, which develops self-belief. When children are relaxed and even half-asleep, their unconscious gradually opens, allowing a wonderful opportunity to instill positive messages that will serve your children faithfully throughout their life.

The four statements Sharma recommends you tell your children at bedtime are:

"You can do whatever you want when you grow up;"

"Never give up;"

"Whatever you do, do it well;"

And last but not least (and no less important), "Remember how much your Daddy loves you."

Love is the most powerful positive emotion in the world, and when we incorporate it into any positive action, a momentum is created that propels us to new heights.

My children are grown up today, but when they were younger I whispered these magic words into their ears at bedtime, and I'm convinced I implanted paradigms in their minds that will help them mature into successful, confident adults.

How Do You Break Records in Sports?
Record breaking results in sports have long been considered more than just a product of fitness and physical training. The following historical event exemplifies that not only is imagination not inferior to "physical manifestation," it is absolutely vital for producing outstanding results:

For years, it was commonly thought that a human being could not run a mile in less than four minutes. Year after year, many athletes failed in their attempt to achieve that, until a Scottish athlete by the name of Roger Bannister did it for the first time on May 6th, 1954: he ran a mile in an all-time record of 3:59.4 minutes. The entire world watched in amazement at this wonder. What made the difference between Banister and many good athletes who attempted it before him was **the imagination**. He ceaselessly dreamt and imagined how he was going to cross the finish line with the stop watch showing 3:59. Again and again, he created this strong vision in his imagination, a mental picture of the final moment—running, crossing the line, the stop watch showing 3:59 minutes, a new record! Then, with the vision imprinted in his unconscious mind, Bannister carried it out in reality—he ran that mile in less than 4 minutes! Indeed, Bannister used his imagination to change the prevalent paradigm in his unconscious mind—that it was impossible to run a mile in less than four minutes—and then executed it. This is another proof of the importance of imagination in programming the unconscious mind for fulfillment.

It was a historical moment, when one of the strongest limiting beliefs regarding the human potential was shattered. Just a year later, 37 more athletes ran a mile in less than four minutes; and the year following it, more than 300 athletes achieved the same. This is to teach us that "it's all in our head" and that our mental side can veto our physical abilities, for better or worse. The four-minute block in the mile run was nothing more than **a psychological barrier**, and it's enough for one person to break that paradigm and show others what is truly possible for other athletes to change their own limiting belief and achieve the "impossible."

Bannister made it possible for all the other athletes. To prove that, when this book was written, the one-mile-run record was set at 3:43, far off from the four-minute psychological barrier. This reminds me once more of Henry Ford's statement—"Whether you think that you can, or that you can't, you are usually right."

Today, the use of imagination is one of the standard methods of coaching in sports and serves as a major tool in manifesting reality, including in the field of medicine for some healing methods. As an athletic person with knowledge in the fields of sports, I believe that the difference between the first place and the few behind it is mainly mental. The person winning isn't necessarily the most talented or experienced athlete, but the one who possesses the highest self-confidence, self-image, and self-belief. This is what makes imagination so important in yielding extraordinary results in sports or in any other field.

◆

Before closing this subchapter, here are two points on how to apply guided imagination to create a change in the unconscious mind:

The first point: The unconscious mind doesn't understand the meaning of the word "no." It interprets "don't be afraid" as "be afraid." If I tell you, "don't think about a yellow banana," you will obviously see a yellow banana in your imagination. Therefore, the unconscious mind must be given positive suggestions. For example, "be brave" instead of "don't be afraid."

The second point: The unconscious mind doesn't distinguish imagination from reality. It interprets any imagery as if it were happening in reality. Have you ever had a wet dream? Or a nightmare that woke you up all sweaty with a racing pulse? It's clear that imagination alone has identical physiological effects to similar experiences in reality. This proves, once more, the power of our imagination in shaping reality.

Einstein Once More

By now, you probably realize why Einstein said that imagination is more important than any knowledge, since any action should begin in the imagination. The imagination is imprinted on the unconscious mind and enlists it in our favor, crafting and paving the road to fulfillment. As children we used our imagination, but as adults we have forgotten this skill as it was pushed aside by the upbringing and culture we absorbed all our lives, causing us to lose our main source of creation.

Therefore, **it's good practice to activate your imagination**, practice using it and making time for it during repose and relaxation within your intensive daily routine. Here are a few points during the day in which I activate my imagination—I recommend you use them too, to train your imagination muscles: minutes before falling asleep and upon awakening; during scheduled breaks throughout the day such as using the bathroom, pouring a glass of water or making coffee, while waiting (for a meeting, a doctor, in line, etc.); any time you can close your eyes, even for a minute or two. It's preferable that they be closed, but even with eyes wide open you can easily work your imagination once you get used to it. Another opportunity to glide into alpha waves is a short afternoon nap. Even when I'm pressed for time, a 10-15 minute relaxation and imagination will awaken, invigorate, and instill seeds of success into my unconscious. Training your imagination and directing it towards your goals at certain points throughout the day is one of the most important actions to contribute to your success. In chapter nine, you will learn how to establish these observation points.

I shall sum up this chapter with another one of Einstein's quotes: *"The intuitive mind is a sacred gift and the rational mind is a faithful servant. We have created a society that honors the servant and has forgotten the gift."*

CHAPTER SEVEN:
The Automatic Pilot—Our Main Roadblock

"In order not to feel apprehension when faced with big, challenging occasions, let's approach them with baby steps to achieve our mission!"

—H.J. Shalev

I have already mentioned that the dynamic reality of business in the second decade of the 21st century forces us to change and reinvent ourselves frequently. What once took years now takes months, weeks, and sometimes even hours. The intense pace of our lives keeps accelerating. Therefore, every person—especially a manager, entrepreneur, or business owner—will be unable to succeed in today's reality without the willingness and openness to constantly change in order to adapt himself and his business to the ever-changing business world.

But how do we bring about a business change? How do we overcome the main roadblock to change—namely, our own human nature?

Gandhi said, "If you want to change the world, start with yourself." Forget about the world; let's start with maybe changing the reality **around you**, which you experience daily. This reality is in many ways a mirror of yourself, so in order to change it, you must first change yourself. But most likely you, as most managers and business owners, have no idea how to do that in a planned, organized, and effective way, leaving little room for the luck goddess. The questions that arise are: How to change? What are the components of change? What do we even need in order to begin to change? How do we overcome the fear of change that is so engrained in us?

Starting in this chapter and through the remainder of the book, I will address these questions and provide a **structured, logical, and methodical prescription** for carrying out a sustainable business change from inside out, as well as tools to implement it.

Increasing the Fulfillment of the Human Potential

The Michael Method[32] instructors' course taught me that on average, people fulfill only 7-15% of their personal potential. This statistic always amazed me and made me wonder why. Why do we fulfill such a small percentage of our ability, and how can we increase it to 20%, 30%, or even 50%? Think about it: it's like doubling, tripling, or even quadrupling our "computing ability," or the speed of our "vehicle." Awesome, isn't it? Therefore, I made it my goal to make every effort to increase the fulfillment of my own as well as my clients' human potential. I have found that the way to achieve this increase entails changing habits and the perception of reality. This is the road I took myself ever since I decided to change careers back in 2005. I can testify beyond any doubt that the changes I have implemented in my life, first

---

32 The Michael Method—fulfilling individual potential to attain excellence—is an organization working on personal development of teenagers within the school system; it is a wonderful framework that instills in the youth a belief in their ability, a positive self-image, a positive internal locus of control, a positive attitude, and many practical tools to succeed in life. I took their instructors' training course in 2007, and had the pleasure of leading youths later on. For more information, visit: http://www.michael.org.il/en

and foremost changing my habits, have significantly increased my ability to fulfill much more of my personal potential and succeed. Suffice it to mention that I had a "short fuse" and would easily anger and complain, while today I am much more *above the line*. This is only one example of the myriad of personality traits I have transformed since 2005.

From my personal experience, as well as working with nearly a thousand clients on roads to transformation, I have discovered a recurring pattern in every process of transformation. The purpose of this chapter, and the next one, is to describe the pattern, which I call the **CO-OP Formula**. This formula can be used to lead the way for managers, entrepreneurs, business owners, or anyone changing careers to implement changes more smoothly.

There are two explanations behind the name *CO-OP Formula*. **First**, the formula answers the question, "what are the **cooperating forces** inside our *operating system*?" The obvious answer is the mind and the heart. Not many know this, but the heart is a very important center of intelligence that is connected to the mind and supports it. If so, what do they contain? How do they work to create our reality? I mentioned earlier that our *TTT*, governed by the unconscious mind, creates **The Reality** we experience. But how does it happen? What are the stages that take place in creating reality? For most of us, the *operating system* is a "black box;" we don't understand how it works, therefore we run on *autopilot*. The **second** explanation for the name *CO-OP* is the acronym of **C**onsciousness, **O**bservation, **O**ption, and **P**ractice. In the next chapter, I will break down these steps, one by one, but first let's examine the starting point for making a change.

Evolution Rather Than Revolution

The CO-OP Formula is an evolutionary formula, meaning it expresses a gradual process over time rather than an overnight change. You may be nodding your head in disappointment right now; modern life in the fast lane has us so used to the "instant," we want everything right now, today—better yet, yesterday. We are impatient, pressed for time, and prefer shortcuts. Popular guides on how to make you rich, guaranteeing overnight success, are a good example. I regret to inform you that this book is not one of them. Rather, it deals with evolution—as is seen with most things in nature—not revolution. According to Darwin, evolution is what created all the fascinating forms of life on earth. Anything big ever created by man is the product of evolution: the Great Wall of China, which spans 5,500 miles and took nearly two centuries to build; structures like the Colosseum in Rome or the Taj Mahal in India; the Egyptian pyramids; and more. At the same time, there is Archimedes' eureka and Newton's apple, but those are exceptions of instantaneous revelations. Most things in the universe are evolutionary, as is the process of transformation brought to you in this book in general, and via the CO-OP Formula in particular.

"Chains of habit are too light to be felt until they are too heavy to be broken"—Warren Buffet

The starting point of the formula is in positioning our existing set of *habits* opposite the results we produce in our life. I am referring to "habits" as a broad term consisting of thoughts, conduct, emotions, and beliefs. In fact, "habits" are synonymous with everything contained in our *Operating System*. I have already mentioned that *habits* dwell in our unconscious mind; however, what I am also referring to here is all our conscious behaviors— that is, the *TTT* we discussed earlier. The starting point shows a direct link between our *existing habits* and the *current results* we produce.

Diagram 7-1 illustrates that:

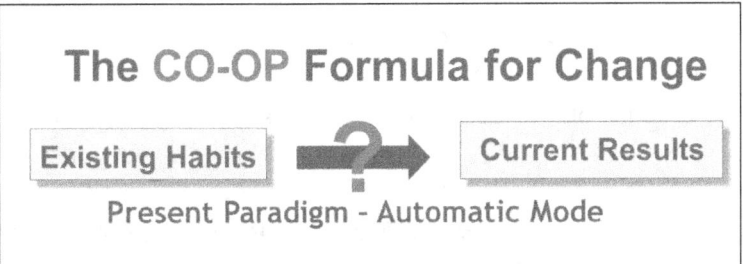

Diagram 7-1 – the link between Existing Habits and Current Results

Let's look at an example: When I am punctual, hardworking, communicative, friendly, positive, and optimistic, all of these are beneficial *habits* that cause me to produce good results. But if I'm not a tidy person, am a procrastinator, non-communicative, angry, perfectionist, blaming others, complaining, resist everything, pessimistic, and have many more impeding traits, these debilitating *habits* hinder the results I produce. It's clear that these *habits* interfere with my energy, power, and precision, as well as my communication level with the people around me on whom I rely for my success. Hence, the damage to the results I produce is obvious. In summation, I will reiterate that **there is a clear connection between a person's *existing habits* and the *current results* he yields in his life.**

As absurd as it may sound, **most people are unaware of the connection between their *existing habits* and *current results***, as the question mark in diagram 7-1 represents. Why? Because how else can you explain the fact that people have *habits* that hinder their success, and yet they stick to them instead of changing them? This lack of awareness causes them to blame their life's *circumstances* for their bad luck: the economy, the government, their parents, their spouses, their bosses—the list is practically endless. When there is someone to blame for their failure to succeed, **most people won't see or understand how they create their own reality**; how their *habits*—their *TTT*—affect, more than anything else, the results they produce. This is the essence of the *Focus Principle* I reviewed in chapter three.

"The definition of insanity is repeating the same mistakes and expecting different results"—Albert Einstein

What is that akin to? To having a habit that harms me and sends me banging my head against the wall with a negative result—a headache. Yet, I still don't understand the connection between banging my head against the wall and getting a headache. I keep wondering why my head hurts, as I continue to bang my head against the wall out of habit, experiencing the pain over and over again. Meaning, I don't see the relationship between the action, the habit, and their outcome.

In this state, my habit has the upper hand and I stick to it, unaware and unable to recognize the results it brings. This, of course, is an extreme, exaggerated case, but think of how many *habits* we repeat over and over in our lives, reaching unsatisfactory results.

Now I shall address the moral of the story: How many people have "headaches"—that is, problems in life—because they "bang their heads against the wall," meaning they possess debilitating *habits* that cause these problems, yet which they are unaware of? I call this conduct being **without a positive EYE**. And what do most people do when they have a "headache?" That's right, they take a painkiller. But the painkiller doesn't solve the problem at its root; it only handles the symptom. Therefore, the "headache" is only temporarily relieved, but recurs again and again so long as they continue "banging their heads against the wall." Similarly, many people handle their life's problems only after they have surfaced, without knowing or understanding how they could have prevented them from the start. Yes, the problems recur and there is no choice but to blame the surroundings for them. A similar phenomenon is taking shape today with regards to antidepressants. Due to the worldwide depression epidemic, whose eradication from the source isn't an option known to most people, or is too long and complicated for them, those depressed take more and more medication that only relieves their depression temporarily, but does not solve the root of the problem. Indeed, they go looking for instant solutions—and didn't we mention that already?

Despite all the negative implications of the *existing habits*, we usually hold on to them. We don't understand that we ourselves have caused the results by how we behave, in our way of thinking and feeling, in our beliefs, and in the way we respond to them—all of these are *habits* that dictate our everyday conduct.

There is no better than Einstein's statement in this subchapter's heading to illustrate just how much most of us behave "insanely" in our current reality.

Hey, Fly, the Next Window Is Open!

This subchapter's title sums up humankind's **automatic behavior**. We've touched on this *program* in chapter two:

If a person is unaware of the correlation between his *existing habits* and the *current results* he produces, it means his behavior is mechanical, unaware, self-activated—like a robot, a golem, or a puppet on strings. While it may be a rather offensive way to describe our daily life, unfortunately, it is indeed the case.

◆

Another analogy to describe this automatic state is when a fly is trapped in a room and tries to leave, banging into the window again and again, thinking he can break through it. The poor fly is unaware of the option to fly out through the open window next to it, and so persistently continues at his task, to no avail.

Here is another example, this time from real life: One of my clients, Ed (alias), had a habit of being too verbose. Ed was naturally unaware of it, and used to exhaust his conversation partners to the point where they began to avoid him. Ed couldn't understand why his social life was suffering. This habit no doubt affected his results, influencing his life for the worse. With my help and the help of the *CO-OP Formula*, Ed realized his debilitating automatic habit, changed it, and began to reap a lot more success in his life in general, and his career in particular.

Here is an additional list of examples for limiting *habits* from the business world, which I often run into in my work. These habits impede their owner's results, without them being sufficiently aware:

- √ A domineering manager who restricts his employees and prevents them from doing their job properly.

- √ Procrastination that prevents the business owner from engaging in important activity (such as marketing and sales), causing him to "escape" to secondary, unimportant activities.

- √ A "short fuse" which causes the manager to respond rudely during important negotiations and delays agreements and progress.

- √ A business owner's limiting belief—"I'm not good enough"—causing perfectionism, stress and overload, bad time management, self-criticism, and back again[33]

√ Automatic resistance to changing economies, getting stuck in the comfort zone, and chronic conservatism that hinders change, growth, and prosperity.

In most of these cases, the executive or business owner is totally unaware of the extent to which the *habits* that don't serve him create the reality he is experiencing. With such awareness lacking, **he has no access to change**, because he doesn't see himself as the cause of his management or business results!

Man Hath No Pre-Eminence Above Beast—Ecclesiastes 3:19

According to the Kabbalah, people **operate on automatic mode 90% of the time.** Think about it—90% of the time, our habits affect the results we produce without us even being aware of their influence and how to find a way out of this loop! Furthermore, you've probably heard the expression, "Man hath no pre-eminence above beast.[34]" But in what way is man more eminent than a beast? It's customary to think that man is superior to the beast in morality and responsibility, two areas whose common denominator is the ability to **choose**. Indeed, we were given the right to choose back in the Garden of Eden, but if we spend 90% of the time on *auto mode*, unaware of the correlation between

---

33 I developed a new model I call the "Excellent Catch-22," which characterizes at least 30% of people and causes blockage. Look out for my new book on the topic, which will illuminate and expand on this catch from all its practical and theoretical aspects.

34 The full verse from Ecclesiastes 3:19 says, "For that which befalleth the sons of men befalleth beasts; even one thing befalleth them: as the one dieth, so dieth the other; yea, they have all one breath; so that a man hath no preeminence above a beast: for all is vanity." Here, the

habits and results, it means that we actually have no *choice* 90% of the time! If so, we're not fulfilling our entire potential because we're simply not choosing enough, **and without *choice*, we are just like any beast**, hence, "man hath no pre-eminence above beast." Therefore, the essence and purpose of any transformation process is to get out of *auto mode* and increase our ability to choose, which we shall see how to implement in the next chapter.

The *automatic program* consists of *existing habits* that don't serve us and lead to inadequate *current results*. Thus, we understand that if our *existing habits* have led us to the *current results* (diagram 7-1), and we want better results, we must **form new, better *habits*** in order to achieve *improved results*.

Diagram 7-2 illustrates that:

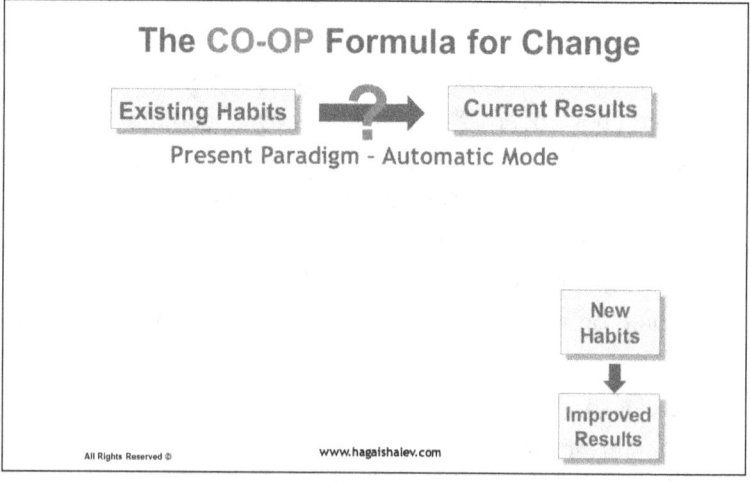

The CO-OP Formula for Change

Existing Habits → Current Results

Present Paradigm - Automatic Mode

New Habits

Improved Results

All Rights Reserved ©   www.hagaishalev.com

Diagram 7-2 – the purpose of the transformation process

idea is that both man and beast are mortal. Today, we use the verse as a partial expression with an opposite meaning in order to emphasize man's spiritual superiority over the beast.

This is the purpose of the transformation process: to achieve better results in order to gain success. Some of the questions that arise are: How can we change our *existing habits* and adopt new, *improved habits?* How do we get out of *auto mode* and acquire and implement *improved habits* that will enable us to achieve *improved results?*

The CO-OP Formula helps us answer these questions with a precise, organized and systematic structuring. All this will be discussed in the following chapter, chapter eight.

◆

I shall close this chapter with a verse by French poet Paul Valéry: *"The best way to make your dreams come true is to wake up."*

PART II

GETTING
USED TO
SUCCESS

CHAPTER EIGHT:
The Change Begins Now!

"Dripping water hollows out stone not through force but through persistence"

—Ovid

Congratulations on reaching the heart of this book. What you've read so far in the first seven chapters was designed to prepare you for this chapter, which describes and teaches you how to make any change in your *TTT* from a practical standpoint. Abraham Lincoln once said, "If I had eight hours *to chop down a tree, I'd spend six hours sharpening my ax.*" I'm a firm believer in this approach and have chosen to implement it in this book. Since every person has automatic mechanisms that resist change in his *operating system*, diving straight into this chapter would have activated these mechanisms in you and sabotaged your opportunity to implement the *CO-OP Formula* with a *positive EYE*.

I already mentioned in chapter four that the degree of transformation in general, and a breakthrough in particular, depends on the balance between the **commitment** to undergo change and the **circumstances** that impede it. In the power struggle between them, only when the *commitment* is stronger than the *circumstances* will a change occur. If so, the challenge faced by the changing person is to reinforce the *commitment* and weaken the *circumstances,* so the *commitment* has the upper hand, forging towards the change and breakthrough. In a nutshell, this is what we have discussed in the first seven chapters.

Before we dive deeper, I shall add another vital component to *commitment*, and that is **openness**. As *commitment's* courageous friend, *openness* is crucial for undergoing change, since it enables the transfer of new information through the human filters I have mentioned in chapter three. Without *openness*, we resist automatically and tend to negate everything that doesn't correlate with our world view, thus blocking any road to change. If so, the first seven chapters aimed to prepare yourself for the "real thing;" having read them, you're probably less skeptical now and more **open and committed** to making your change while coping with your *circumstances* and overpowering them. I'm convinced that the "six hours spent sharpening your ax" will pay off once you start "chopping the tree" of habits that debilitate you, cutting it down completely by the end of the book.

In chapter seven, I presented the starting point: our *existing habits* dictate our *current results*, mostly automatically. I also said that the essence of any transformation process is exchanging the *existing habits* for new, *better habits*, in order to gain *improved results* (see diagram 7-2).

Therefore, the million dollar question is: how do we recognize the *existing habits* that don't serve us and replace them with new and *better habits?* How can we acquire and apply *new habits* that will bring us *improved results* that fit our desires and goals in life and in business?

Let's start breaking down the process of transformation to its stages.

"Self-knowledge is the starting point of personal excellence"—Robin Sharma

The first step in changing our habits is raising **self-awareness** [35](diagram 8-1). Oxford dictionary defines awareness as, "knowledge or perception of a situation or fact." To make it simple, we can say that awareness means being in a state of knowledge when we have the proper information. The question is, what is the proper information? **What do we need to know in order to begin undergoing change?** Awareness of what?

◆

I distinguish between three levels of awareness, all of which are required in order to undergo change:

The first level of *awareness* is recognizing the *habits* that don't serve us, acknowledging and accepting them. As with anything we want to change, we must first become aware of, recognize, and accept the existing situation. In this regard, we must also be aware of the correlation between *existing habits* and *current results*, as is represented by the question mark in diagram 8-1. In order to achieve change, we must **be aware of the cause and effect relationship between the cause (the habit) and the effect (result) it produces.** As absurd as it may sound, as with the "banging the head against the wall" example in chapter seven, I must be aware that if my head hurts, it's because I just banged it against the wall. If I don't see that connection at all, then I'm surely unable to change. In this case, the only solution is a painkiller, and that, as said, only treats the symptom and not the cause, and is thus ineffective in removing the headache for good.

---

35 For semantic reasons, I'll refer to awareness as Consciousness in the CO-OP Formula and its diagrams.

Another example: an angry manager who wishes to motivate his employees towards achieving better results should be aware of the correlation between his anger and responses and how they affect his surroundings and the results he and his team achieve. As long as he is unaware of this correlation, he won't understand the reason for his team's poor function, won't know what to change, and therefore will not be able to change anything. Such lack of *awareness* usually causes the manager to blame his environment for the results because he doesn't acknowledge his responsibility for the situation. In chapter three, we called this state an *external locus of control*, which is one of the main factors that impede change.

Even if I'm aware of the correlation between banging my head against the wall and my headache, the *habit* may overpower me, so I may stick to it despite its destructive results. If so, we need some more levels of awareness in order to change the *habit*.

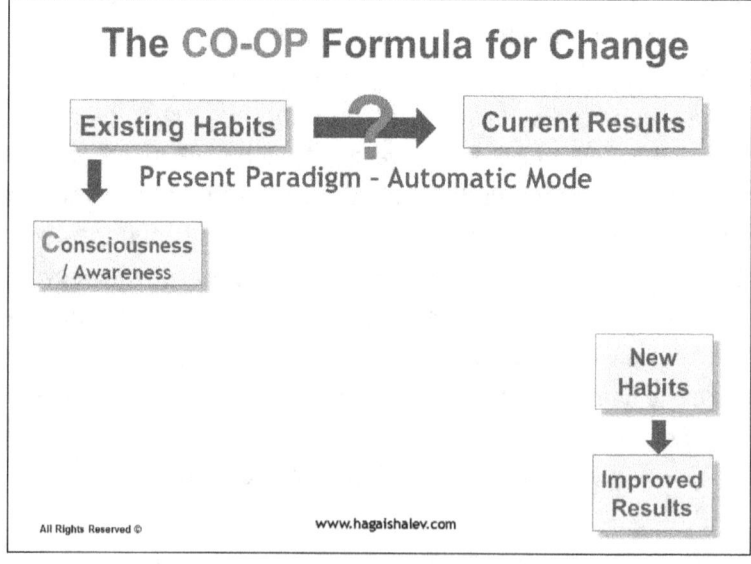

Diagram 8-1 – Awareness is the key to any change

The second level of *awareness* required is that any ***habit* is changeable.** This is not obvious to most people. For example, the irritable manager may claim, "This is who I am and you must accept me as I am." Just so you know, cranky manager, you can change your character and learn to be less reactive and more *above the line*. I mentioned in chapter three that Dr. Bruce Lipton proved in his research that, by changing our belief system, we can change the function of our genes. And if this is true about our genes, the very building blocks of our bodies, why wouldn't we be able to change our *habits*, too?

With banging our head against the wall, it could be quite frustrating knowing what causes the headache while being unaware of one's ability to change this *automatic habit* and stop the banging. This could lead to helplessness, self-judgment, and self-blame, thus sabotaging the change. Furthermore, it's clear that automatic behaviors have no *positive EYE* and cause one to drop *below the line* and impede results. To prevent that, I have **to know** I can change my banging *habit*, thus opening up to optimism about the possibility of change. Sometimes the power of habit can be strong and durable, like an entrenchment, but even if it's a very old *habit*, automatic and well engrained in your unconscious mind, **know that you have the power to change!** This is the second level of *awareness* vital to any change.

The third level of *awareness* required to undergo change is the knowledge of **how** to change *habits*; not just acknowledging that we can change *habits* that don't serve us, but learning and finding out the **way** to actually change them. In chapter six, I mentioned a number of methods to change *habits* in the unconscious mind. In this chapter, I will teach you my methodology for changing *habits*, the *CO-OP Formula*, so you can soon acquire the third level of *awareness* needed to undergo any change.

The Vital Link to Transformation That Is Missing in Most Awareness Methods

In short, the following **three levels of awareness** are required in order to open a window to change: *awareness* of having *existing habits* that don't serve us and of the linkage between them and our *current results*; *awareness* of being able to change these *habits*; and *awareness* of how to change them.

So far, I've dealt at great length with developing your awareness: the *above and below the line* model, the *Fulfillment Pyramid* model, the *focus principle*, *positive attitude*, and the five principles for undergoing a successful process of transformation in chapter four are a few important foundations for success that have surely expanded your *awareness*. Sometimes, *awareness* alone can cause change. In my client Ed's case, it was enough to bring his attention to his talkative nature (gently) for him to "get it" and transform himself accordingly. His newfound *awareness* was enough to draw his attention to his communication *habits* and led him to becoming less verbose. If the fly banging into the windowpane again and again knows that the next window over is open and that it can exit from there, this *awareness* alone will probably be enough for him to skip the closed window and exit through the open one.

However, while *awareness* is a prerequisite for change, **it's usually not enough to bring about change. In most cases, *awareness* doesn't generate choice.** For most people, knowledge itself isn't enough; they need more in order to uproot a long-standing *habit*. After all, how many times have you said, "I want to but it doesn't work out?" How many times have you decided to do sports, or go on a diet, or cut down on watching TV, or exchange any other *habit* that doesn't serve you for a better *habit*? Every kid knows what is needed in order to lose weight—eat less and exercise more—yet the obesity epidemic is spreading wider and wider.

People's *awareness* in these matters isn't enough to motivate them to act consistently and diligently to transform themselves.

If so, *awareness* alone, as important as it is, will not suffice. I have met many aware people in my life who, unfortunately, were also poor, because it required much more than their *awareness* to make a change. The next vital step on our way to *choice* after becoming *aware* is **self-observation**, as shown in diagram 8-2. One of the things that separates man from the beast is his ability to observe himself. When we are aware that something is happening to us, we can also **observe ourselves** as it happens. For example, if I'm aware that I cause myself a headache when I bang my head against the wall, the next time I get a headache, my *awareness* will allow me to **observe myself** while **actually** banging my head. Of course, this *self-observation* will allow me to stop doing that, which is already a *choice*—the beginning of the change.

By the way, *self-observation* doesn't always happen in real time. Sometimes I engage in it only in retrospect. For example, I may only realize today that I was angry yesterday, behaved inappropriately, and as a result caused antagonism with my partner in conversation and didn't achieve the results I wanted. We shall soon see how even **self-observation in retrospect** promotes change. However, it should be noted that, in order for us to actually complete the change, we must eventually be able to *self-observe* **in the present**, which is something we have to practice.

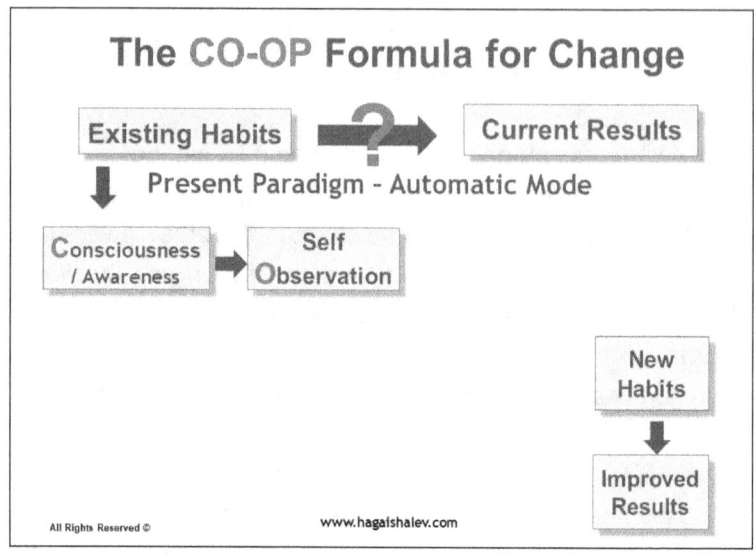

Diagram 8-2—Self-observation is the missing component in most awareness methods

The more you practice **awareness** and **self-observation**[36], the more you can upgrade the observation to occur in real time, in the present. How do you practice *self-observation*? More about that in this chapter and in the following chapter.

In my extensive researches into transformation insights and tools, I have learned many awareness methods. Indeed, while I didn't master every single one of them, even a partial knowledge made it clear that most awareness methods have one major flaw: **they are overly abstract and theoretical, lacking practicality, and unable to properly link between theory and practice**, between their core idea and daily life. These methods strongly emphasize awareness, but to some degree neglect self-observation, which can bring theory into practice—the *choice*. If those awareness

---

36 For semantic reasons, I'll refer to Self-Observation as Observation in the CO-OP Formula's diagrams.

methods do include self-observation (such as in Buddhism), it's not sufficiently prominent and structured from the get go, such that every student can adopt it right when they start their practical experimentation and implementation. I would like to clarify that I am not criticizing those awareness methods, but am simply expressing my opinion as to what I think should be emphasized in order to accelerate personal development and create quick changes with a *positive EYE—self-observation*, which is exactly what I do in the methodology I have developed.

Self-observation is the main factor and the escape from the *autopilot program,* the same *program* that is usually stronger than you and reverts you back to your evil ways. It's like an automatic pilot steering your airplane to an unwanted destination while you try to manually turn it around. As long as you keep manually steering, you will take command of the airplane. But if you let go for even a moment, it will go back to its automatic direction against your will. **This is the main obstacle people face: for most of us, willpower alone isn't enough to persist in manual steering.** The inability to continue consistently is the main hurdle in modern life. We have so much to handle that if we let the *autopilot* back in even a bit, it will return to its evil ways and we'll be left with the disappointment or even trauma of "we tried, but it's impossible..."

This is where *self-observation* enters the picture, enabling us to constantly observe the *autopilot* through our *aware* eyes. *Self-observation* **enables us to actually translate *awareness* into *choice*;** it is the bridge between theory and practice. It's as if you're constantly in the company of a good friend whose eyes and perspective enable you to see yourself; as if you have constant cellular reception with a fly on the wall who reports your whereabouts and what your *autopilot* is doing at every moment. Sounds exhausting? Don't worry, you'll soon learn how to create a **new autopilot program**, a new *habit*, an excellent *habit* of constant *awareness and self-observation*.

No Chase and No Chance—But Choice!

Self-observation in itself also does not bring about change. However, *self-observation* restores our **choice**, and this is its significance. As I mentioned in chapter seven, when on *autopilot*, we don't fully exercise the **choice** given to us, not really rising above the beasts. Therefore, **the purpose of any process of transformation is to restore our** *choice* and enable us to choose as much as we can, moving from change by chance to change by *choice*. This is one of the main factors that will enable people to increase the fulfillment of their potential.

When self-observation happens in the present, we are presented with **choice**, which is the next stage in the CO-OP Formula, as seen in diagram 8-3[37]. If I'm already aware of the correlation between banging my head against the wall (and the two other levels of awareness I discussed above), and I'm observing myself in real time while carrying out this bad habit, I have regained the ability **to choose**. Choose what? Naturally, to stop myself from banging my head against the wall—a choice to stop the debilitating habit. It's worth noting that at least at the onset of the transformation process, I recommend making **small choices**, even tiny ones, taking **baby steps**[38] from choice to choice. It's not the place or time for procrastinators to launch a project they

---

37 For semantic reasons, I'll refer to choice as Option in the CO-OP Formula and its diagrams.

38 From here on, I shall use the term "baby steps" to illustrate an increasing succession of small choices, from easy to harder, one after another.

have been putting off for two years, or those with stage fright to get on stage and give their best lecture. You see, the autopilot is a strong, stubborn enemy, and a powerful head-on battle will only strengthen and entrench it even more. Evolution, not revolution, is the name of the game. Any new habit should be broken down into intermediate steps and **begun with the tiniest first step.** This approach enables us to slowly break through the program's dam, until the drops turn into a steady wave that breaks open the dam and enables the new habit to flow freely without being stopped. Indeed, as Ovid said in the opening of this chapter, **"Dripping water hollows out stone not through force but through persistence."** Drop by drop, we infiltrate our unconscious mind and plant in it a tiny change before the "gatekeeper" entrusted to its entrance can notice us. Indeed, with as strong and tenacious an enemy as the autopilot, only guerilla war can lead to victory.

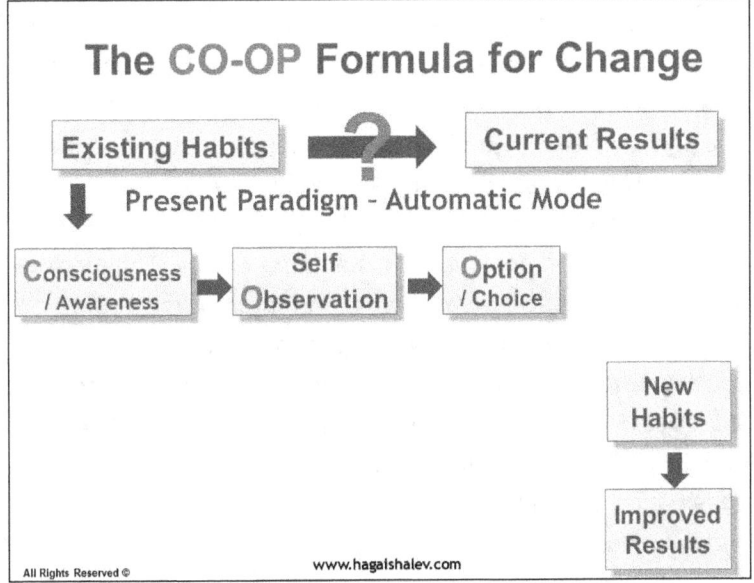

Diagram 8-3 – Choice is the beginning of Change

As I've said, *self-observation* doesn't always happen while **performing** the unruly habit; sometimes we only notice it in retrospect. For example, I may only notice my headache half an hour after banging my head against the wall. Being already *aware* of it, I *observe myself* in retrospect and see how banging my head a half an hour earlier caused my current headache. In this situation, it's best to first **accept** the rowdy behavior. Accept it, because it's already happened, and making it "wrong" is not going to take away my headache; I would only be making matters worse, dropping *below the line* and blocking change. Unlike the *autopilot program* in most people, there is no point in resisting the past, in blaming or self-judging; those are likely to worsen my headache. I must first accept the past (having already banged my head against the wall), and immediately think of **what** I can learn from it and **how** to avoid repeating the bad habit in the future (*questions of opportunity and possibility*—see chapter three). It's clear that, according to the *Focus Principle*, I am focusing on the solution instead of the problem, thus opening up to solving it faster. The solution is a *future choice*: while it's too late to stop banging my head as a choice, I can decide that the next time the *autopilot* returns and has me banging my head against the wall, I will notice it in real time so that I can choose, in that **future moment**, to avoid doing it. This is a *future choice*. The more we practice **observation in retrospect** and **future choice**, the more we can shorten the time between performing the bad *habit* and noticing its results, until we begin implementing **present moment** *self-observation* in the unconscious mind to make *choices* in **real time**. This is the practice needed in order to develop *self-observation* skills and abide by them, as a gateway to restoring *choice* in our life.

◆

To sum up so far: We learned the 3 levels of *awareness*, we *observed* ourselves in real time and *chose*, which then opened up a major gateway to change! This is the outline of the *CO-OP Formula* and the required, essential practice in order to implement it successfully.

As we near the end of this subchapter, here is an insight about *choice*, which may seem obvious: We want to make **conscious choices**, ones which aren't automatic, but are made with a *positive EYE*: Efficiency, Yield, and Expediency—choices that drive us towards the *improved results* we want to achieve. If you do that, you will move from change by chance to change by *choice*.

Robin Sharma's words are a perfect way to close this subchapter: "Believe it's all destiny, but act like it's all choice."

An Important Reminder

You probably know people in your work environment with an *existing habit* that is harmful to them. Have you ever encountered a manager that doesn't trust his employees, demands to be involved in the smallest details of their work, demanding to approve every matter and becoming a bottleneck? Perhaps you're like that yourself?

Well, with your knowledge of the steps in the formula, it's clear that it is an **existing habit** of the manager's which disempowers his employees, restrains them, prolongs his team's execution process, and therefore damages his and his team's **current results**. Furthermore, from what you've read so far, you can conclude that if the manager would become **aware** of this habit and **observe** *himself* and his team while on *auto mode*, he could **choose** to change the habit bit by bit. However, while all of these are essential conditions for undergoing change, they are not enough. In order for our manager to transform himself, he must be **open** to receive feedback, to learn new things, and of course, to **want** them and be **committed** to implementing them. This is where the human ego stands in the way, and many times blocks any change. I discussed this in length in chapter four.

Therefore, I am reminding you that in order to undergo change, you must **first be open and committed** to the transformation process, even before you implement the *CO-OP Formula*. You must acknowledge the importance of the change, be willing to put aside your ego, accept feedback, be flexible with your thoughts and habits, and focus on the *improved results* you wish to achieve. Indeed, this change isn't simple, but as you can see from the book, I am breaking it down to its components, since each in itself is much easier to perform. The main question is, how much **are you willing to change yourself and seeking to change yourself**, and how **open and committed** are you to that? All the rest is mainly technique, persistence, and perseverance.

How to Preserve the Choice?

Even if you are open and committed to change, *choosing* a *new habit* once isn't enough, because your life's routine will easily throw you back into your *existing habit*, the *autopilot*. As I mentioned in chapter six, implementing a *new habit* in the unconscious mind is an evolutionary process, requiring repetition and perseverance through *baby steps*. Therefore, you must repeat the **choice** again and again and again[39]. This is the next step in implementing the *CO-OP Formula—***practice.** Research shows that in order to

---

39 In chapter nine, I will give more details about the recommended frequency of performing the choice and how to execute the practice.

create a *new habit*, you must practice it consecutively for thirty days[40]. This allows for the old habit to change and a new, better *habit* to form.

This is the full circle (diagram 8-4): **Awareness** of the connection between habits and results enables real-time **self-observation**, which opens us up to regaining **choice** and fulfilling it in *baby steps*, again and again and again, until after a 30-day **practice**, a **new, better habit** is formed, producing **improved results**.

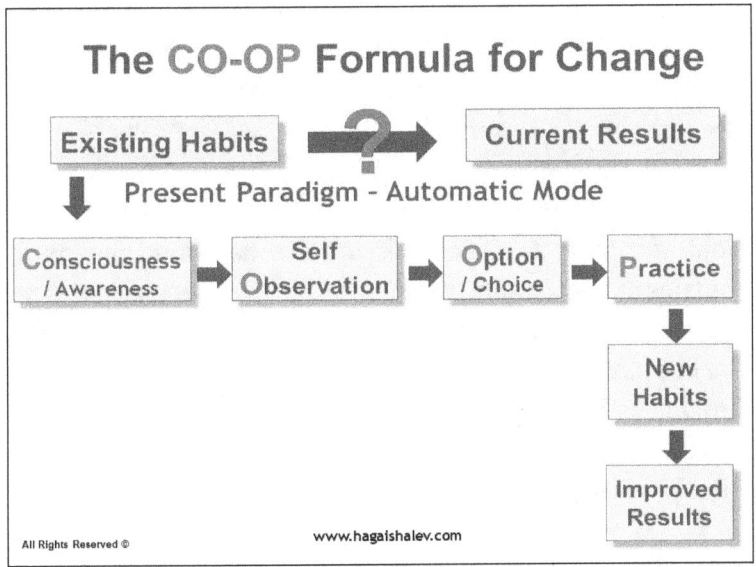

Diagram 8-4–The CO-OP Formula's complete path from Awareness to Improved Results

---

40 Research findings are not uniform here: some say 21 days of repetition is enough to implement the change while other say 28 days. To remove any doubt, I choose 30 days. However, if 30 days aren't enough either, I recommend extending the implementation period by a few days. These few extra days are nothing compared to the effort you've already invested in the change, and surely nothing compared to the benefit of the improved results it will bring you

This sums up the theoretical aspect of the *CO-OP Formula*. From now until the end of this chapter, and more intensely throughout the rest of the book, I shall expand on and demonstrate how to make the formula applicable and practical; as a result, you will be able to use it in your daily life with any change in your *TTT* so you can fulfill The Reality that is ideal for yourself.

Tools, People, Tools

The next stage in the *CO-OP Formula* is the **tools**. Before I introduce the *tools*, I would like to mention that the acronym "*CO-OP*" stands for the formula's components: **C**onsciousness (awareness), self-**O**bservation, **O**ption (choice), **P**ractice, and... Tools (diagram 8-5).

What are the *tools*? **The *tools* are the hands-on means to implement the formula in practice.** The formula's outline—*self-awareness, self-observation and choice*—are all abstract terms. The question is, what do we do with them? How do we implement the formula in daily life to bring about change? The answer is with the help of the *tools*. The latter enable us to break down the formula into implementable actions that generate change.

Aside from calling them by name, I have already reviewed quite a few *tools* for you in this book, mainly in chapter three. The time has come to connect them to the formula in order to illustrate its application. In fact, all the characteristics *above the line* discussed in chapter three are *tools* for implementing change according to the *CO-OP Formula* (see diagram 3-3)—the *focus principle, positive attitude, accepting the past*, and *questions of opportunity and possibility* ("what and how?") are all such *tools*.

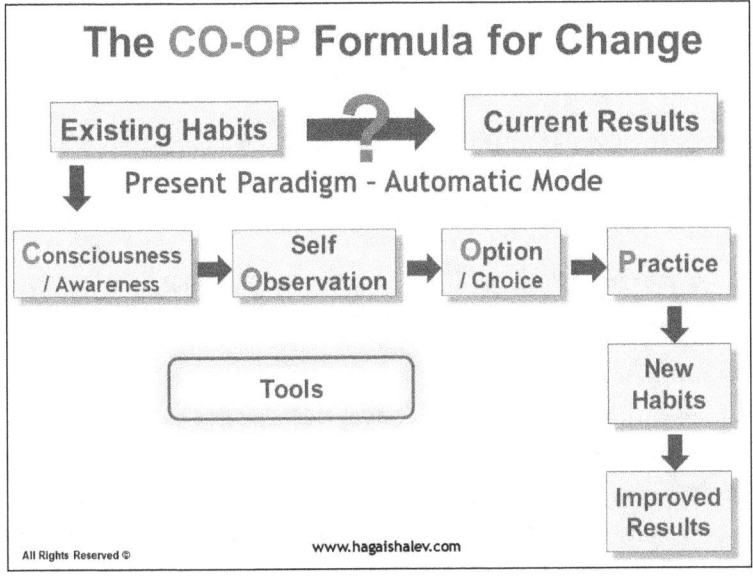

Diagram 8-5 – The Tools supporting the Formula's outline: Awareness, Self-observation and Choice

For example: Let's say I have a habit that doesn't serve me—I "live in the past." I think about the past a lot, sometimes nostalgically, but mostly with frustration due to all the mistakes I have made and at everyone who has ever stood in my way of getting what I deserve. I blow off steam, complaining and blaming the past and everyone around me for my current miserable fate. In chapter three, I called it "resisting the past." It's clear that such *TTT* is an *existing habit* that drags me *below the line*, sabotaging my *current results*. It's also focusing me on the negative past, thus preventing me from focusing on the present and the positive future I wish to create for myself. With a lack of *awareness*, this habit is automatic and I can't see the correlation between it and the unsatisfactory *current results* I am producing in my life. This is the first part of the *CO-OP Formula*—the *autopilot*—which you learned about in chapter seven.

In order to transform myself, I must work according to the main elements of the formula, as detailed in this chapter:

1. Develop **awareness** of that habit; acknowledge that it exists within me, harms me, that I should and can change it, and that I have a way to do it using the formula.

2. **Observe myself** each time I automatically slip into the past and, as a result, express myself with a negative *TTT*.

3. **Choose,** each time I observe and identify it, to change my *TTT* with a *positive EYE,* taking *baby steps.* Meaning, let go of the past, stop dwelling on it, accept it instead of resisting it[41], forgive myself and others, focus on the present, and ask myself how I can advance today in order to achieve better results in the future.

4. **Practice** these choices at least twelve times a day by taking *baby steps,* even if only for a few seconds each time.

5. After 30 days of practice, I've created a **new habit**: I accept the past, I don't dwell on it or resist it, I let it go and focus on the present in *TTT* with a *positive EYE* to the future, thus finding myself more *above the line* and achieving **improved results** in my life.

---

41 The absurdity is that even if I really want to, I can't change my past, so I have no choice but to accept it. Accepting the past doesn't necessarily mean agreeing with it. "Accepting" means it's already happened, I can't change it. "Not agreeing to it" means after I've accepted the past, how can I change it in the future? What can I do today to make my future different? If that past has brought me to a present which I'm unhappy with, I don't agree to it and say, "This is it," but I take initiative in the present and choose to be proactive and responsible in order to change the automatic future derived from the past.

Similarly, **you can take any** *habit* **that doesn't serve you and change it using the** *tools* **I am sharing with you in this book**. The *tools* illuminate and indicate what in your automatic behavior may hinder your results. They direct you to automatic failure points in your thinking and behavior, providing a real checklist. When you go over it while knowing yourself, the automatic *habits* you wish to change will surface. Sometimes you need a coach or a person that knows you well in order to shine a flashlight on the *habits* that are debilitating you. After locating them, apply the formula to them, mainly its crux*: Awareness, self-observation,* and *choice.* In my workshops and private coaching sessions, I teach about fifteen main *tools* to make a change and guide people on how to implement them using the *CO-OP Formula.* Throughout the book, I cover about ten *tools* in detail. The attached bookmark[42] (diagram 8-6) includes these *tools* and a few others, most of which are partially addressed in the book. Learn how to implement them, practice them, and you will be able to create the necessary changes in your life to fulfill your potential and accomplish getting used to success.

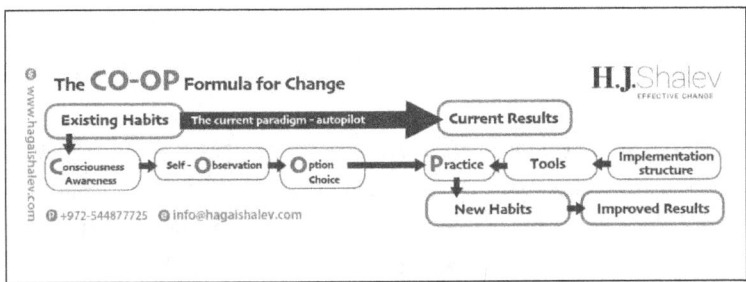

Diagram 8-6-1 – Tools Bookmark #1

---

42 See the Tools Bookmark attached to this book. If you haven't received it with your copy, please send a message to office@hagaishalev.com and write on the subject line, "Please send me the English version of the Tools Bookmark," and I'll sent it to you.

"The price of greatness is responsibility"— Winston Churchill
Here is another example for implementing another tool:

I once worked with a very talented manager named Fred (alias) who failed to fulfill his business potential. He experienced recurring problems and his results didn't take off. After a few months of working with my methodology, I was surprised to find out that nothing much had changed. Since Fred was open and committed to the coaching process, it seemed odd and atypical to me. Usually, when my clients are open and committed, I don't even have to be at my best—the results come. But since every cause has an effect, I wracked my brain trying to find the source of Fred's standstill.

One paradox stood out the entire time: Fred's manager told him that he was not taking enough responsibility for the matters that were under his care. In contrast, Fred seemed on the outside to be the epitome of assuming responsibility: he was always accountable, he took initiative, took a lot on himself, was involved in every matter his subordinates handled, and was highly motivated. If so, then what did his boss want from him, and what did he mean by "irresponsible?"

Finally, I realized Fred **complains and whines a lot** and that this was the source of the paradox. I suddenly realized just how tricky our ego can be, like a Trojan horse inside us, catching us off guard. **Every time we whine, complain, and blame, we're unconsciously shrugging off some of our responsibility.** If so-and-so is to blame for an erroneous figure, and if so-and-so is holding me back from carrying out my task, then I'm not fully responsible for my results! And if I'm so dependent on others, then as long as **they** don't change and deliver the goods, I won't be able to achieve the results I want! That is, complaining and grumbling automatically program our unconscious mind to believe that our power is limited and that we cannot solve our problems on our own. Thus, the unconscious mind, the super-computer that determines 95% of our results, tells us to give up *Doing* and remain in our comfort zone. If so, it's clear why we don't fulfill our potential and why we yield unsatisfactory results.

Hence, the relevant *tool* is a full *internal locus of control*, taking 100% responsibility for our actions and results, avoid blaming others for what doesn't work for us, and giving up on complaining and grumbling[43]. When Fred became **aware** of this habit of whining and complaining, realizing that it was holding him back, he could **observe** himself in

---

43 In my work, I have found that this is one of the greatest challenges of humankind. The habit of complaining and grumbling is so engrained in us and accepted in our culture that no one realizes how much it impedes success. Notice your tendency to complain and whine. Avoid doing it, and you will experience a significant upgrade in your performance.

Tools

1. Openness and commitment to change
2. The Focus Principle – focusing on what is working and enhancing
3. Positive attitude
4. Asking questions of possibility and opportunity: How and What, instead of Why
5. Emotion as an indicator – choose to be Above the Line
6. E.T.F.B Model as a tool for controlling thoughts and emotions
7. Changing paradigms that don't serve you
8. Choosing Internal Locus of Control and proactivity, applying no to circumstances
9. Don't resist automatically, accept what you cannot change
10. Let go of the need to control and to know all the details
11. Choose to want instead of need or must or have to
12. Accept the past, be in the present and don't fear the future
13. Give up self-judgment, be proactive and responsible, don't blame
14. Forgive yourself and others
15. Give up perfectionism
16. The Fulfillment Pyramid – act out of the Being according to the be-do-have principle
17. The Being question: When I [...] how do I feel, think and act?
18. Choose the higher-self consciousness instead of the ego
19. Give up grumbling and complaining
20. Choose gratitude
21. Business planning as a tool for fulfillment and success
22. Use the imagination and program the unconscious mind to success
23. Meditation – a tool to access the unconscious mind to create change in it
24. Unconditional self-love and love of others

Diagram 8-6-2—Tools Bookmark #2

real time while complaining and grumbling. Only then was he able to **choose** a **tool** and stop it. After some **practice**, he indeed created a **new habit** and managed **to improve his and his team's results** significantly.

Fred implemented all the steps in the *CO-OP Formula* while using the full *internal locus of control tool.*

Those were two examples of implementing the *tools* in the *CO-OP Formula*. Other examples and explanations for tool implementation will be presented in the following chapter and throughout the rest of the book.

And Now, to the Hidden Iceberg

Before we dive deeper into the *CO-OP Formula* and implement more of its *tools*, I would like to connect what you learned in chapter six with this chapter.

In chapter six, I mentioned that since the unconscious mind is the source of all *habits*, and because it's not easily accessible, any transformation process should include a structured method to access the unconscious mind in order to generate the proper changes to support our goals.

Here is a reminder of what it said:

"By now you will realize that the challenge facing anyone who wishes to fulfill his potential, thrive, and succeed, is harnessing his unconscious mind to benefit his conscious wishes. To do that, he must find a way to access the unconscious mind, despite its inaccessibility, and program it to promote his goals. The average person, subject to automatic programming during his life, cannot make a meaningful change in his life without reprogramming the unconscious mind. Accessing the unconscious mind is crucial in order to pave new paths and assimilate new and better *habits*. Thus, **any process of transformation must first include a change in the limiting perceptions of the unconscious.** Otherwise, without being able to influence the real human *operating system*, a change made on the conscious level alone is doomed to fail."

◆

Take a look at diagram 8-7. It represents a transformation process according to the *CO-OP Formula* while reviewing what happens in our brain during the transformation. In chapter six, I said that there is another method to creating change in the unconscious mind. It may be less glamorous or quick to yield results than other methods, but it's highly effective and brings sustainable results. **This method for transforming the unconscious mind is based on the fact that when we repeat something in the conscious mind, it slowly trickles into the unconscious mind, where it's imprinted as a change.** For example, when someone takes driving lessons, he gradually acquires the skills needed for driving from lesson to lesson. Each lesson assimilates another aspect of the driving *habit* into his unconscious mind. When the new *habit* is fully assimilated into the unconscious, that person will never forget how to drive.

The *habit* is so strongly imprinted that it cannot be forgotten. Similarly, we can learn how to ride a bike, touch type, and even how to become more positive, eradicate procrastination, be tidy, manage our time properly, control our negative emotions from the source, and many other physical and mental *habits* this book is reviewing for you. These *habits* require a change in character and improved conduct with a *positive EYE*.

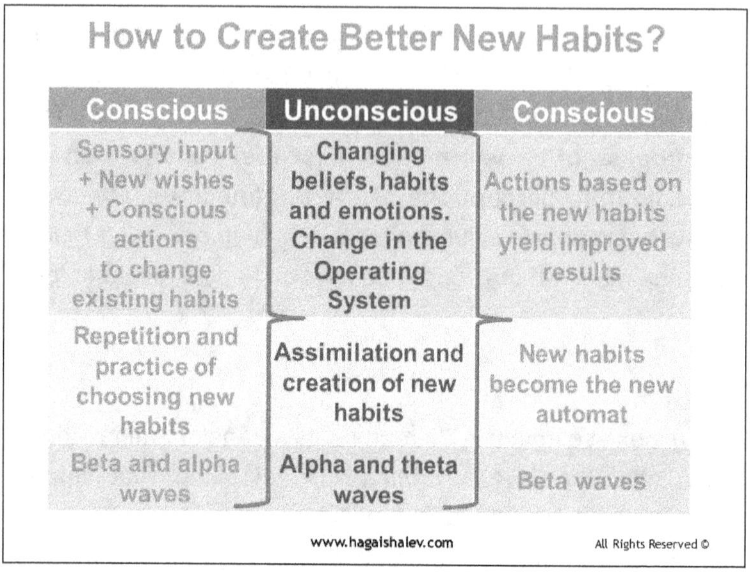

How to Create Better New Habits?		
Conscious	**Unconscious**	**Conscious**
Sensory input + New wishes + Conscious actions to change existing habits	Changing beliefs, habits and emotions. Change in the Operating System	Actions based on the new habits yield improved results
Repetition and practice of choosing new habits	Assimilation and creation of new habits	New habits become the new automat
Beta and alpha waves	Alpha and theta waves	Beta waves

www.hagaishalev.com   All Rights Reserved ©

Diagram 8-7 – Changing habits based on CO-OP, from conscious to unconscious and back to conscious

This process is illustrated in diagram 8-7. Any transformation process begins in the left column with the conscious mind: we decide what we want to change and use our senses to choose conscious, determined, and lasting actions to change our *existing habits*. To do this, we use all of our *TTT*'s, where the **T**asks derive from the **T**houghts and the **T**erms. All of this is done with brain waves reflecting complete wakefulness—mostly beta waves. *Practice* and repetition of these *choices* with *baby steps* causes them to gradually seep into the unconscious mind.

A transformation in the human *operating system* then begins within the unconscious mind, in beliefs, habits, and emotions. The longer the conscious actions last, the more the change in the unconscious is reinforced and assimilated, until it finally becomes *new habits*. These changes in the unconscious are processed in the alpha and theta wave states, and thus accelerate when we conjure up these *new habits* in our imagination, during relaxation, in meditation, before falling asleep, and upon waking up.

After implementing the *new habits* in the unconscious mind, they surface in the conscious mind and play out in daily life. The actions we take are founded on the comfortable "bed" of the *new habits*, allowing these actions to be performed with a *positive EYE* and yield *improved results*—just like how, when computer applications run on a new, upgraded operating system, clean of viruses and bugs, the computer performs better; or when a business owner who once disliked sales and marketing changes his belief system about it and now sees himself as the head sales manager of his business and his sales and marketing efforts become far more effective.

When *new habits* are assimilated into the unconscious, they become the *new program*[44], which serves and promotes you, replacing the old *autopilot program* that impeded and delayed you, thus enabling *improved results*.

◆

The way to apply all this relies on the *CO-OP Formula*: you become *aware* of the *autopilot* that is impeding you; *observe yourself* in real time while performing your *existing habits*; *choose* to change them using the proper *tools*; *practice* these *new habits* over and over with *baby steps* for 30 consecutive days; and then gradually assimilate these *new habits* into your unconscious mind, where they are yours forever. Bingo: you've succeeded in making the change and the new *program* has assimilated!

---

44 From now on, I will use the term ***"new program"*** to express the succession of *new habits* after they have been assimilated into the unconscious mind.

Another small yet important detail: assimilating the *new habits* into the unconscious mind is more efficient when we're *above the line*, that is, feeling positive; that's another reason, aside from those I discussed in chapter three, why it's best to keep *above the line* as much as possible. More on that in the following chapter.

◆

I shall end this chapter with a quote by Michael Oliver, founder of the *Natural Selling* method: "Watch your **deeds**, they become **habits**. Watch your **habits**, they become **character**. Watch your **character**, for it becomes your **destiny**." People often speak of luck or destiny; Michael Oliver clearly states that we create our own destiny. It begins with actions motivated by our conscious mind, which, when repeated, become our unconscious *habits*, imprinted on our unconscious mind as they become character. Character manifests in our results through our new actions, and the results ultimately shape our destiny. Now you've learned that this entire mechanism, automatic in most people, is really in your hands if you implement the *CO-OP Formula*. It all begins with actions you consciously take, with *awareness, self-observation*, and *choice*. These actions, when done *above the line* with a *positive EYE* and in *baby steps*, slowly trickle into your unconscious mind, creating the changes that will enable you to achieve *improved results* in your life in general, and in your business, management, and career in particular.

In the following chapter I shall introduce one last component of the *CO-OP Formula*, which greatly helps to implement it properly, and will teach you how to practice a few more *tools* in the formula.

CHAPTER NINE:
The Practical Implementation of the Transformation Process

"I listen and forget, see and remember, do and understand"
—Chinese proverb

In chapters seven and eight you learned the *CO-OP Formula*, and you are now familiar with all the steps to carry out any transformation process. In this chapter, I will take you one step further in applying the formula in practice while adding its final component, which makes it far more implementable. In addition, I will present a few more examples to illustrate how to apply the formula in specific situations.

How to Ensure the Tools' Implementation

Chapter eight introduced you to the *tools*. You saw that the *tools* are the primary vehicle for turning the *CO-OP Formula* from theory to practice. The *tools* show you how and with what to apply the formula's outline—*Awareness*, *self-observation*, and *choice*—to create a change in your *habits*.

However, *tools* are not enough, because **who will guarantee that you will use them? How will you remember to use the *tools* in your busy daily routine?**

When I first started my professional coaching career, I witnessed more than once that in the second session, my client hadn't practiced the *tools* enough during the first week of working together. "I had a very tough week," he told me, presenting me with the endless *circumstances* that befell him and distracted him. A week earlier, on our first session, the client learned the *CO-OP Formula* and the basic *tools* to implement it. At the end of the session, he chose one *habit* that didn't serve him, which he was aware of, and took it upon himself to start changing in according to the methodology. I gradually learned that good intentions and commitment aren't enough in order to apply the formula. The common "explanation" by the client for the failure sounded like this: "On Sunday the formula worked perfectly. I was very much *aware*, constantly *observed* myself and really managed to make *small choices* that began to make a difference. I even felt *above the line*. On the second day it didn't work as well as the first, but I still applied the formula. But on the third day, everything went haywire. The day started badly; a client didn't receive his merchandise despite my promise, he was very angry, and I was going crazy trying to fix the issue. I'm sorry, but the whole *CO-OP Formula* thing just slipped away with all these unusual *circumstances...*"

This is when I realized that I needed another component in the *CO-OP Formula*: the **Implementation Structure,** which I will reveal to you later on in this chapter. But before that, in line with my methodical format, let's try to better understand why we even need the *implementation structure*: what is the infrastructure that will enable the *implementation structure* to best serve us, yet support the rest of the formula's component in the most optimal way?

The Missing Basic Habit for Affecting Change

I have already mentioned that **self-observation** is the missing link in most awareness methods for affecting change with a *positive EYE*. Although *self-observation* is possible for any person, it is the weakest link in every transformation process. This is because

most people don't have the practical ability to observe themselves. Why? Simply because we aren't taught it. In fact, when we were young, our parents taught us to look at others. They knew very well how to watch others and gossip about them in our presence. You surely remember their conversations, which you weren't even supposed to hear, such as, "Did you see how Sara was dressed?" or, "What do these neighbors think, just leaving their garbage bags laying around by their door?" or, "This government, this teacher, your aunt, and so on..." You got the hint. From a young age, we were taught to observe others. But observing ourselves? Very little, if at all, and usually in an accusatory, judgmental tone that only pushed us *below the line*. "Look at you! When did you last look at yourself in the mirror?"

This is why therapeutic modalities were developed. The therapist observes the client and reflects back the *TTT* which the latter is unable to notice because he lacks the *awareness* or because he doesn't know how to observe himself. Furthermore, as someone who is consistently seen by various therapists and coaches (about 15 of them since 2006), and has a high level of *self-observation*, I can attest that my therapist has a greater ability to observe me than I can observe myself. Hence, the therapist's added value and benefit to the client is clear.

And so, most people observe others better than they observe themselves. Therefore, we mostly find the causes for things outside ourselves: that is where we're looking for them and that is where we find them. It reminds me of a joke about a person who lost his wallet and went looking for it under a streetlamp; when asked why he was searching under the streetlamp of all places, he answered, "Because here there's light." Similarly, you can probably pinpoint exactly what the problem is with your spouse, parents, mother-in-law, and all your beloveds, and why they're unable to achieve their goals. But what about yourself? What is the problem that's keeping you back? This is a whole different story, and you probably don't have a good enough answer because you don't know how to observe yourself. Do you know how many times I reflected something to a client and he said, "That's exactly what my wife says about me?" Over the years, my spouse, Osnat, has told me that I react to things too rigidly. **But do we listen to our spouses and use their deep knowledge of us and their ability to observe us?** Unfortunately, the answer is usually no, whether it's because we are unable to see what they see in us, or because our *autopilot* first and foremost resists them.

Thus, because most of us don't have the practical ability to self-observe, we cannot change. ***Self-observation*** is a fundamental *habit* so crucial to success, yet it is so absent in most people. It is the weak link in most transformation processes, and the one that usually sabotages them. Some people may have a great degree of *awareness*, but as long as they don't have a built-in habit of self-observation, they can't see how their *TTT* created The Reality they are experiencing, and so they cannot transform themselves. In other words, **as long as we don't know how to observe ourselves, and *self-observation* isn't a *habit* assimilated into our unconscious mind, we stand no chance of transforming**. This is because there is a rift between *awareness* and *choice*, leaving the latter unreachable. So, as a result, we don't *choose* enough, we get stuck on *auto mode*, we don't fulfill our human potential, are frustrated, *below the line*, and end up not making the kind of money we want to—and can—make.

So what do we do? We learn to self-observe and make self-observation a **fundamental *habit*** that is the basis for any transformation process. How do we do it? By using ***implementation structures.***

How Does the Implementation Structure Restore Our Freedom of Choice?

The implementation structure, or rather, implementation structures, are our daily reminders to observe, to use the tools and activate the triangle that resides at the core of the formula: Consciousness (awareness)—Observation—Options (choice).

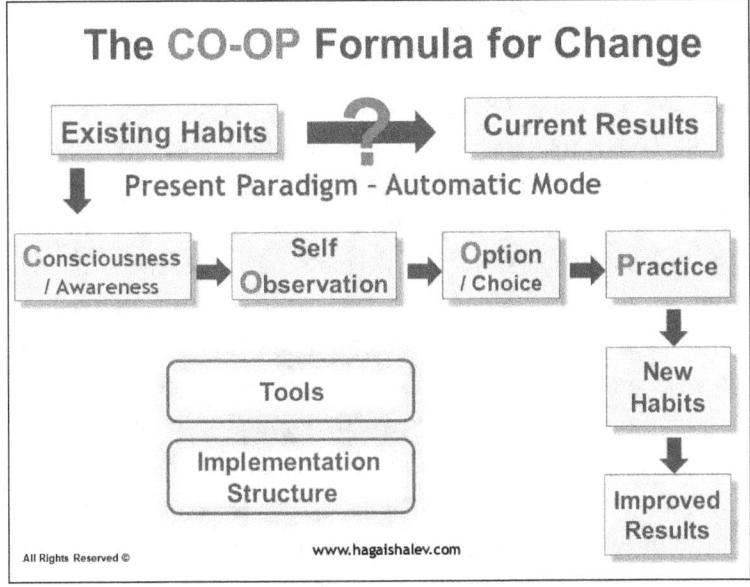

Diagram 9-1 – Implementation Structure supports Self-observation

Examples of implementation structures: reminders in one's diary and/or cell phone; notes posted around the home or office (on the mirror, computer, near the mouse, near your favorite mug); little post-it notes on your cell phone and keyboard; customizing your screen saver; different symbols in the car (pendants, key chains and stickers); finding a friend or a coach who will support you in the process; each time you go to the bathroom, wash hands, or shower; each time you have a glass of water or a cup of coffee; etc.

Since we are frequently exposed to all these accessories and daily actions, sometimes even hundreds of times a day, we can tie each one of them to *self-observation*. The *implementation structures* work very well as a trigger for *self-observation*: whether we write "self-observation" on these post-it notes or our screen saver, or add a smiley ☺ that reminds us of it, or even a tiny blank sticker in our favorite color, meant only for us, reminding ourselves, "Stop and observe yourself now."

The idea is simple: we don't know how to *self-observe* because we don't have the *habit*. **The *implementation structures* remind us to *observe*.** If we can stop at least 12 times a day, 7 days a week, every hour between 8:00 am and 8:00 pm, to adhere to the *implementation structures* we put around ourselves, to leave what we are doing for a few seconds, *self-observe*, pull out the right *tool* and *choose* to change one of the *habits* that hinder us, we will be one step closer to creating a *new* and *better habit*. Remember, one simple choice isn't enough to create change, but if we *practice* it, use the *implantation structures* to continue *observing* and making *small choices* 12 times a day for 30 days consecutively, then **bingo!** We will have assimilated a new *habit* in our unconscious mind and created a permanent change—a *new automatic program*!

The Ideal Implementation Structure

More than anything else, the smartphone serves as the ideal device to support an *implementation structure*. There is a group of free apps in every operating system called Hourly Chime[45], which

---

45 Here are specific Hourly Chime apps you can download: for iPhone users, HourMate or Soft Chimes Orchimf. For Android users, Caynax Hourly Chime or BellMan or Time Signal. Note that these apps were

enable the smartphone to chime a short reminder every hour on the hour. Being that the smartphone is with you at all times, this is an excellent solution for reminders you can't miss. The "chime" can be a simple beep, a bell, a tweet, the sound of waves, or any other sound you connect to. Of course, no one around you needs to know the meaning of the chime unless you choose to tell them.

The instructions for using this *implementation structure* are simple: each time you hear the smartphone chime, it's a reminder for you to *self-observe*. You stop your daily routine for a few seconds in order to briefly *observe yourself*. You *observe* your existing automatic *habit*, which you're aware of and chose to work on that day in order to change it. This *observation* is very quick: 20 or 30 seconds, a minute or two at the most. No more than that. While *observing*, you should notice if you are acting according to the *existing habit* at that moment. If so, don't judge yourself[46], but immediately make one simple *choice* to change the *habit* using one of the *tools* and then go about your day. If, while *observing*, you notice that you're not acting on the impeding *existing habit*, give yourself positive reinforcement; "Well done, wonderful, I'm acting with a *positive EYE.*" Furthermore, **look back** at the hour since the last chime and ask yourself if, in that hour, you acted according to this limiting *habit*. If not, give yourself further positive reinforcement; "Great, I've been acting according to my new positive *habit* for the last hour." On the other hand, if you see that you spent the last hour automatically repeating the *existing habit* that doesn't serve you, give up judging and make a **future choice**. Tell yourself, "The next time the *automatic program* returns and the limiting *old habit* is activated, I want to notice that in real time

---

available when the book was written, and may have changed by the time you read this due to the dynamic app market.

46 Self-judgment drags you *below the line.*

so I can *choose* at **that future moment** to avoid it and implement the *new habit.*"

If the smartphone chimes and you're too busy to stop for *self-observation*, do it as soon as your finish your task, whether it's a phone call, a meeting, etc. Incidentally, sometimes when you're interacting with other people, a brief *self-observation* will actually show you the *existing habits* that are least beneficial to you; if possible, you should also *observe* during intensive activities.

Although chime apps are the ideal *implementation structures* to me, any cue I mentioned in the last subchapter that reminds you to stop and *observe* is a legitimate *implementation structure*, so long as you notice it and actually stop for *self-observation*.

An Example for Applying an Implementation Structure
Let's use an example to illustrate this from Fred's story in chapter eight. As mentioned, Fred had a limiting *existing habit* of **grumbling and complaining**. Let's take this *habit* to an extreme: Fred is constantly complaining about others, blaming *circumstances* for his unlucky fate. He asks a lot of "why" questions: "Why does this always happen to me? Why aren't they more considerate? Why is the standard of living so expensive?" We called this behavior *external locus of control*. It's clear that this attitude drags Fred *below the line* and hinders his results. What is the solution? Stop grumbling and complaining, apply an *internal locus of control*, and switch the "why" questions to "how and what[47]": How do I cope with this negative situation I am currently experiencing? What can I do to improve my situation? These are the *tools* with which Fred can transform himself.

---

47 This is the "questions of possibility and opportunity" *tool* I mentioned in chapter three.

Using the *implementation structure* in order to apply the *tools* works as follows:

1. When his smartphone chimes as planned, Fred stops for a brief *self-observation* of his *TTT* and asks himself if he is grumbling and complaining right now, whether in thought, speech, or action.

2. If so, he first accepts the situation without judgment, *chooses* to immediately stop the *habit*, and picks a *tool* to help him handle it. Instead of asking "why," he can ask himself *questions of possibility and opportunity* in order to change his approach. He can also recognize that he's now in an *external locus of control*, and *chooses* to take 100% responsibility for the *circumstances* instead of blaming them (i.e., the surroundings) for his situation. I call this *choice "no to circumstances"*: Choosing to **say no** to *circumstances* and choosing to move **beyond** the *circumstances.* It's important to mention that the *choice* should be minor, taken in *baby steps*, unintimidating, so it can be implemented within seconds.

3. If he notices that he's **not** grumbling and complaining, Fred gives himself a positive reinforcement.

4. Immediately following, he *looks back* at the last hour to see if he grumbled and complained during it.

5. If the answer is no, Fred gives himself more positive reinforcement!

6. If the answer is yes, Fred once more accepts the situation without judging and uses *future choice*: the **next time** the *old habit* of grumbles and complaints kicks into *automatic* mode, he will make a *future choice* to implement the *internal locus of control* as well as *possibility and opportunity questions*, while cutting the *habit* short. Furthermore, he tells himself that

if and when it happens again, he wants to notice it in real time and then make a *small choice* with a *positive EYE* in order to eradicate the *existing habit* and replace it with a *new habit*.

7. When Fred implements all these steps every day for 30 consecutive days, 12 times a day, the *existing habit* will be transformed and replaced by a *new habit*—a *new automatic program* and a full *internal locus of control* without grumbles and complaints.

The *self-observation* process and *choosing* the observation points are illustrated in diagram 9-2:

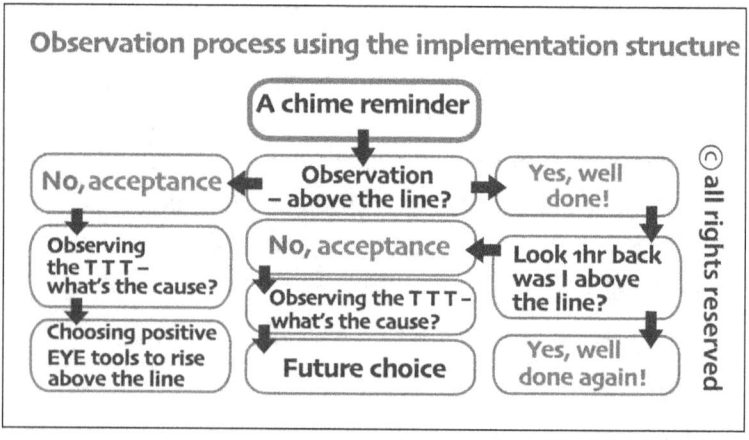

Diagram 9-2—Observation process and choosing in observation points[48]

Note that even if the steps of *observation and choice* last a full minute, they still don't take up more than 12 minutes a day. Now ask yourself: "Is it worth dedicating 12 minutes a day to eliminate a limiting *existing habit* and instead acquire a *new habit* that will lead me to success?" I believe the answer is very positive. I have

---

48 This diagram appears on the bookmark, so you don't have to memorize it.

often experienced it when changing my own *habits* and in working with close to a thousand clients who have transformed their *habits* and succeeded.

So the **purpose of these chime apps is to remind us to take structured points of *self-observation*, so that you don't just rely on your memory to *observe*.** Over time, when the *self-observation habit* is well assimilated into your unconscious mind, you won't need the apps because you will have acquired a *new habit*: the ability to *self-observe* **without** needing reminders. According to the *CO-OP Formula*, this will happen after 30 consecutive days of *practicing* your *new habit* of *self-observation*.

Effectively Applying the CO-OP Formula and the Implementation Structures

Remember that *self-observation* doesn't come naturally to humans; factoring in our engrained resistance to change makes it even more challenging. This resistance even creates daunting chemistry in our body every time we try to move out of the comfort zone. "Butterflies in the stomach," "It makes me sick," "I feel paralyzed," are only some of the expressions we use to describe the effects of our intentions on our physiology. Hence, know your *automatic program*: it is stubborn, dislikes changes, and believes that the current status quo is best for you, regardless of how bad you feel. Growth and development are not on its list of interests. The *automatic program*'s job is to ensure your survival, and as long as you're alive it is doing its job, even if you're *below the line*[49]. Therefore, you must use all of your commitment, determination, and grit to apply the *implementation structures*

---

49 More about how to cope with our automatic *resistance* to change in chapter 13 using the "Ego and Higher Self" *tool*.

and follow them. They are the gateway to *self-observation* and *choice*, and, ultimately, to any transformation.

I have already mentioned the importance of applying the *CO-OP Formula* in *baby steps,* both during *self-observation* and while *choosing.* This is in order for you to experience small instances of success that will reinforce and motivate you. Michael Jordan, one of the greatest basketball players of all times, once said, "I handle everything step by step." In other words: "Grasp all, lose all." The *baby steps* approach is also congruent with evolution in nature. **Patience and grit are qualities that yield success.** This is the way to let changes seep into the unconscious mind while applying the *implementation structures.*

◆

Here are a few examples of implementing *baby steps* with a *positive EYE:*

A person suffering from **procrastination** should not launch the life project he's been putting off for a year when starting to apply *self-observation.* This could be too hard to apply and just as easy to give up on and say, "I tried, but it didn't work." This could also develop a trauma rooted in failure, whose very presence prevents further attempts. Instead, I recommend you stop postponing **one small thing with each *observation* point.** Assuming you tend to postpone certain chores, try the following: if the sink is piled up with dishes, wash one plate; if you have 100 documents to file on your desk, file one; if you have dozens of phone calls to return, return one. Thus, you slowly acclimate your *operating system* to overcoming procrastination a little at a time. Your belief in your ability to overcome procrastination will gradually increase, allowing you to expand your *choices* to perform more and more tasks you used to postpone. Another example is **physical exercise.** Unless you already exercise regularly, now isn't the time to get up every morning at 6:00 am and spend two grueling hours at the gym. This will only lead to muscle contraction, injury, and mental strain that may defeat you. Instead, set a practice of 15 minutes 3 times a week, at home or nearby, when you have free time, and gradually increase the frequency, scope, and intensity.

Similarly, I don't recommend trying to tackle all of your limiting *habits* and deciding you want to transform them all at once. Instead, use your strong motivation and apply the *CO-OP* to one or two *habits* at one time at most. **Patience, determination, and perseverance are the right attitude for making successful changes.**

Applying the *CO-OP Formula* is purely technical at first: the smartphone chime reminds us to take a *self-observation* point, allowing us to make one simple *choice* with a *positive EYE.* As you recall, this is how each *TTT* done with a positive *EYE* seeps into our unconscious mind, creating a small change, which grows into a big one over time. Once the change is assimilated and reinforced in the unconscious mind, the technical actions become the positive, *new program.* At this point, your super-computer takes care of everything, just like any acquired *habit,* such as driving. This is why skepticism is expected and allowed at the onset of your transformation process. You may doubt whether you will succeed in the transformation process, but remain disciplined enough to carry out the technique accurately. With time, and especially when you begin to see results, your skepticism dissipates and your belief is formed, allowing the change to empower and fortify you. Remember the following conditioning: **without an *implementation structure*, there is no *self-observation*; without *self-observation*, there is no *choice*;**

and without *choice*, there is no *change*. Don't underestimate the *implementation structure*; it is small in quantity but high in quality, and without it, the transformation technique in this book is usually unattainable.

Your **commitment** plays a key role throughout the transformation process. As I emphasized in chapter four, the balance between *commitment* and *circumstances* is what determines your ability to break through and achieve your goals. As long as the *circumstances* overpower the *commitment*, it will be hard for you to overcome the *automatic program* and apply the *CO-OP Formula* with a *positive EYE*; you will always have reasons not to act, and they will thwart any initiative. Only when you choose full *internal locus of control* and say *no to circumstances*[50] will your *commitment* rise above the *circumstances* and allow you to succeed.

I like to visually illustrate this when meeting my clients:

I instruct the client to lift his fists to shoulder height like a boxer. "You have *commitment* in your right hand," I tell him, "and *circumstances* in your left hand. Now you can decide—which hand is higher and stronger?" The idea is clear: the more the client focuses on his right fist, placing it higher and stronger than the left, the more he reinforces his *commitment* beyond *circumstances*. Remember, you can *choose* that at any given moment. How? By using the *CO-OP Formula* in this book. I shall sum up with the following statement: "Circumstance stands no chance as long as you stand against."

---

50 Choosing to **say no** to *circumstances* and choosing **beyond** the *circumstances*.

How to use the bookmark

Another *implementation structure* is the *tools bookmark* attached to the book, which can be folded into any wallet or pocket. Review it again and you will see that it includes everything you need in order to successfully apply the *CO-OP Formula*. You don't have to remember that formula by heart, since it appears on one side of the bookmark, along with a diagram showing the order of actions to be taken with *observation* points (diagram 9-2). On the other side is the list of *tools* to implement the formula, some of which are covered in this book, so you don't need to memorize the *tools* either. The bookmark frees you from the need to remember the transformation process by heart; it turns your attention to the important details and enables you to focus on the first important action at the base of any change you want to make: *self-observation*.

When the reminder chimes, pull out the bookmark and look at the *CO-OP Formula*. Read its outline: *Awareness, self-observation,* and *choice*. Remember your existing *awareness* and the change you would like to implement (you can write it down as well, so you don't have to memorize it); *observe* yourself and follow the actions on the *observation* diagram; choose a suitable *tool* from the list of *tools* on the bookmark; and make one simple *choice* in your *TTT* with a *positive EYE* using *baby steps.* This way you can persistently *practice* the formula and acquire the *new habits* that will yield the results you want, assimilating a *new automatic program*.

This is the entire method in a nutshell.

More Examples of Applying the CO-OP Formula

In order to further illustrate the application of the formula, I chose two real cases studies from among my clients in order to demonstrate how the *CO-OP Formula* instigates substantial transformation when implemented. One case study is personal and the other is business-related. Note that although my work focuses on business-managerial coaching, the formula is valid and applicable for any type of change, since all humans share the same *operating system* during the process of transformation.

Case Study #1—Nail-Biting

Jonathan (alias) approached me to promote his business—unique online marketing services. During the preliminary evaluation, I noticed a few behavioral and character habits Jonathan could change in order to break through, but before I began to work with him on changing these *habits*, I opted to give him a sense of immediate success by changing a rather simple *habit* using the *CO-OP Formula.* When I asked my usual question at the end of the first session—"Which habit would you most like to change?"—forty-year-old Jonathan said that he hasn't been able to get rid of his nail biting *habit*, which bothered him a lot.

My instructions for Jonathan were simple:

√ Enter hourly reminders in your smartphone for *self-observation*; 12 reminders between 8:00 am and 8:00 pm, 7 days a week. The idea is that the smartphone will chime or beep briefly to draw your attention and remind you to *observe* yourself.

√ Leave everything you're doing for a few moments (up to a minute) and *observe* yourself and your nails. If you're biting at that moment, accept the fact without judgment, *choose* to immediately stop and remove your nails from your teeth. If you weren't biting at the moment of *observation*, give yourself a positive reinforcement and then *look back* to see if you bit your nails in the hour since your last *observation* point. If not, give yourself another positive reinforcement. If you did, accept it and don't beat yourself up, but make a *future choice* not to bite and apply it in the next hour.

√ Practice this 30 days consecutively until you acquire the *new habit* of not biting nails.

Within a week, Jonathan stopped biting his nails. What he hadn't been able to do for years, he did within days by using the *CO-OP Formula* and without any extraneous effort. Furthermore, this accomplishment built momentum for the success of his entire coaching process.

Case Study #2—Procrastination

We're all familiar to some degree or another with one of human-kind's most debilitating *habits*: **procrastination**. I assume you've run into it and suffered from it, whether it was yours or someone else's around you.

Sharon (alias) is an executive in her late 30s who approached me to help her make a career change.

As with Jonathan, I encouraged Sharon right from the onset of her coaching process to experience immediate success in applying the *CO-OP Formula* through changing one prominent *habit* that bothered her. Sharon chose to grab the bull by the horns and eradicate her procrastination at work.

◆

Here, too, my instruction for Sharon were simple:

✓ Enter hourly reminders in your smartphone for *self-obser-vation*; 12 reminders between 8:00 am and 8:00 pm, 7 days a week. The idea is that the smartphone will chime or beep briefly to draw your attention and remind you to *observe* yourself.

✓ Leave everything you're doing for a few moments and *observe* yourself to identify the things you're procrastinating on. If, indeed, you identify procrastination when *observing*, accept it without judgment, and *choose* to immediately perform one or two small tasks that you have been putting off. Give it a few minutes only.

Note that Sharon was instructed to fulfill only **minor postponed tasks**, things that would take up a minute or two. The idea was to give her small experiences for success that, when added up over time, would change her being and her procrastination paradigm. Another example is from my other client, Nora (alias), who had a cosmetic treatments business: Nora used to avoid getting phone calls—she simply didn't answer most of her incoming calls. She was *aware* of the *habit* but couldn't get rid of it. This chronic procrastination *habit* would prevent her from answering her cell phone, thinking she would call them back later, but in actuality, Nora usually didn't return calls, most of which were from her clients. You can imagine what a client would do after not being able to reach Nora numerous times; that's right, they went somewhere else! Eradicating this procrastination while making *small choices* to answer more and more calls made Nora's clients happier and steadier, which translated into a lot more money in

Nora's bank account[51].

Back to Sharon:

√ If you weren't putting off anything during the *observation*, give yourself positive reinforcement and then *look back* to see if you postponed anything in the hour since your last *observation* point. If not, give yourself more positive reinforcement. If you did, accept it and don't beat yourself up, but make a *future choice* not to procrastinate, and apply it in the next hour.

√ *Practice* this for 30 days consecutively until you acquire the *new habit*: eradicating procrastination.

A week later, Sharon reported a significant improvement in her procrastination *habit*. The improvement continued in the following weeks, as she stopped putting off bigger tasks, until the *new habit* of doing things on time was assimilated. Since procrastination is a common *habit* among many, I have had the pleasure of helping dozens of clients eradicate it the same way over the years.

To Jonathan and Sharon's credit, they were both very *open* and *committed* to applying the *CO-OP Formula*'s principles diligently and consistently.

---

51 I recommend expanding on this *habit*. In the competitive era we live in, clients lack time and patience. Being unresponsive with no voice mail drives our clients away. Business owners who don't leave a welcoming greeting on their voice mail are sure to lose clients and leads. When I tell business owners without voice mail that their clients are getting an annoying busy signal, they say, "Let them text." "Yes," I respond, "But what if they're driving? Or have no time or patience to write a text message? You just lost a client."

Does the Physician Heal Himself?

There are plenty of examples of successful and unsuccessful implementations in life. Each one is a learning opportunity. Although I am fluent in practicing the CO-OP Formula, I, too, may falter sometimes; here is one recent example I remember vividly:

I do cross training every Saturday morning. I wake up at 5:30 a.m., earlier than any other day of the week. After my regular morning meditation, I leave for the sports center nearby to practice with my group, "Early Risers," at 6:30 a.m. After about two hours of running and power endurance training with Raz, our lovely instructor who volunteers to train us, we have the traditional potluck breakfast. By 9:30 a.m., I am back home, full of adrenaline and satisfaction (and with a full belly), careful not to wake up my family. One Saturday, I was surprised to find my wife Osnat at home, knowing that she had planned on going to the beach with a friend that morning. Apparently her friend couldn't make it and Osnat had no one to go with, so I immediately offered to accompany her to the beach. She accepted my offer happily, asking me to change into swim trunks. "What for?" I asked her. "I'm going to get sand all over anyway, so I may as well keep my shorts on," I continued. "What's the difference between trunks and shorts?" I added. To my surprise, Osnat insisted I wear swim trunks for whatever reason. Here, my automatic resistance took over. "Why should I bother? She's just being stubborn and I'm not going to let her have it," I thought, "What's more, I'm doing her a favor by accompanying her to the beach instead of her friend." So I refused to change into my trunks and walked down to the garden to read the weekend papers and sunbathe like I usually do after the Saturday practice. On my way down, *awareness* hit me with all its might. I *observed myself*, and immediately noticed that I was resisting Osnat for no reason. "What's the big deal to change into swim trunks?" I thought. I noticed that it was my *automatic program* talking to Osnat just minutes earlier. Knowing her, I remembered that aesthetics are very important to Osnat and that she's right; I look better in my trunks than in my gym shorts. Within seconds, I got a grip on myself, *chose* to walk back up, apologize to Osnat, put on my trunks, and make the rest of the morning an enjoyable date on the beach.

It's clear that if it weren't for my *self-observation* ability, I would not have noticed the resisting *automatic program*. The *choice* to return, give in, and act with a *positive EYE* was the smartest decision and it paid off. Luckily, I woke up in time to *choose* differently and cancel the automatic decision I had made just a few minutes earlier.

◆

My following statement poignantly sums up this chapter: "I brake, awake, break (off), shake (off), and take a stake to make my new *automatic program*."

In the following chapter, we rise to a higher level in the intensity of the *tools* as we learn three mega *tools* for a very broad implementation of the *CO-OP Formula.*

PART III

PRACTICAL TOOLS
TO GET USED TO SUCCESS

CHAPTER TEN:
Three Mega Tools for Effectively Implementing Change

"The real voyage of discovery consists not in seeking new landscapes, but in having new eyes."

—Marcel Proust

So far, you have acknowledged that change is a necessity in the dynamic, modern day reality in order to thrive and succeed. You learned the required conditions to facilitate change and the methodology to implement it. Now, you are ready to **carry out the change in real life** by using the *CO-OP Formula*. Using the *implementation structure* I reviewed in the previous chapter to enable *self-observation* is a basic prerequisite for applying the *CO-OP Formula*. Beyond that, the *tools* do the rest. Therefore, in this chapter and the ones to follow, I shall give you a list of *tools* that will expand your resources for practically implementing change in your life using the formula.

Routine Self-awareness Protocol
Before giving you the additional *tools*, here is a **summary** of what you've learned so far in order to free yourself from the *automatic program* and bring more *choice* into your life:

Remember, there will always be *circumstances*. Shit happens, as they say. Yes, no one can escape being faced with unpleasant or unwanted *circumstances* sometimes; so why are we so surprised when they show up? After the initial automatic resistance, accept the *circumstances*. Accept them because they're here, they've already happened. You can't prevent them or turn back time, and you can't move forward looking into the rearview mirror all the time. In addition, the future is where you're going to spend the rest of your life, so you'd better give it your fullest attention. "Accepting" the *circumstances* doesn't mean "agreeing" with them, because right after your accept them, ask yourself *questions of possibility and opportunity*—**how** to cope with the *circumstances* and **what** to do to change them. Remember that you are capable of handling the *circumstances*, so don't let the *automatic program* weaken you into giving up. You may not be able to change the *circumstances* that have already happened, but you can **choose how to react** to them, and most likely change them for the future. Have an *internal locus of control* and do your best with utmost commitment to changing the situation. Use your *awareness* to *observe* the situation, identify your *TTT* at that moment, *choose* an appropriate *tool* to change your response, and apply it with a *positive EYE* and *baby steps* to create a *new automatic program*. Until your *self-observation* becomes automatic, use *implementation structures*. *Practice* your *choice* until it's assimilated and made into a *new habit* within 30 days.

More than Anything, Keep Yourself Above the Line

I already mentioned in chapter three that the short road to success is keeping *above the line* as much as possible: being *above the line* helps us keep a *positive attitude* and *focus*, and keeps us proactive, taking initiative, communicating well, and experiencing more self-love and love from others. *Above the line* we work effectively, vigorously, enthusiastically, with high awareness and more. All these clearly lead to and promote success. So far, we've discussed this model as a mental state to **be in**. Now, you can work to **create it**, using all that you've learned in this book to raise yourself *above the line*.

The **above and below the line model is the first mega-tool I will present to you in this chapter.** As a *tool,* it's not just a mental state to aspire to, but a reality that can and should be created using the *CO-OP Formula.* Once you're *aware* of the importance of being *above the line* and its related components, *self-observation* will enable you to identify the moments when you're *below the line.* This is an easy task to complete, since it entails identifying an emotional state, and you're already proficient at recognizing your emotions. Next, you can check what in your *TTT* causes you to be *below the line.* This is another step in *self-observation.* The list of characteristics *below the line* in diagram 10-1 will help you with that. Do you automatically resist something you can't change (people around you, the weather, what happened in your past, etc.)? Are you currently *focused* on what's not working in your life? Are you in an *external locus of control*? Are you blaming someone or something for your bad luck? This way, you can go over the list of components comprising the *below the line* and recognize them in action in your *TTT.* After the recognition step, it's crucial that you accept that these are the facts and immediately move on to the *choice* step—*choosing* a *TTT* with a *positive EYE* that will raise you *above the line*[52]. Focus on the half full cup and your current possibilities and opportunities

---

52 While being *above the line* is crucial for success, it's certainly legitimate to choose to be *below the line,* at least for some time. This state will enable the expression of negative feelings, which some say must be released prior to any change. In my work, I have found that choosing if and for how long to remain *below the line* differs from person to person. Hence, while I recommend minimizing the time spent being *below the line* and acting swiftly to rise *above the line,* I suggest you choose the point of change best suited to you while remaining fully *aware* of the situation and of your possibilities for change. Just beware of being sucked into an *external locus of control,* which is an automatic habit

in life; give up judgment and blame, including of yourself; let go of resistance to things that aren't in your control; and *choose* an *internal locus of control*—decide that you are the cause of what's happening in your life and ask yourself *questions of opportunity and possibility* to pave your way in the future. All the *above the line* characteristics in diagram 10-1 are means of *choice* and implementation in order to actually rise *above the line*.

Above the line	proactive	presence	happy	praise & empowerment
internal locus of control	desire positive focus	acceptance & letting go vision	"what, how" questions forgiveness	high responsibility strong commitment love
high results	effective	awareness	positive attitude higher self	high integrity
positive emotion	high energy	enthusiasm	good communicator	vibrant
poor responsibility	need for control	limiting paradigms	"why?" questions	stuck in the past
fear	judgmental	Suffering	reactive	
poor integrity	negative focus	victim needy	blame	weak commitment
ineffective	poor results	automat ego	unaware	negative attitude
Below the line	negative emotion	low energy	uncommunicative	tired

www.hagaishalev.com   All Rights Reserved ©

Diagram 10-1 – Above and Below the Line Characteristics

Notice that when you're *below the line*, the *autopilot* usually keeps you stuck. There's a tendency to withdraw, give up, sink into depression, and become passive and vulnerable. The experience is of a downward spiral into a bottomless pit. According to the *CO-OP Formula*, stopping this fall is challenging yet possible: it requires *self-observation* and identifying the situation, accepting

that may paralyze you.

reality, being *aware* that it doesn't have to continue this way, realizing you can overcome *circumstances*, and knowing that you have a *choice*—even if you've hit rock bottom. From here, you can start to rise *above the line* while *choosing* to cope. Start changing the current components that are *below the line*. Think: What is the solution? What are the options? This is how you gradually begin to direct your *TTT* towards clearing the fog and finding answers. The more you turn your resources to *above the line* characteristics, the more you'll broaden your horizons, and new directions of action will open for you. Finally, *practicing* this scenario over and over again will turn it into a *new habit*. Sometimes dropping *below the line* is inevitable, but you can very quickly get back *above the line* and walk the path of success. Yes, it's possible! In fact, I see it in my own life and the lives of my clients every day. I'm sure you know what it's like to be on *autopilot* and drop *below the line*, but then things get better and you climb back *above the line,* even without knowing how to implement the *CO-OP Formula*. What the mind doesn't do, time does over hours or days. The *tool* I'm teaching you here will allow you to get there much quicker, sometimes within minutes, saving you lots of turmoil and energy as you move with a *positive EYE* towards your goals.

"Luck is when preparedness meets opportunity"—Earl Nightingale

In chapter three I said that most people don't live up to their fullest potential because they lack a *positive attitude and focus on what is enhancing* their lives; they are more focused on the dangers and risks, the negative, the fears and the possibilities of failure than on the chances to advance, the opportunities, the positive, their successes and what is working for them. This is akin to a tightrope acrobat walking the rope and constantly fearing that he might fall. Indeed, he will eventually fall; in the absence of sufficient *positive attitude*, success, prosperity, well-being, satisfaction, and happiness in life are all compromised. By now, it should be clear to you that a flawed *automatic program* isn't a decree that you must accept. As with any automatic state, by using *awareness, self-observation*, and *choice*, you can change it. **A *positive attitude* and *focus* on what is enhancing your life is another mega-*tool* in your transformative abilities.**

You're already familiar with the *CO-OP Formula*'s outline: first, be *aware* of the automatic *existing habit* and your negative tendency; second, *observe* yourself during your daily conduct, identify the *TTT* reflecting the negative attitude and focusing on problem;, then *choose* to change to a *positive attitude* and *focus* on what leads you to success. For example: instead of dwelling on the problems, look for the opportunities; instead of judging and criticizing, praise and empower (yourself included); instead of resisting, accept and let go; instead of listening to the news, look for empowering stories; and instead of getting angry, respond moderately. Do that 12 times a day while using the *implementation structure* (reminders). By *practicing* it for 30 days straight, you will slowly begin to adopt a more *positive attitude* and *focus* on the possibilities and opportunities in your life, until the *new habit* will be assimilated into your *operating system* and become the positive *new automatic program*. This is how you use this important *tool* to steer yourself towards success. With a *positive attitude* and *focus* in your toolbox, you will be more open to recognizing opportunities that come your way. This readiness comes from your positive mental state. Your life's opportunities will be the same, but your ability to notice them is what will turn "luck" your way. This is what Earl Nightingale means in the quote that opens this subchapter. If needed, go back to chapter three and remind yourself of the powerful effect *positive attitude* and *focus* can have on your life.

Enlisting Children by Using Positive Attitude and Focus

The incident I remember most clearly in which I applied *the positive attitude* and *focus tools* was in late 2006, shortly after I became familiar with it. I remember reflecting on my relationship with my teenage kids, Daniel and Shelly, when it dawned on me: not only was I not around enough to develop a relationship with them beyond the formal parent-child relationship, our communication mostly involved criticism. "**Why** isn't your room tidy? **Why** haven't you done your homework yet? **Why** do you come home so late?" The "why" questions are a *below the line* characteristic, so they clearly dragged my relationship with my children *below the line* and only amplified their resistance to me, which is typical of adolescence. Recognizing this situation as a result of *self-observation* caused a flash of *awareness* that opened my eyes. I immediately set out to change the situation. **I decided that from then on, I would stop with the annoying "why" questions and communicate with them with *positive attitude* and *focus* alone.** The "why" questions were replaced with a genuine interest in their well-being; searching for "what to fix" was replaced by focusing on their good, strong qualities and the brief exchanges were replaced with going out together and sharing common interests. I was surprised at how quickly the results came. I suddenly began to see my children in a different light. I suddenly noticed how smart, mature, and perceptive they are; how worldly and knowledgeable, with communication and relationships skills far beyond what I possessed at their age. We became closer and developed a friendship. They realized there was more to me than just their "nagging father," and opened up to me in a way that made us much more collaborative. **Instead of focusing 80-90% of the time on what needed fixing with them, I focused on what was working, their strengths and capabilities.** Sure, I still had to draw boundaries for them, but instead of doing it all the time, I chose to do so only when it was truly necessary. And when I did draw boundaries, they were accepted with far more understanding from my children than their former automatic resistance. Simply put, I changed the dosage so that a mostly negative style of communication became mostly positive; the results were quick to come.

This realization resonated deeply within me. It became an example of the amazing power of the *positive attitude* and *focus tools*. It was then that I realized that you can achieve the same thing in any type of relationship, including romantic, work, or management ones. Imagine what would happen if the average manager replaced his "what to fix" approach with reinforcing his employees' strengths while focusing on possibilities and opportunities. Imagine what would happen in politics if the criticism and inflated ego approach could be replaced by a kind, positive attitude with integrity. I believe that transformation is also inevitable in politics. My father of blessed memory used to say, "What isn't achieved through the mind is achieved through time..."

Finally, with regards to romantic relationships, here too I noticed that changing the attitude and focus to the positive paves the way to a healthier, better relationship. These are powerful *tools*, which will improve your life in every dimension, far beyond business, management, or career.

"You are where your thoughts are. Make sure your thoughts are where you want to be."—Rabbi Nachman of Breslov
You have probably heard of the expression, "Thoughts become reality." Indeed, in chapter six you saw that imagination is the fuel that feeds the unconscious mind, your super-computer that determines your results. Therefore, it's important that you are able to control your thoughts and guide them to places you would like

to be, as Rabbi Nachman says in this subchapter's heading.

The question is, "How can we control our thoughts? Can thoughts even be controlled?" Because no one has ever taught us to do that, most people don't know how to control their thoughts. Thoughts are mostly automatic, taking up a major role in the *automatic program* of the *human operating system* which I have discussed in this book.

Can we escape our cognitive *autopilot*? Can we control our thoughts and harness them for our success? The answer is yes, **and this is the third *mega-tool* you will receive in this chapter.**

◆

In order to teach you how to control your thoughts, I will use a classic tool from cognitive psychology called the ***E.T.F.B*** model[53], which I will develop into a practical *tool* you can use with the *CO-OP Formula*[54]. **The model shows the cause and effect relationship through our emotional system.** I can't say enough about the importance of the emotional system in success and fulfillment. I won't exaggerate if I say that this is the most influential system in the reality we create for ourselves. I have mentioned the *below and above the line* model throughout the book; I said that being *above the line* is the key to success and that remaining *below the line* often guarantees failure. Your emotions express, more than anything, where you are in relation to the line. The important,

---

53 **E**vent, **T**hought (interpretation), **F**eeling (emotion), **B**ehavior (response or reaction). I will occasionally replace the major words in capital letters with those in round parentheses.

54 The *E.T.F.B* model is presented here with much of my own additions and interpretations.

major decisions in life are emotional and only later do we justify them rationally. Indeed, the heart chooses and the mind approves in any area of your life. An excellent example for that is buying clothes and other products: how many times have you bought something and never used it because you don't really need it? Did you know that 80% of your closet you only wear 20% of the time[55]? Therefore, understanding your emotional system—and, even more so, your **ability to control it**—is one of the pillars or success. What we are referring to here is **emotional intelligence**[56]. One of the interesting definitions of emotional intelligence is "the ability to act against the automatic control hierarchy of the emotions over the mind." Meaning, emotional intelligence is the ability to choose rationally even if it goes against negative feelings. For example, if someone hurt me, I won't automatically lash out at him. It's not an easy challenge for a person who hasn't learned to control his thoughts and emotions and acts *automatically*. How do we do it? We'll soon see.

From Cause to Effect Through the Emotional System

The first step in analyzing the cause and effect relationship is an **event**; another name for an event here is *circumstances*. The *event* reflects objective facts as something that happens outside of us: someone said something, something happened around us, etc. The *event* is usually not in our control, at least not directly. It reaches our consciousness and we immediately turn it into **thoughts** (interpretations): it's good/bad, worthwhile/ not worthwhile, pretty/ugly, etc. Another word for *interpretation* is thoughts. Every *event* that happens around us and is known to us

---

55 According to the Pareto principle, also known as the 80/20 rule.

56 In short, emotional intelligence is a person's ability to identify, evaluate, and manage his and other people's emotions.

arouses thoughts in us. Between the *event* and the *thoughts*, there are the **three filters** we discussed in chapter three, which are based on our senses: 1) Our senses don't perceive the entirety of reality; 2) The *focus principle*—the things we focus on greatly determine the reality we absorb; 3) Our world view distorts the reality we experience; our paradigms, which are the glasses through which we see the world, determine what our senses will absorb. These filters don't appear in the original *E.T.F.B* model, but I'm adding them in order to emphasize the gap between the objective *event* and the subjective *interpretation* (see diagram 10-2). This point is critical in understanding the model, yet most people are unaware of it; these *filters* distort the objective *circumstances* on their way to our subjective thoughts. The *event* has a cause and it's based on facts, while thoughts depend on *interpretation*. And here lies the big difference between people: **every person has his own filters from which his individual, subjective interpretation emerges.** Let's take workload for example: ten new orders have come into the business (*event*—an objective fact.) One person may interpret it as, "It's so stressful, I'm really suffering," while another may say to himself, "How great, marketing are doing their job." Two subjective *thoughts* (interpretations) of the same objective *event;* what sets them apart is the *three filters*. It's noteworthy that most people usually don't distinguish between facts and interpretation. Most of us believe that our interpretation is the true reality. So, for example, it's hard for us to understand how one person is cold when we're hot; how my friend can wear such a horrible outfit; and how my manager doesn't see the problems I run into at work, which I believe prevent me from fulfilling his instructions; and so on.

After *thought* (interpretation) comes *feeling* (emotion). This context is highly important; it teaches us unequivocally that **feeling is always the result of interpretation**; of our *thoughts*, our *focus*, and our *attitude* to life. Let's say the *event* is checking your bank account and realizing your balance is way lower than you thought. Your automatic *thoughts* will surely involve a negative interpretation—"How will I make ends meet this month?" The *feelings* (emotions) automatically derived from this *thought* will be negative—worry, fear, anxiety. On the other hand, if the *thought* that follows the *event* is, "But I've taken many actions already and they will yield results soon," you will have a sense of optimism and satisfaction, perhaps even pride and serenity. Same facts, different interpretation, and accordingly a different emotion. The first *thought* will find you *below the line*, while the second *thought* will find you *above* it. **This is what makes the E.T.F.B model so important: the axiom that negative *thoughts* (interpretations) always lead to negative *feelings* (emotions) and that positive *thoughts* (interpretations) lead to positive *feelings* (emotions).** Most people aren't aware of this strong connection. There are a few reasons for it, the most prominent one being that interpretation, i.e., *thought*, is very elusive. It's as quick as lightening and mostly goes unnoticed but for the *feeling* (emotion), which is very dominant in our being.

Here are two statements that illustrate this:

1. "I was offended because he didn't say hi to me in the hallway." The *event*: he didn't say hi. The emotional outcome: insult. And where is the *thought*? Quick and hidden so that we often don't notice it. It's clear that if the interpretation was, "He couldn't care less about me," so the insult makes sense. However, according to the *E.T.F.B* model, if the *thought* were, "He was very busy and preoccupied," I would probably not have been insulted.

2. "I'm frustrated because my boss didn't copy me on an email." The *event*: my manager didn't copy me on the email. The

emotional outcome: frustration. And the interpretation? Hidden and elusive once again, yet probably negative, as if to say, "He doesn't appreciate my work," or else there would be no negative emotion, such as frustration. Here, too, a positive interpretation such as, "I guess he's considerate of my valuable time," would have left the emotion in positive territory.

We will expand on the interpretation-emotion pair in a moment, but first, I would like to complete the *E.T.F.B* model and explain the acronyms: *Event—Thought* (interpretation)—*Feeling* (emotion)—*Behavior* (response or reaction) (diagram 10-2).

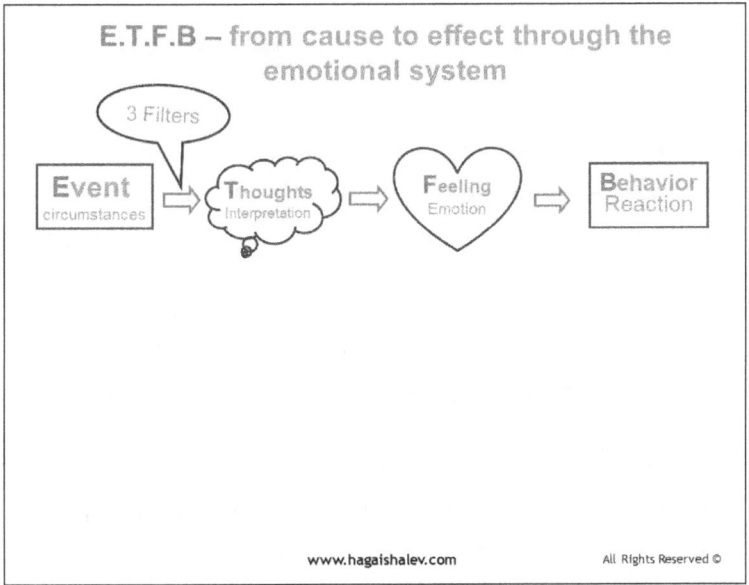

Diagram 10-2—the E.T.F.B Model Outline

The *behavior* (response or reaction) is expressed in a statement or action. So far, the model steps were internal, involving *thoughts* and *feelings* (emotions); now comes the external part—how we react to the *event*. Here, too, a negative inner flow of the interpretation-emotions duo will result in a negative *behavior* (reaction), while positive interpretation-emotion will yield a positive *behavior.*

The *behavior* affects the results, which don't appear in the original *E.T.F.B* model. It's clear that a positive *behavior* will usually yield a positive result, while a negative *behavior* will usually cause a negative outcome. For instance, if we yell at someone or, god forbid, hit him (negative *behaviors*), good won't come out of it. However, if we support, help, and encourage those around us (positive *behaviors*), our results will most likely be positive and beneficial to us.

◆

This sums up the relationship between the model's parts. Now I shall examine and analyze their meaning and how to use *E.T.F.B* in order to achieve better results.

Since the positive flow in the model is beneficial and promotes *improved results*, I won't discuss it any further, but will focus on the negative flow so you can learn how to handle it, turn it into a positive flow, and later on learn to avoid it entirely (diagram 10-3). First, I shall reiterate the main relationship in the model: **negative *thoughts* lead to negative *feelings.*** Secondly, the buck usually doesn't stop there, because a negative *feeling* creates more negative *thoughts*, deepening them, as they in turn cause more negative *feelings.* Thus, a negative loop is created, rolling us like a snowball *below the line* (diagram 10-6). This automatically negative emotional conduct is common among most people, reinforced by conflicts and quarrels with others and sometimes feeding off of the latter. Thirdly, *thoughts* involve *choice*, which we will address shortly.

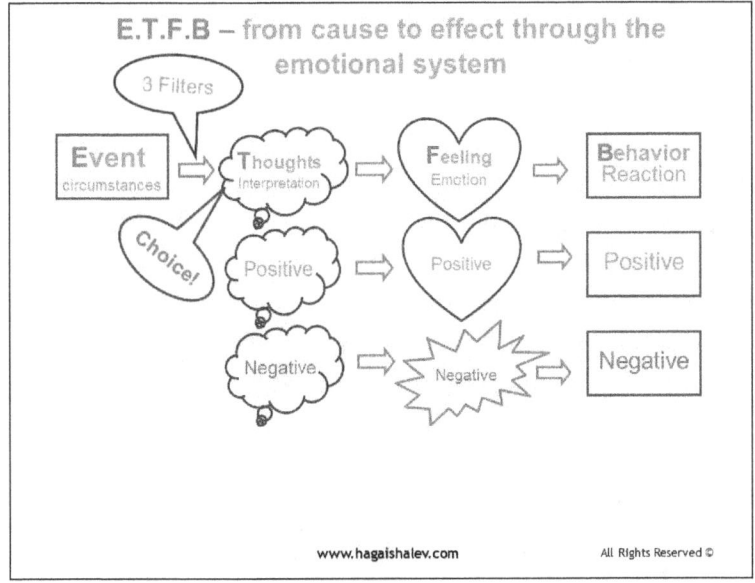

Diagram 10-3—Positive and Negative Flow in the E.T.F.B Model

How Can We Control Negative Emotions?

Before I show you how to get out of a negative emotional loop, let's get a better understanding on the cultural-environmental background to our emotional conduct. Let's begin by examining just how much we can influence the components of the *E.T.F.B* model: *Circumstances, events,* what is happening around us— those are usually not under our direct control. As far as *thoughts* go, we normally don't have the necessary skill to direct them to our benefit. Usually, no one in any educational framework teaches us how to control, manage, or regulate our *thoughts*. The same goes for *feelings*—**the emotional conduct of most people is automatic,** reactive, and uncontrollable. We get angry, worried, or frustrated because someone or something around us caused it, and we have nothing left to do but to react. The only component of the *E.T.F.B* model that we have learned to manage is our *behavior*. This is because, from a very young age, we're taught what to say and do and how to behave. We are told, "This is nice, this isn't, this is allowed, forbidden, don't talk like that, don't raise a hand, it's not polite to shout, say 'thank you' and 'please,'" and so on. The outcome is that we acquire the skill of reaction (*behavior*) and learn to control it (diagram 10-4). If we're inside a negative loop, we have a negative interpretation (*thought*) of the *event*, which elicits a negative emotion (*feeling*)—thus, the automatic tendency is to react negatively. Here, the **mechanism controlling our *behavior* enters**. The more tamed we become in controlling *behavior*, the more we can hold back negative emotions without expressing them.

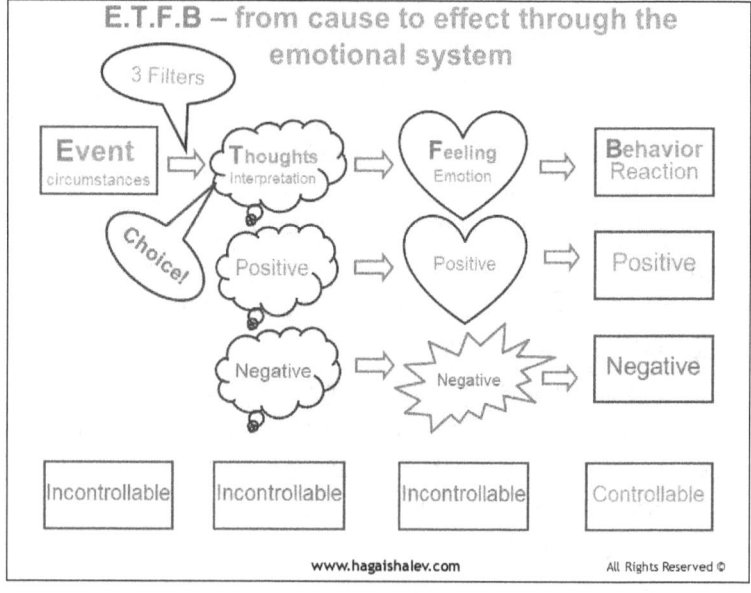

Diagram 10-4—Automatic Conduct in the E.T.F.B Model

Two main scenarios are then made possible. **In the first one**: We hold back our negative emotions so long that they eventually "burst," like lava shooting out of a volcano, or a jet of steam. We can no longer keep the negative emotions pent up inside us, and they release uncontrollably. These are the incidents which we usually regret in retrospect. **The negative reaction bursts out in all its might.** These extreme situations are legally termed "temporary insanity." Ordinary, normal people suddenly commit irrational acts, including physical violence. **This is obviously a bad solution to a negative emotional loop.** The consequences are grave both to the person acting out negatively and to the people around him.

One of the most prominent examples of a negative emotional conduct with a severe outcome comes from the final match of the 2006 FIFA World Cup. The world's eyes were set on the French star and captain, Zinedine Zidane, whose team had reached the FIFA finals for the second time in history, with an excellent chance of taking the cup. But then, in response to some swear words used against him by the Italian defender, Materazzi, Zidane head-butted him and was suspended from the game. France remained with ten players—a disadvantage that jeopardized its ability to win. Indeed, it was Italy who won the sought after cup. Not only did Zidane lose his chance at becoming a world-renowned champion, he also ended his career after that game with a terrible sense of frustration and regret. If it weren't for his automatic negative reaction) *behavior*), he might have been the one raising the world cup, the most positive ending to his grand career. Instead, he ended on a bad note, both personally and for the team which he captained. This is what a momentary outburst of uncontrollable negative emotion (*feeling*) can cause.

The second scenario is when we are tamed so well that we can control our *behavior* all the way, a complete self-restraint without a negative reaction. This may seem like the ideal situation, since no damage is caused to our surroundings, but it is an illusion; deep inside, we're frustrated, angry, worried, or flooded with these and other negative emotions; those emotions gnaw at us from within, with no release or outlet. It's no fun being in this state; we're way *below the line*, facing severe consequences to our results and success; finally, the pent up negative residues may become a source of deep frustration and may even lead to disease. If so, **even controlling the *behavior* while harboring negative *feelings* is not a satisfactory solution.**

So what is the solution? The solution is controlling the source; the thoughts (interpretation).

Like an Advil for a Shoulder

What do I mean by that? Say my shoulder hurts and I go to the doctor. The doctor tells me, "No problem, just pop an Advil and you'll be as good as new." I answer, "Doctor, it's great that you want to help me reduce my shoulder pain, but that won't solve the problem. There's a reason why my shoulder hurts and Advil isn't the answer. Let's look for **the source** of the pain; perhaps it's an injured joint, an inflammation, or an overstretched ligament." The message is clear: in order to alleviate the pain for good, one must treat the **source of the problem**, not just the symptom. Advil will only take away the pain for a few hours, but without treating the root of the problem, the pain will return, so what's the point? **This phenomenon of treating the symptom instead of the source repeats itself in many areas of life.** We live in an "instant" era—everyone wants everything now, immediately, yesterday if possible, fast, simple, and easy. We have neither time nor patience to wait, because time is money. One outcome of this phenomenon, which I mentioned earlier, is the flourishing industry of antidepressant drugs. Depression is an epidemic taking over the world. Why? Because something in the modern lifestyle is detrimental to human happiness. **Despite abundance,**

progress, and convenience, people are not happy. The key to their unhappiness lies in their *thoughts*, in their conduct, in the *automatic program* controlling their daily lives and their lack of sufficient *choice*. People "bang their heads against the wall" all the time, so no wonder they have a "headache." Depression is spreading like wildfire and most people take antidepressants to treat the symptoms instead of finding the source of their depression—what in their automatic thought pattern caused it; what in their *TTT*, conduct, focus, attitude or resistance of the past is keeping happiness away from them. This is the source from which one should change and uproot the depression.

This book was written with the mindset that the shortest route is the longest, evolutionary one. I believe it to be the only way to achieve results: upgrading the *operating system*, treating the part of the iceberg that is underwater, changing beliefs, *habits* and emotions from their **source** in the unconscious mind to create the proper foundation for transformation—the *Being*—that will support the *Doing* with a *positive EYE*.

"Give a man a fish, and you feed him for a day. Teach a man to fish, and you feed him for a lifetime"—Lao Tzu

So, many times we treat the symptom instead of the source, either because we don't know how to treat the source or because we hope to find a quick remedy to our ailment; the latter is usually a false hope. In fact, the only step in the *E.T.F.B* model that isn't in your control is the *event*, the *circumstances*; those are the things that happen around you without your direct or indirect influence. Everything else, including the interpretation—the *thoughts*, leading to *feelings* and *behavior*—can be in your full control (diagram 10-5). The *E.T.F.B* model teaches us that the source of *behavior* and *results* is *thoughts*. If you control your *thoughts* and channel them positively, it will enable a positive flow through the model, yielding positive *feelings*, positive *behavior*, and ultimately, better *results* as well. The ability to control your *thoughts* is the "fishing rod" that you want to buy so you can satisfy your hunger for results and success throughout your life.

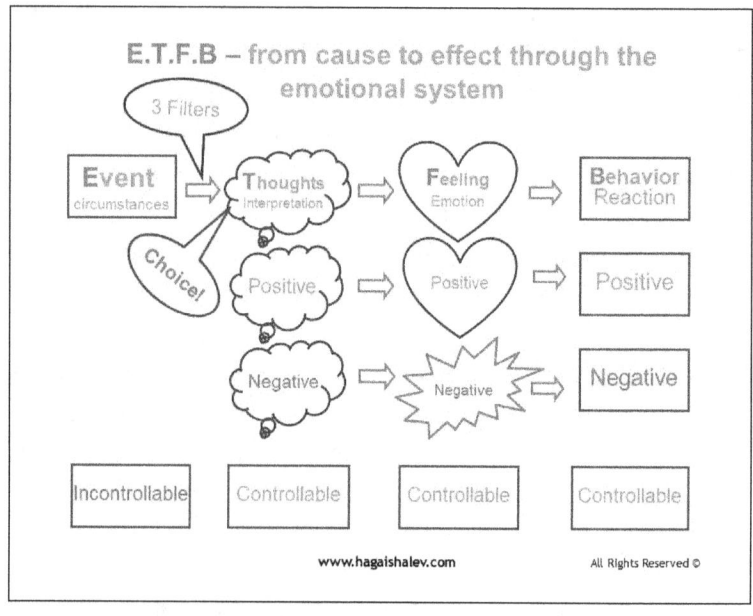

Diagram 10-5—Conscious Conduct in the E.T.F.B Model

Before I move on to a detailed account of how to control your *thoughts*, let's examine two metaphors that will shed a practical light on the *E.T.F.B* Model, showing us how to implement it with a *positive EYE*. By now, you know how fond I am of metaphors; I believe they are excellent, implementable *tools* because they simplify complex models, creating easy-to-remember analogies and helping us free ourselves from limiting paradigms.

How to Exit the Vortex?

I've already mentioned the negative loop created when a negative *thought* produces a negative *feeling*, only for that to produce more negative *thoughts*, and so on. This way, the negative *feelings* intensify automatically, foreshadowing a stronger negative *behavior* (reaction) later on. We can imagine that as a downward spiral as illustrated in diagram 10-6. If you use your imagination and look at the spiral from above (not from the side), you will see that it resembles a vortex in the ocean.

What is our instinctive reaction when we encounter a vortex at sea? Resistance. We stress out or even panic, try with all our might to stay above sea level so we can breathe and lift out of it. I recall my first lesson about the ocean my Dad taught me: "If you encounter a vortex, don't resist; most likely, its force will be greater than yours. Instead, fill up your lungs with air and let the vortex pull you down. Don't worry, I'm not teaching your how to drown, but how to save your strength for the lower levels of the vortex, where it's weaker. For when it does weaken, you can seize the moment to exert the energy you maintained in order to break sideways with all your might and save yourself from the vortex."

And now to the lesson:

Firstly, the metaphor well exemplifies how our natural, automatic tendency to resist only sinks us deeper. Just like being at sea, when we encounter an emotional vortex or any other duress in life, we first resist the *event*, ask "why" questions and mourn our fate, thus perpetuating the negative *event* and getting stuck in it without being able to overcome it. Indeed, **what you resist, persists!** Therefore, just like at sea, the idea is not to automatically resist the *circumstances* around us, which we cannot change, but to first accept them, for an automatic resistance to *circumstances* guarantees "downing." Of course, the first reaction could be blurting out some juicy swear words, but from there on, it's important to *observe* and *choose* conscious steps, not automatic. For example, you may ask yourself (quickly), "What can I do to exit this vortex?" or, "How do I handle it?" both of which are *questions of possibility and opportunity.* On the one hand, you should acknowledge being in a vortex; on the other hand, remember how you exit it: without resisting, by accepting the situation, letting go, and letting the vortex carry you **temporarily** until you can break sideways, change the negative thoughts, and free yourself.

The same goes for an emotional vortex. Instead of resisting the negative *thoughts* and *feelings* it brings, accept the situation and allow yourself to drop *below the line* temporarily—but as soon as you can, use your full power of *awareness* and *choice* to change the interpretation and *thoughts*, step out of the emotional storm, and stop the negative loop.

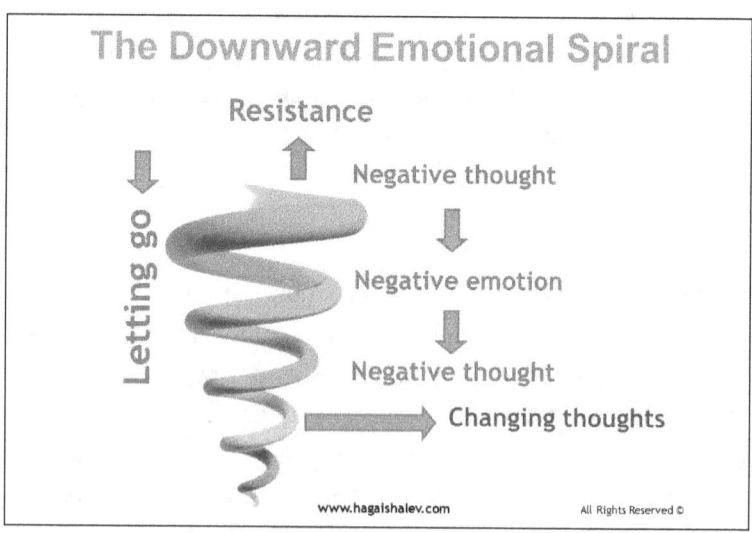

Diagram 10-6—An Emotional Vortex is like an Ocean Vortex

To emphasize: changing *thoughts* doesn't imply resisting the negative automatic interpretation; the idea is not to negate the automatic interpretation or to judge and criticize yourself for your negative thinking. Doing that only perpetuates and fixates the negative interpretation. It's like telling you not to think of a pink elephant, knowing that your imagination will automatically conjure up a pink elephant to occupy your thoughts. Instead, *observe* the vortex you've encountered, accept the resistance, and let go of judgment; then replace the negative *thoughts* with positive ones; simply change your *thoughts* by thinking about something entirely different from that *event* or negative *circumstances*. You will receive the *tools* to do that shortly.

Like Clouds in the Sky

The second metaphor I would like to present for understanding the implementation of the *E.T.F.B* model is "clouds in the sky." *Thoughts* are like clouds in the sky. Suddenly, a dark cloud appears. Why and where it came from, I do not know. I'm not familiar with the science of cloud formation, and honestly, I don't care about it, since I have no control over it. All I know is that the heavens have a natural mechanism that creates dark clouds. The same goes for the lesson at hand: the dark cloud is analogous to negative interpretation and *thoughts*, which come out of nowhere, from a source that cannot be controlled.

So, when a dark cloud appears, I grasp it. The same happens with a negative thought—my *automatic program* doesn't know how to release it, so I hold onto it. In nature, similar forces attract, and the dark cloud I'm grasping attracts another dark cloud and another one...thus, that small initial cloud suddenly grows into a large, threatening one. Since it's above me as I'm holding it, it brings down rain on my area and I get unpleasantly wet. The same happens with negative thought loops; they automatically gather into a dark, heavy, condensed "cloud" that brings down "heavy rain." The result leads to us dropping *below the line* and "drowning" in the "sea" of negative *feelings* (emotions).

Therefore, the right way to handle dark clouds gathering from uncontrolled sources is utterly different: when a dark cloud appears, I greet it; I'm not surprised that it showed up nor do I resist it, because that is nature's way. Once in a while, I encounter worrying *circumstances*; a client doesn't show up, or a deal I worked hard to close doesn't materialize. If I do my best to avoid the negative *circumstances*, all I have left to do is accept the cloud—the *event*. If so, the dark cloud arrives and, unlike the *automatic program*, I don't grasp it, but let it pass. The slang for it is "Hi and bye." Instead of getting stuck with the dark cloud, I look out to the horizon in search of a white cloud. Just like the heavens form dark clouds, they also form white ones. I don't have to search for or understand how this mechanism works in order to use it; just like I don't have to understand how electricity is produced in order to enjoy using it. All I have to do is look for the closest white cloud. Once I find it, I invite the white cloud to come closer. The moral is, search for and embrace positive interpretation and *thoughts*. Only then will the dark cloud pass, making room for the white one. Note that in chapters three and six, I mentioned that the conscious mind can only hold one single thought at a time, whether it be positive **or** negative; they can't co-exist. Now, it seems that's great news for me, because the moment I found the white cloud, the dark cloud passed; the negative thought dissolves and is replaced by a positive one. A dark cloud may reappear later on, but I'll simply apply the same method—I won't grasp the dark cloud, but let it pass and find a white cloud to replace it. The more I practice it, the more easily I can replace dark clouds with white ones. **From now on, remember that thoughts are like clouds in the sky,** with one exception: you have the power to determine what type of clouds fill up your sky.

"Think before you act"—Proverbs 13:16-25

Now on to the implications. Implementing the E.T.F.B model is done just like any of the other *tools* in this book: by using the *CO-OP Formula*. It all begins with *awareness*. Awareness of what? Awareness of thinking before you act; **awareness that your results are a direct outcome of the interpretation (*thoughts*) that you are in control of.** Although it can be very elusive, hidden, quick and automatic, ***thought* involves *choice*.** It's very hard to discern it because no one teaches us to observe our *thoughts*, nor are you quite aware of how much it is the source of the emotions, reactions, and results you produce in your life. This is unlike *feeling*, which is so dominant, sensory, and influential. However, as you learned from the E.T.F.B model, every *behavior* begins with interpretation, and when you learn to control your *thoughts*, you will also be able to control your *feelings* (emotions), your *behavior*, and the results you achieve. If someone has annoyed you, it's your interpretation (*thoughts*) alone that has caused your anger. Although the *event* is the primary cause, your *thoughts* about the *event* are what determines your *feeling*s most of all.

◆

It you're not quite convinced yet, here's a simple example: let's say you and I are working together in a project management company, and we're both equally responsible for a certain project. Let's also assume we didn't meet the objectives of this project and left the client disappointed, as well as causing the company a great financial loss. Now we're sitting opposite our boss, who is reprimanding us angrily for our lack of initiative and poor performance. You, the reader, take the reprimand with responsibility and courage, withstanding the outburst and responding with calmness and acceptance. "I take full responsibility for the failure. I'm very sorry it happened and I promise this type of a disaster won't happen again," you tell the boss. I, on the other hand, am well *below the line*, full of complaints against the boss, feeling hurt, betrayed, and frustrated; I have lots of excuses and reasons for the failure and I blame my boss for his lack of sufficient cooperation and so on. Your *feelings* and *behavior* are **different** than mine, whereas the *circumstances* are completely **identical**. What is the reason for that difference? It is our *operating systems*, of course. While your interpretation, your reaction, was to accept the situation and take responsibility, mine was victim-like, judgmental, and hit sensitive areas in me that aroused negative *thoughts*, such as, ""I'm not good enough; he doesn't appreciate me; it's my fault[57]." Everything originates from our subjective *thoughts*, which are the source for all the chain reactions that occur in our *operating system; feelings, behaviors,* and *results.*

◆

Let's go back to the *CO-OP Formula* to examine how to cope with a negative loop and overcome it. As I have said, everything begins with *awareness. Awareness* of what? Of the fact that every emotional process begins with a *thought* that can be changed.

---

57 My friend, Rachi Wertheimer, calls these sensitive areas "scratches" in her excellent book, "Relationsheep—Healing Your Relationships." If you want to delve deeper into the *E.T.F.B* model and further develop your emotional intelligence, I highly recommend you read this book. In the book, Rachi explores inherently negative personal interpretations and introduces the best model I know for developing emotional intelligence. I use the Sheep model in my work with almost every client.

The next step is *self-observation*; first of the emotion, so we can recognize being *below the line*; next, we observe our *thoughts* and interpretations in order to identify the thought pattern that caused the negative *feeling*. The axiom the *E.T.F.B* model shows us is that, if we're *below the line*, there has to be some negative interpretation (*thought*) in the background that has caused it. Once we identify the automatic, elusive negative *thought,* we move onto the *choice*—choosing to manage our *thoughts* and change them, control and steer them to the white clouds in our sky, with a *positive EYE* and *baby steps. Practicing* the *choice* 12 times a day for 30 days will create a *new habit* of guiding out *thoughts* in positive, beneficial directions. As a result, we'll be able to control our emotions (*feelings*), enabling us to be more *above the live*, react (*behave*) more positively, and achieve *improved results*.

Tools for Controlling Thoughts

Now let's go on with our practical implementation, looking more closely and extensively at **choice** in order to learn how to change the automatic interpretation. I shall review **three sub-*tools* for changing *thoughts*:**

1. Immunization and prevention. The first sub-tool with which we can influence interpretation is immunization and prevention of the automatic negativity of *thoughts*. As I've mentioned in chapter three, from infancy to adulthood, through all aspects of our lives, we don't place enough emphasis on keeping a *positive attitude, focusing* more on problems and hardship than on possibilities and opportunities. This results in an ever-increasing automatic negative reaction to any event with negative circumstances. Meaning, when we're flooded with negativity, every little thing sets us off into a loop of negative emotions, all of which stem from our *thoughts*. How do we prevent that? By gradually developing *positive attitudes* and a *focus* on what is working in our life. When you develop more *positive attitude* and *focus,* your *operating system* will slowly get used to being more positive and respond with fewer automatic negative *thoughts*. Being more positive, you will be more *above the line*, having more positive *thoughts* and becoming less sensitive. The outcome will be less negative interpretation, and thus less negative *feelings*. The more you practice it, the more you'll be *above the line*. One of the best immunizations around, which is common among all religions, is **gratitude**: simply expressing gratitude for all the good things in our life. For instance, the first commandment in Judaism is to, upon waking, recite the "Modeh Ani[58]" ("I give thanks") blessing. This statement carries so much wisdom. Instead of the *automatic program* trying to stay in bed and postpone getting up to face a new day's work, the gratitude immediately replaces the dark cloud that appears upon waking with a white one, at once focusing us on the positive, the half full cup. And there is so much good to be grateful for, including the small things most of us take for granted—a place to live, food to eat, work that brings us income, people to love and be loved by, and the most obvious fact: we are awake, therefore we are alive! Giving thanks in the morning, as well as during other *self-observation* points during the day, evokes positive emotions, increases our positive threshold, builds a positive setup for the day, and prevents at least some of the automatic negative interpretations in response to negative *circumstances* we run into in everyday life.

From what you've already learned in this book, it's clear

---

58 The full "Modeh Ani" prayer: "I thank you, living and enduring king, for you have graciously returned my soul within me. Great is your faithfulness."

that *practicing* **gratitude in the long term programs your unconscious mind for positivity,** and I've already mentioned that the more positive you are, the more *above the line* you find yourself, ensuring that your road to success is paved.

2. Specific choice. When a negative *thought* lodges in our minds, it's usually a specific one. It may be a concern (for a person, a financial situation, our health), a fear (of change, of the future, of a person) or a negative personal interpretation (I'm not good enough, no one likes me, I'm a loser, I'm unsafe). It's always specifically linked to *circumstances*. In other words, any *event* elicits a *thought* once the facts move through the *three filters* and settle in our *operating system* as a paradigm.

But realize that the coin has two sides: one is the negative, automatic *thought*; the other is a different, positive *thought* about those same *circumstances*. Buddhism maintains that everything is empty and meaningless, aside from the meaning we lend to it. Note that there's hardly any bad without good. The more I look at negative *circumstances* in my life, the more I understand how complex and sophisticated the world we live in is; a universe that has survived and existed for 14 billion years cannot be any different. We humans find it difficult if not impossible to fathom this complexity, nor have we fully discovered all the laws of the universe. For example, how many times has something happened to you that started as negative but turned out to be positive, even if it was long after the fact? This is what I experienced when I quit my job under pressure of *circumstances*, only to find out that, in retrospect, it allowed me to undergo an incredible transformation and fulfill my life's purpose. **The more you look for the flip side of the coin, the more you will notice it.** For example, I noticed that usually when a client cancels an appointment without advance notice, my automatic reaction is anger, but it all works out in the end, as I'm able to schedule another client in that opening, one who called just minutes after the cancellation; or it allows me the rest that I truly need at that moment; or I have time to complete a task I have been putting off.

If so, instead of automatically focusing on the half empty cup due to specific negative *circumstances*, look for the positive and ask yourself q*uestions of possibility and opportunity.* How do I overcome the problem? What can I do to improve my *circumstances*? What is good about the new situation? What does it enable me to do? How can I make lemonade out of this lemon? The moment you turn your *focus* from the problem to its possible solutions, you're replacing the dark cloud with a white one, **because when we look for solutions, we always find them— always.** Sometimes it happens immediately; other times it takes longer. According to quantum physics, we have an infinite amount of available possibilities at any given moment; instead of focusing on the problem, look for the solution. This is how you make your *thoughts* and interpretations more positive, and your *feelings* inevitably become positive as well. This is a mindful use of the *E.T.F.B* model: *choosing* to change the *focus, attitude,* and types of questions you ask yourself ("what and how" instead of "why") in order to create change in your thought pattern and rise *above the line*[59].

---

59 Notice the synergy between the *tools*: *E.T.F.B, positive attitude* and *focus*, being *above the line,* and *questions of possibility and opportunity.* Indeed, all the *tools* in this book for implementing the *CO-OP Formula* are **"communicating vessels."** Each *tool* you choose is connected to other *tools* that emerge intuitively and come together to create harmony for effectively implementing the *CO-OP.* Furthermore, each additional *tool* reinforce the positive effect of the other *tools.*

3. General choice. Sometimes we find ourselves on an emotional rollercoaster, and it's very difficult—if not impossible (mainly for a person untrained with *E.T.F.B*)—to make a specific positive *choice*. In this case, you can make a **general choice** to change your *thoughts*. This choice is based on an axiom we already established: "The conscious mind can only entertain one single thought at any given moment." Whether it is a negative or a positive thought, they cannot co-exist. Therefore, what is initially perceived as a weakness and limitation of the human *operating system* becomes an advantage. Even if your head is full of negative thoughts, you can always replace them with available positive thoughts—ones you jot down on a piece of paper in your wallet, or on some app on your smartphone—chasing away the negative thoughts. Here are a few examples for thoughts you can choose to focus on instead: people you love, places you love, a good book you've read, a good movie you've seen, a success you experienced, a fun vacation, etc. Moreover, you may make some physical change that will break the negative loop: go out to the garden, go for a walk or a jog, do 20 pushups or sit-ups, go to the beach or a nearby park, prepare your favorite dish, call a good friend, and so on. I advise my clients to call me when they're in an emotional low they can't pull themselves out of. In our conversation, I try to change their *focus* and *thoughts* to help them rise *above the line*. *Choosing* anything that makes you feel good breaks the negative loop, the *automatic program*, lets in possibility, light, and positivity, opening up new ways to further escape the *autopilot*.

The principle is easy to understand, yet not always easy to perform; still, distracting the negative thoughts with new, positive thoughts or actions will cause the former to scatter. True, this thought exchange is somewhat contrived, and we often find the negative thoughts returning shortly thereafter. In this case, one must repeat the *choice* of positive thoughts again and again. Sound tiring? Perhaps, but remember that thoughts are like a muscle; *practicing* a repetitive *choice* in *small steps* with a *positive EYE* trains the muscle so it can create a *new habit* and improve your life.

I believe it's one of the most worthwhile *choices* to *practice* and implement. Try and see for yourself!

E.T.F.B Model—Summary and Conclusions

The *E.T.F.B* model illuminates the connection between cause and effect through the human emotional system. The significance of the model lies in locating **thoughts as a source of emotions**. It mainly enables us to handle negative emotional loops by *choosing* to change the thoughts and moving from *below the line* to *above the line*.

In order to implement the *E.T.F.B* model with a *positive EYE* in your life, be *aware* of the model's principles and *tools* as presented above, and use *observation points* to *observe yourself*, your emotions, and your thoughts. Identify the negative *feelings* and the negative *thoughts* at their base, and choose to change the *thoughts* using the *tools* in the previous subchapter. *Practice* this *choice* again and again with a *positive EYE* and *baby steps*, until it's fully assimilated into your unconscious mind and creates a new thinking *habit*, more positive and more controllable, to enable you to remain *above the line* and achieve *improved results*. Finally, remember the cloud and vortex metaphors to make the implementation easier for you.

How Andy Implemented the E.T.F.B Model to Create Change

Here is an example of the effect and power of the *tools* I just reviewed in this chapter, as reflected in my client Andy's (alias) life, as he wrote to me at the end of the coaching process:

"Thank you for helping me out of the snowball I was trapped in, consisting of negative thoughts that led to negative results and vice versa. Although my life's circumstances haven't changed for the most part, my interpretation has changed completely as well as myself; I think positively and thrive. The CO-OP Formula worked for me like a miracle remedy; within seven sessions, I became a different person—optimistic, happy, looking at life from a mature viewpoint, instead of being driven by my ego. Every aspect of my life changed dramatically. The peak was when I received a quarterly outstanding award at my workplace, which I was planning to leave only two months earlier. I think it's very hard to help someone who is focused on what is wrong, in being a victim of life; H.J. completed the mission with great success."

I shall close this chapter with my own saying: "*When you are in great gratitude, you shift your attitude, and you manifest in multitude.*"

CHAPTER ELEVEN:
How to Set Goals and Achieve Them Effectively

"When the 'what' is clear, the 'how' is clarified"
—H.J. Shalev

In this chapter, we shall put the *Being* tools aside and discuss the *Doing*. So far, you've acknowledged the importance of *Being* as an essential mental foundation for achieving results. Without it, the *Doing* will remain powerless and usually destined for failure; since you've made it this far with me in this book, I'm convinced that you pretty much recognize that. However, the purpose of this book is to serve as a practical guide to achieving results. Without detracting from the importance of *Being* as the basis for action, the rules of the world we live in do require action in order to get things moving and achieve goals, and *Doing* in order to yield results. As such, it's about time we turn our attention also to the matter of *Doing*. The laws of nature force us to sow in order to harvest. I won't get into any New Age theories like the law of attraction, and how some believe that if you stick to it, you can produce results even with idleness. While I usually support such theories, I believe that the more appropriate road of manifestation should combine an enabling state of being (*above the line*, acceptance, being unattached to results[60], self-confidence, etc.) with the right amount of activity[61]. Thus, before I give you more *tools* for

---

60 Can also be described as surrendering.

61 I won't expand on what the "right amount of activity" is. I will only mention that over-doing is the common state, which I have experienced firsthand. Here, our will and desire are so strong that we do not have

changing beliefs, *habits*, and emotions to continue supporting your actions, let's take a look at one of the most important *Doing* principles there is: business planning.

What Motivates Us to Achieve Goals?

I shall open with the following statement by Dr. Hedva Braunstein-Bercovitz, head of the masters program in occupational psychology at the Academic College of Tel Aviv: "When you're working in a job that suits you for profound inner reasons (not for financial reasons), your feeling of satisfaction gives you the strength to cope with different types of pressure and reinforces your mental strength and durability." Dr. Braunstein-Bercovitz refers to a satisfaction that stems from "profound inner reasons" that reinforce us when coping with challenges, enabling us to persist and succeed. What are these "profound inner reasons?" This will be the focus of this chapter, but before we dive any deeper, let's look at what they **do not entail**: "Not for financial reasons." Of course, there's nothing wrong with money; it's very legitimate to aspire to wealth and work for it; ever since money was invented, it's no doubt been a motivator and a catalyst of economic growth and prosperity. However, man cannot succeed on money alone. Seeking wealth only isn't a sufficient catalyst for results, we are told by Dr. Braunstein-Bercovitz. I see it daily in my work with entrepreneurs motivated only by aspirations of getting rich; as soon as they hit the first hurdle, they realize that there's probably no way of making quick cash in their current enterprise, and they tend to give up and search for easy money elsewhere. Thus, these entrepreneurs overlook the two important qualities that breed success: persistence and determination.

---

enough patience for evolutionary processes, which are nature's way. This is also where our focus is highly subjective; we're certain we know what the right way is, are inattentive, and are not open enough to opportunities and other possibilities around us.

If so, **what are those "profound inner reasons" that help us succeed?** A study conducted by MIT sheds light on them. The study, titled, "The Surprising Truth About What Motivates Us[62]," examined what motivates people towards performance and achievements, and to what extent does monetary compensation motivate them to yield results. According to the study, if the task involves more than just mechanical skills or basic cognitive skills, but also creative thinking, **higher pay resulted in lower performance.** Yes, you heard right! We live with the assumption that the more we get paid, the more motivated we are to perform, yet studies show that this is true only for basic mechanical skills.

What does increase performance and satisfaction at work when performing more complex tasks, then? According to the study, the three factors are **Autonomy, Mastery,** and **Purpose.** The common thread between them is the "profound inner reasons," the "why": why do we do what we do? What need is it important for us to fulfill and how does it relate to our values? To our DNA? To what inspires us? To the good we wish to do for others and in the world? What is our passion at work? And what about you—what were you destined to do? What do you love doing? What excites and moves you? All these are factors that motivate you much more than money in the long run. I feel it myself, as I write these lines late at night. If so, as business owners and executives seeking success and fortune, we should tap into our "profound inner reasons" so we can better achieve our goals and, at the end of the day, earn more. Just to reiterate, there's no harm in wanting to make money; **but money need not be the end goal, as it is always the outcome of performance based on autonomy at work, aspirations to mastery, and a worthy, valuable purpose.** When we are driven by these causes, we can be highly beneficial

---

62 See the short video https://www.hagaishalev.com/en/blog/motivation.

to many people, so that the monetary compensation they are willing to pay us becomes almost unavoidable. I have already stated in this book that we are first and foremost emotional creatures motivated by feelings. Indeed, the emotional connection is the fuel; it's the power source that motivates and drives us towards fulfillment and achievement. This holds true for work as it does in any other area. Think about what you're willing to do when you're in love or what a mother is willing to sacrifice for her children.

Great examples from the business world of how money isn't necessarily the motive for performance are worldwide projects such as Wikipedia, Linux, etc. Here, one can see talented, exceptional individuals who contribute their time, effort, and knowledge to benefit society with no monetary reward. As one who volunteers for many organizations, I can attest to how much satisfaction there is in community service. In general, there is an increasing trend of doing community service around the world. Any social gathering around a worthy purpose is a good example of the values that motivate people. Furthermore, in recent years, the term "social business" has emerged, showing us that **there is no contradiction between a social-environmental approach and financial gain.** On the contrary, the most successful businesses usually combine the two very well.

I shall end this subchapter with a quote by Confucius: "Choose a job you love, and you will never have to work a day in your life."

"If you don't know where you're going, any road will take you there"—Cheshire Cat, Alice in Wonderland

So that we can connect to the "profound inner reasons" motivating us towards fulfillment, results, and ultimately money, we must find them, define them, and plan how to realize them. I meet many people wandering around aimlessly in this world, like ships that sail without captains or destinations, moving only according to the direction of the wind and the condition of the waves. Such a ship's ability to reach a specific destination relies on chance. My recommendation: steer your "ship" to "Rome." Why? Because "Rome" is a wonderful city and all roads lead to Rome. We each have our own "Rome," and when you reach yours, don't forget to do as the Romans do. If you aim for Rome, there are much better chances you will get there. Indeed, most people in general—and business owners in particular—don't really plan. When I talk to them about planning, they say, "I don't know what's going to happen tomorrow morning, yet you want me to tell you where I'll be in a year?" I answer, "Yes, of course, if you do want to reach your 'Rome' and not get side-tracked like Alice."

It's odd that non-planning—a concept that would never work in large corporations—is a common practice among small business owners and employees in their careers. This despite the fact that size doesn't matter here. Indeed, planning brings *focus*, commitment, and fulfillment with a *positive EYE* among small business owners and career professionals, just the same as with big corporations. Why, then, do business owners and employees refrain from planning? **Firstly**, because they seem to think they don't need planning: "It's all up to me anyway, and I'm always planning in my head, so what's the point of writing it down?" they say. **Secondly**, planning serves as a commitment that must be fulfilled. It's easier not to commit; so long as the planning isn't in writing, the commitment isn't announced, so it's easier for the business owner or employee not to keep his word and "forget" that he has committed to doing something. In the daily grind we live in, where one thing follows another, new replacing old, with the dynamic pace of life and business, who can ordinarily remember setting any given goal? **It's easy, too easy, to forgo unwritten**

commitments. Therefore, from time to time, I publish an annual goals plan on my blog. **Thirdly**, ignorance prevents planning; how do you plan, anyway? Business owners tell me, "I've never learned how to plan and I don't do it right; so I'll just skip it."

If so, the purpose of this chapter is to guide you on how to plan properly and with a *positive* EYE.

Business Planning with a Positive EYE

Business planning should be done in writing: a written goal is three times as likely to be achieved as a purely mental one. Setting goals down in writing brings focus, specificity, commitment, and effectiveness, since you know where you're going and how to gather and adapt your resources to get there. Setting goals down in writing leads to fulfillment, higher income, and larger profits.

Proper planning should be done from the viewpoint that any business goal is possible. This is not the time to be "realistic;" to me, "realistic" is a code word for "inferior." When we're "realistic," we are aiming lower from the get go, and our chances of attaining and fulfilling our biggest dreams lessen. According to the *focus principle*, we've learned that what you focus on increases; we've also seen that your *TTT* determines your reality, and that your paradigms define what is possible or impossible for you. Add it up, and you'll realize that "realistic" is highly subjective. Meaning, **your focus and intention very much determine your ability to achieve your goals.** As the saying goes, "Shoot for the moon. Even if you miss, you'll land among the stars." **Proper planning means aiming high from the viewpoint that anything is possible.** Having been a CFO and having worked with American executives, I couldn't initially understand their tendency to always set such high standards when planning. Today, I fully understand that and believe it's one of the main traits that made America one of the strongest economic superpowers in the world.

My business owning clients often ask me, "Do you think my goals are realistic?" I answer, "Who am I to know? I'm not God, and I never tell a client he's aiming too high." Let's say a client tells me he wants to make ten million dollars in a year. Yes, it's highly ambitious, but it's not impossible. Aren't there other business owners who have made ten million dollars in a year? Then why can't you? Therefore, I respect my clients' goals and see myself more as a guide, a mentor, a facilitator, and a catalyst for them to reach those goals, rather than a realistic critic of their ability to attain them. I believe wholeheartedly that any business goal is possible; I focus more on how to accomplish them than whether they're possible. At the same time, I use my skills as an economist to guide my clients towards the area and the niche that will give them the greatest opportunity to fulfill their highest business potential. The world is full of ordinary people who have achieved extraordinary things, and I believe that everyone has the potential to achieve the extraordinary. This is the first rule I learned as a novice paratrooper in the IDF: the body can achieve much more than the mind thinks it can. "Seek and you shall find," the scriptures say. In his book, *Think and Grow Rich*, Napoleon Hill writes, "Whatever the mind of man can conceive and believe, it can achieve." This is great news for you, because if you conceive and believe in the things you want to achieve, you will probably do so. We will soon find out the meaning of "conceive and believe." I wholeheartedly believe in it, and see it as my mission in the world to help any person fulfill their dreams. Sometimes, especially when you plan them out ambitiously, dreams do come true!

What Isn't Measured, Isn't Managed

An effective goal should also be concrete. The tendency to not commit causes many to plan in a non-concrete way. "I want to succeed and make a lot of money," my clients tell me. "Wow, great," I answer, "What do you mean by 'succeed'? What, to you, is 'a lot of money?' What are the measurements for that?" **It's important for a goal to be quantitative, measurable, and descriptive of exactly what you want.** A good goal should answer the questions **who, what, when, and how much.** Testing it is simple: when you get there, it should be very clear to you, beyond any doubt, whether or not you have achieved your goal. Indeed, what isn't measured, isn't managed. As long as we don't measure things, we can't really manage them properly, as we leave too much to the imagination; again, concreteness brings clarity and focus, as well as greater commitment to act and accomplish.

Furthermore, planning reduces the margin for error. Those who have experience making errors and having to fix them know **it takes ten times longer to fix an error than to do things right the first time.** I'm not saying you can completely avoid errors, but you can certainly minimize them, and proper planning helps us do that.

◆

We've seen, then, that effective action requires planning, but one may ask, how do we plan? What is an effective business planning method that can lead us to ultimate fulfillment? The best planning method I know is called *"Breakthrough."* It's the most effective methodology for setting goals and achieving them, and one which I mentioned in chapter four. *Breakthrough* is a known and acceptable term in the business world. Many successful firms, including Apple and Google, implement it as the backbone of their businesses, reaping much success. *Breakthrough* methodology has

a number of characteristics: the **first characteristic** is a significant, drastic increase in results in a relatively short time period.
A breakthrough isn't supposed to happen in the normal course of
business, as represented by the red line in diagram 11-1. The red
line reflects "business as usual," while the green graph shows the
new field of possibilities that a *breakthrough* enables; the green
arrow pointing upwards reflects the sharp increase in results in a
relatively short period. The **second characteristic** is that a *breakthrough* is perceived as an "impossible" achievement. It shows a
very ambitious standard of achievements, in keeping with the effective planning principles I discussed earlier in this chapter. The
third characteristic is that a *breakthrough* begins with a present
declaration of where we'd like to be in the future, without having
planned how to get there yet. First, we verbalize **what** we want to
achieve, and only then do we think about **how** to achieve it. The
reason for this is found in the title of this chapter: "When the 'what'
is clear, the 'how' is clarified." Let's break this down:

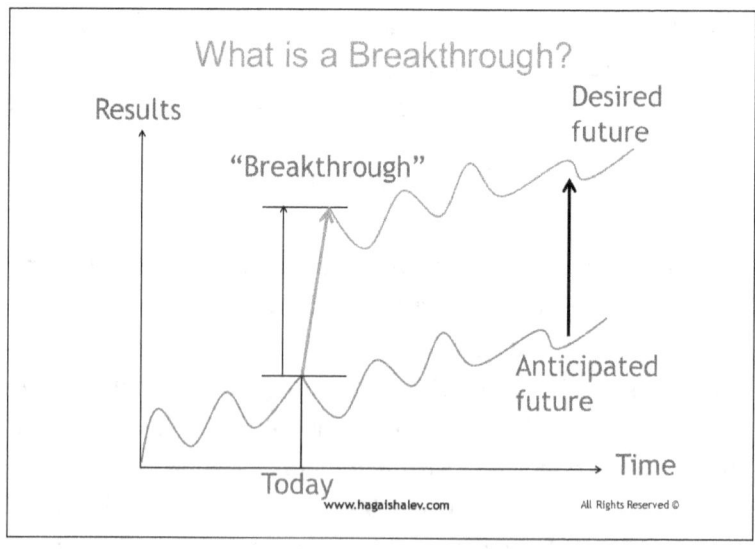

Diagram 11-1—What is a Breakthrough

How to Land a Man on the Moon

The best example of a *breakthrough* comes from May 5th, 1961, when then-president John F. Kennedy delivered a message before a joint session of Congress, broadcast on TV: *"I believe that this nation should commit itself to achieving the goal, before this decade is out, of landing a man on the moon and returning him safely to the earth."* When Kennedy declared that, the technology needed in order to send a man to the moon was yet to be invented; the metals required to build spaceships were not yet available; landing a man on the moon seemed like a fantasy, like science fiction, like something "impossible." It was a highly ambitious goal. Still, Kennedy's declaration created a shift in humanity's approach to space: the American nation joined the effort, the congress allocated budgets, and NASA deployed to fulfill the dream. When, in 1969, Neil Armstrong stepped on the moon for the first time, it was literally a *breakthrough* for humankind. Indeed, Kennedy's declaration created a gravitational pull, a center of attraction and an inspiration, arousing energy and emotion that ignited the fulfillment of that dream. This is the great significance of the *breakthrough* approach in general, and the declaration in particular: the motivation and impetus that it generates by affecting people, organizations, and nations.

The *breakthrough* approach is also evident in Israel's history of fulfillment and success: the declaration of independence of the State of Israel was held on Friday, May 14th, 1948 in Tel Aviv. The great risks of going through with the declaration were clear, due to the Arab armies' threat to invade the emerging country, as well as the extensive objections by the U.S. and other countries. Indeed, it was a declaration of the "impossible" and the onset of a battle of David against Goliath. It was primarily the spirit of the Israelis and their yearning for independence that led this battle to its happy end.

◆

The planning method of the *breakthrough* approach is contrary to the natural way most organizations and business owners plan, if and when they plan at all. Most businesses first and foremost ask themselves, "Where were we yesterday?" and then, "Where are we today?" and only then, based on the answers to the previous questions, "Where could we get to tomorrow?" This is logical, linear thinking typical of humans. The *breakthrough* approach is entirely different.

"You can't invent something new based on experience"— Albert Einstein

The planning method that takes the past through the present and into the future is called **past-based planning**. This is the most common planning method in the business world: financial executives copy the previous year's data, paste it onto the following year, and then change figures, mostly increasing income and expenses at a lower rate than income growth so that the reflected profit improves. Sometimes they even reduce costs to reflect cost reductions and better efficiency. The most important thing is that the forecast budget looks nice and reasonable, so as to survive the arduous road leading to approval by the board of directors. As a CFO, I experienced this many times, and though not all organizations plan that way, it is a common approach.

Such planning is deficient at its core, since it's based on the past. This past may include all the achievements and good things that happened to the business, but it also includes all the business' past paradigms. These paradigms contain all the limiting perceptions and beliefs of the past that underlay these organizations. This past-based planning takes the past and reflects it on the future in order to create more of the same results, even if it is an improved version of the past.

This approach has led organizations to the verge of bankruptcy and even extinction. This is one of the main reasons the Kodak Company found itself in Chapter 11 bankruptcy "all of a sudden" when the camera film market that had earned the company so much money for years, vanished in favor of digital cameras. The linear thinking of "what was will be," while sticking to the past paradigm, probably made Kodak believe that camera film would exist forever. As this book is being written, what was left of that mega-corporation is a shrunken version, busy reinventing itself as a digital printing company. There are countless similar examples in many fields. Here are some from the dynamic cell phone market: Motorola, which invented and dominated the cellular market, is nonexistent in it today; Nokia, which rose against the backdrop of Motorola's fall, found itself crashing as well when it failed to predict the emergence of the smartphones; and finally Apple, which fell before it rose. I shall discuss Apple in more detail shortly.

"The best way to predict the future Is to create it"—Peter Drucker

I've already mentioned that small business owners and salaried employees usually don't plan; when they do plan, they think about tomorrow, next week, next month. Okay, the strict ones also think about next quarter, perhaps even next year, but they usually do that in a linear way, thinking from the past, through the present, and into the future—past-based planning. They often use the term "realistic planning." **A far better planning method is the *breakthrough* approach, also known as *future-based planning*.** According to this method, we first turn to the future and ask ourselves, "Where would I like to be in a year or so?"

Not, "Where can I get according to my past," but, "What do I **really want**? What will fulfill my dreams, my vision, and my potential?" In other words, define the future *what*—what are the goals I aspire to? What is the optimal future I would like to create for myself? According to this method, **we first jump into some future point in time and define the ideal reality we want to experience there.** Only after that do we go back to the present and begin to build the bridge we need to cross into that future; and we do all that without involving the past. We don't ignore it—it exists, it's important, and it's the source of our experience, but it's not the starting point from which to plan the future. Remember, setting future goals—the *what*—doesn't have to be "realistic." While defining the *how*, you may find gaps and holes between the present and the future you're planning. For example, you may discover that you'll need more time to get from point A to point B, or that the road is blocked and you need to find a different route. Indeed, this is the life of the planner, and there is no planner who hasn't experienced one hitch or another which required him to change plans. We call that *circumstances*. You've probably heard the saying, "Every plan is a basis for change." I truly believe that and see it as an inseparable aspect of fulfillment. A frequent change of plans characterizes the *breakthrough* method, since we're aiming high towards "impossible" goals to begin with.

◆

I shall now return to diagram 11-1 and explain it in detail:

Focus only on the red line for a moment: the line shaped like an ascending sine wave describes people's normal behavior along the time axis. It has two main characteristics:

First, it has inclines and slopes that reflect the fluctuations that usually characterize human endeavors. In fact, everything in nature moves according to the sine wave pattern: Day and night, the seasons of the year, tidal ebb and flow, life cycles, and more. So are we, humans, subject to emotional, mental, and physical fluctuations, according to this sine wave pattern.

Second, the red graph is on an incline from left to right, showing us that people advance through life and improve all the time thanks to the knowledge and experience they accumulate. Usually, we can say that people in general and businesses in particular usually yield better results the further they are along the timeline.

Nonetheless, the red line doesn't reflect a change in our daily life. It assumes "business as usual," a past-based way of planning, and therefore its right end shows our "anticipated future"—that is, where we are expected to reach if we continue our current conduct.

Those who wish for higher future results need to change their thinking and conduct in order to attain their desired future. The entire upper portion of the diagram reflects this change, which I call *future-based planning*:

One can see that while undergoing a *breakthrough* kind of change, the red line upgrades through the green arrow, turning into the green line. This is made possible by a significant, sharp increase in results over a fairly short time period, as expressed by the green arrow pointing upward. Suddenly, the green graph reflects a new field of opportunities, leading us to our "desired future," with a higher level of results in every future point in time. It may seem like the *breakthrough* is happening in one instant, but that's not the case; while the leap is sharp and comparatively quick, it does still reflect an evolution across a large number of *baby steps*. In my standard coaching plan, a *breakthrough* occurs within around six months. Nonetheless, a *breakthrough* usually deviates from the usual course of business, creating a new field of opportunities. It is powerful and looks like an extraordinary leap on the timeline of the business, the business owner, or the career planner.

To sum up, **a *breakthrough* change enables us to reach a future that was not attainable until now.**

◆

I shall close this subchapter with another quote by Albert Einstein: "We cannot solve problems by using the same kind of thinking we used when we created them." By saying, "the same kind of thinking we used when we created them," Einstein means the way of thinking we used to act on in the **past**. It cannot be the key to solving the very problems it created. In order to bring about a new and better reality that would constitute a *breakthrough*, we must learn to think **differently**.

How Can a Small Business Owner Succeed Like Apple?

One of the most prominent examples of a *breakthrough*, or better yet, a *breakthrough* company[63] is Apple. In 1997, *Apple* was close to going under Chapter 11; it competed head to head with Microsoft and Intel but couldn't withstand the competition. During those years, Apple was selling only Mac computers. It had a very small market segment, reflecting a minor portion of the worldwide PC market. Its target audience mainly consisted of geeks and

---

63 A company for whom *breakthroughs* are a way of life, generating a series of *breakthroughs* in a persistent and consistent manner.

designers who bought its computers. A change occurred when Steve Jobs came back to run Apple that same year and started to implement, among other things, the *breakthrough* methodology. Jobs asked himself and his management team, "How can we use all of our wonderful assets: top-notch technology, a 'cool' brand and amazing design, in order to create other products in entirely different markets than the PC market?" He looked at the entire market and identified an opportunity in the music market to come out with products that were completely based on digital music. That is how he invented the iPod. Jobs first defined the product, the **what**, and only then asked the company engineers to develop it. How to develop it was the engineers' challenge; Jobs defined the **what** and the engineers defined the **how**, in that order.

Apple launched the iPod in 2001; iTunes in 2003; the iPhone in 2007; and the iPad in 2010. Each product represented a *breakthrough*, because it was a new product that changed previous paradigms in the market. The outcome: from a company on the verge of bankruptcy in 1997, as this book is being written, Apple is one of the companies with the highest market cap in the world, somewhere above 700 billion dollars as of early 2015. It overtook Microsoft in terms of market value starting in 2010; its stock went up from $0.60 in late 1997 to about $130 per stock in March 2015—over 200 times as much!

For the sake of comparison, after nearly wiping Apple off the market in 1997, Microsoft's stock went up only 3 times more during that same period[64]! **Notice the huge difference—200 time more versus 3 times more!** There are many reasons for this giant gap in both companies' stock performances, which I won't go into here, but from a business planning standpoint relevant to us,

---

64 From $16 to $48 per share.

it's clear that while Apple's strategy was *future-based planning*, Microsoft used past-based planning. It is evident that during the relevant period, Microsoft hardly broke into any new markets and mainly dealt with improving its existing products—those which had earned the company its *breakthrough* in the 1980's, when it reached almost every PC around the world. These changes mostly included *Windows* and *Office*, which saw many upgrades and versions. Indeed, there's nothing wrong with that; to this day, Microsoft is one of the most prominent technological giants in the world. Still, the difference between the two approaches to planning is so striking that it cannot be ignored. **The substantial difference between the two planning methods significantly affected Apple and Microsoft's business results, as reflected in the major gap between their stocks' performances.**

This, then, is the right business planning strategy to reap success: **what holds true for Apple holds just as true for the small business owner and the career planner.** There is nothing preventing you, me, and all other small business owners from implementing the *breakthrough* methodology in our businesses. In fact, I have been using this planning strategy in my business since 2006, and it's been a blessing. Of course, I also teach my clients how to use *future-based planning* in their businesses, and have noticed their success as a result. I can assure you, **this is the best planning method around, and I highly recommend you adopt it as a way of life!**

Business Planning in Practice
Vision

How can you take the planning principles of the *breakthrough* approach you've learned in this chapter and implement them in your specific business or career? To do that, I invite you to use the following form I have outlined, which helps structure and manage your *future-based planning* with a *positive EYE* (see diagram 11-2). The form is available for download from my website through the following link: https://www.hagaishalev.com/en/blog/breakthrogh-form.

On the website, you will also find a number of blog posts dealing with the *breakthrough* methodology and which offer instructions and guidance on how to fill out the form, including examples from my own plan, showing how I implement the form in my business. For more information, start with the following blog post: https://www.hagaishalev.com/en/blog/business-plan-a.

H.J. Shalev
EFFECTIVE CHANGE

Goal Plan – Breakthrough Project

Plan name: _____ (idiom, memory, person, etc. that gets you excited and touches you emotionally)

Name of planner: _____ Date of preparing plan: _____

Due date for achieving the goals (usually up to a year): _____

My business vision/dream (what and for what; what is the impact I would like to make in the world, assuming "anything is possible"):

Guiding questions for the vision:

Who am I? What is my DNA? What are my strengths?

What do I do? What is my uniqueness? How do I benefit my clients? How do I make the world better?

What do I like about my work? What excites me? What am I passionate about regarding my business or career?

My Basic values:

What are the **results/goals** I will achieve by the above due date that will be worthy of my time, money and efforts? (Be specific, write clear and measurable results - who, what, when, how much; assume that "anything is possible" and you have no limitations or fears. Please don't write about all the achievements on the way, but only a brief, quantitative and measurable picture of the due date):

- ✓
- ✓
- ✓

The **strategy** for achieving the goals (roadmap, conceptual plan, high level overview of how I will achieve the goals):

- ✓
- ✓
- ✓

The major milestones regarding the future, in which I will check the direction and pace of my progress towards achieving the goals (answer the "how" to reach the goals question in **detail** - at least 8-10 points each month, including tasks to perform and intermediate goals to achieve. **The milestones are an expansion and breakdown of the strategic principles, answering the "who, what, when and how much" questions):**

Date (last day of the month)	Milestones (tasks & specific intermediate results and measurements. **Please take any strategic principle and break it down into specific actions along the timeline)**	Follow up on execution of Milestone (please mark execution in Green and non-execution in Red)
	✓	✓
	✓	✓
	✓	✓
	✓	✓

HS   Copyright 2010-18 ©All Rights Reserved to H.J. Shalev | www.hagaishalev.com

Diagram 11-2—Goal Plan Form

From this point until the end of the chapter, I shall describe the form in general guidelines and instruct you on how to fill it in. This is **not** a typical 20-page colorful business plan laden with text and graphs, as you may sometimes imagine when you hear the term "business plan." Most times, you won't need outside, professional help in order to fill in the form. Any business owner, career planner, or manager can write this plan by himself. As an avid believer in "keeping it simple," the goal plan form I use is a one-page, very simple outline. However, please note that it is usually designed for your own needs rather than external needs such as raising capital.

The form has five parts. The **first part** at the top is mostly technical. It includes the name of the planner, the date on which they are preparing the plan, the due date for achieving their goals (the future date at which you aim your goals, the *"what"*), and the plan's name. You can make a three-year plan and a five-year plan. For those who haven't engaged in planning so far, I suggest you first prepare a one-year plan or less—perhaps only 6-9 months from the date of planning. I suggest you choose a name for your plan that touches you emotionally and motivates you—an idiom, memory, person, or other association. In the opening of the chapter, I mentioned the importance of purpose in business achievement—that same worthy purpose that is part of the "profound inner reasons" motivating people to perform far more dedicatedly than when motivated by money alone—and the name for your goal plan should connect you to your "profound inner reasons." This way, you are emotionally connected to something or someone that inspires and motivates you. **This emotional drive is one of the major forces that will get you up in the morning with the passion to fulfill your plan and achieve your goals with joy.**

Your Vision Alone Will Get You in the Zone[65]

The **second part** of the form is the *vision*. The *vision* builds emotional depth, serving as the cornerstone of any business accomplishment. If the plan's name provides the emotional connection, the *vision* provides the emotional anchor. This is where purpose sits in its entirety: all the "profound inner reasons," the emotional engine, the motivation to act, the passion, fervor, energy, and power at the basis of fulfillment. Man cannot succeed on money alone, remember? These are all mental components embodied in the *vision*. The *vision* answers the "what" and "for what" questions: what is the impact you would like to make in the world? The assumption underlying the vision is that anything, truly anything, is possible. The vision is your compass, your North, your conscience. The goal plan form includes three questions in the *vision* section, which are **guiding questions for writing an optimal *vision*:**

1. Who am I? What is my DNA? What are my strengths? The idea here is to connect to your skills and strengths rather then automatically focusing on problems and weaknesses.

2. What do I do? What is my uniqueness? How do I benefit my clients? How do I make the world a better place to live in? All of these are sincere serious questions. They don't discuss money, but rather connect you to your "profound inner reasons." If you benefit people using a *vision* that inspires you and motivates you in helpful, enjoyable endeavors, you will make money, for money is always the **outcome** of great benefit provided to others.

---

65 I use this expression to describe a business owner or manager who is connected to his "profound inner reasons," which help him remain in the right *Being* to act with a *positive EYE* and succeed.

3. What do I like about my work? What excites me? What am I passionate about regarding my business or career?

All of these are emotional anchors that propel you to action and to extraordinary results.

Finally, the last part of the *vision* section includes your basic values. These are the fundamental moral standards of your life, from which you usually do not divert. If I wake you up at three AM and ask you what your life's principles are, what you unequivocally believe in, the basic values will be your answer. They may include humaneness, professionalism, love, fulfillment, generosity, or integrity—all of which are values. They are the foundations of your sacred *vision* and the guiding lights to its fruition. In any future dilemma or conflict, your basic values will guide you to a solution, so I recommend you don't deny them.

A Goal is a Dream with a Deadline

The *vision* is the overall *what*. It is eternal, and as such, need not be specific. The *vision* serves you for many years, and so it usually depicts a wide scope of intentions. Everything you do is supposed to fit into your *vision* and connect to it. Within the broad framework of the vision are the *goals*—the third section in the form. **The goals also discuss the *"what,"* but now it's a specific *"what."*** Here, you "fit yourself" into the due date of achieving the *goals*, that same future date your wrote down in the first section of the form. You ask yourself, as if you are at that same future date, what is the new reality you've created and now "see" around you. Indeed, both in the *vision* stage and here, you are asked to use your imagination—the language of your unconscious mind—in order to program it to your goals and harness it to help you achieve them. The questions you should ask yourself are: "What do I see? What will be an adequate return for my time, money and energy? What concrete results will fulfill my *vision*?" **While the *vision* is general and emotional, the goals are very specific.** As described earlier in this chapter, the *goals* are concrete and measurable. What isn't measured isn't managed, remember? The *goals* answer the questions **who, what, when, how much, and where?** They reflect your true desires. This is where you write down income and profit; yes, we're finally talking money. The *goals* show you how many clients you have; the services and products you sell; the structure of your business, how many employees you have, and other specific, quantitative business figures. Don't forget to aim high! One can apply this form to career planning as well, with some necessary changes.

If we look at NASA's *vision*, for instance, we learn that its essence is to "conquer outer space." This definition fulfills the requirement that the *vision* be eternal, since outer space is infinite; the more we travel through outer space, the more we realize its vastness, and so this vision is eternal. On the other hand, NASA's results and *goals* are the stars in the sky. Today, we can be on the moon, tomorrow on Mars, and in X amount of years we may even reach a different galaxy; all the above are specific, concrete *goals* on the timeline, and they fit perfectly into the bigger *vision* picture of conquering outer space. If so, **vision is the overall *what* and the *goals* are the specific *what***, which fits in well with the larger *vision* framework.

"When the 'What' is Clear, the 'How' is Clarified"

In keeping with the *breakthrough* method of planning, only now, after defining the *what*, do we turn to discussing **how** to reach our *goals*. There is a major difference between past-based and future-based planning: instead of focusing on how to improve my past

(past-based planning), the focus here is on how to reach the ideal future I want to create for myself (*future-based planning*). The first method derives from the past, with all its shortcomings and limiting paradigms; thus, it focuses on what's missing, and usually drags one *below the line*. On the other hand, the second method focuses on possibilities and opportunities, and thus is usually *above the line*. Note that the *focus principle* and the *questions of possibility and opportunity* are helpful *tools* here to expand your field of options.

As with the *what*, the *how* is also divided into two parts. The first part is the overall *how*—the **strategy** for achieving your *goals*. **A strategy is the roadmap to reaching your goals; it's the conceptual plan, the high-level overview.** It answers questions from today, from where you're at right now, up until the due date of achieving the *goals*: how will you achieve these *goals*? What needs to happen on the way? What do you want to **do** along the journey in order to accomplish the *goals*? What are the important steps or basic principles to guide you to your *goals*? This doesn't mean writing down all the detailed actions needed to achieve your goals, only the general components for performing this plan of action. For example, a great question to ask yourself in the *strategy* stage is, what is the hardest thing for me to do now, which can move me quickly and effectively towards my objectives?

◆

After defining the *strategy*, you move on to the **milestones**. *Milestones* are the fifth and final section in the plan, outlining a **detailed plan of action toward reaching your goals.** They answer the question, how will you reach your *goals* **in detail**? The *milestones* break down every line in the strategy into specific actions you want to perform along the timeline. I recommend breaking them up on a monthly basis, with at least 8-10 steps each month, which can later be broken down further into weeks or even days. Accordingly, the left column on the form lists the months and the middle column lists the planned tasks. The *milestones* concretely define what you are going to do. For example: ten phone calls to potential clients in November, three networking meetings, launch a campaign on Google AdWords (and what specific actions to take to reach the launch date), etc. Here is where you also write all the people whose help you wish to solicit—consultants, friends, family, etc. **Milestones expand on and specify the *strategy* you wrote in the previous section. They answer the questions who, what, when, how much, and where.** This is where you take every strategic rudiment and break it down into specific tasks to perform along the timeline.

Aside from performing concrete tasks, the **milestones also include intermediate objectives.** As their name suggests, intermediate objectives are partial *goals* within the fulfillment process between your current state and your final *goals*. For example, if your current sales come to $20,000 per month and your goal is to reach $30,000 per month within a year, your *milestones* should include the stages to getting there; you could write $21,000 in January, $21,700 in February, and so on, setting your intermediate goals through to the final *goal* in December. **You need a clear, specific, and measurable definition for your *milestones*, just as you did with your *goals*.** You should be able to tell beyond any doubt at the end of each month whether you've reached the intermediate goal and performed the tasks you planned out.

Congratulations, you've completed the *goal plan*! Now you can move forward with its execution. I recommend referring back to the plan unfailingly at least weekly and preferably daily, especially when tracking your milestone performance. I check on my plan every Sunday night or Monday morning, examining what I've already executed this month and what I have not, and then I plan my tasks for the current week accordingly. The main advantage of this plan is the certainty it provides: at every moment, you know what the next required steps are to move towards your *goals*. Every so often, it's important to reread the *vision* and allow its inspiration to energize you and strengthen your spirit, faith, and persistence on your road to fulfillment. All of these support the mental basis that is so important for manifesting your plans, and through them prospering and succeeding. If you're founding a new business, I suggest you read the *vision* every morning. Similarly, you should recall the *goals* every so often. Don't go over them daily, since your distance from them and their high challenge may weaken you, but you can contemplate your *goals* during meditation or while visualizing at bedtime. This will help you assimilate them into your unconscious mind, and so will help you achieve them.

Every Plan is Subject to Change

After outlining the entire plan and beginning to execute it, it's time to change it. Of course, this isn't mandatory, but it's oftentimes inevitable, and that's absolutely fine. The dynamics of life create ever-changing *circumstances*; some are positive and some negative, demanding your attention in order to keep the plan relevant. The plan isn't set in stone; it's yours, and the "goal setting police" won't be coming after you if you didn't reach your goals. **It's important to keep the plan flexible and updated** in order to avoid a situation where you drop it because it's become disconnected from reality. Furthermore, **new opportunities arise all the time, and you must be alert and ready to take advantage of them.** For instance, in early 2014, I was planning to begin this book project by the end of the year. However, in February I noticed a professional workshop that supports book writing, and I looked into it. I quickly realized that I had an excellent opportunity here to fulfill my dream in an effective way that would save me a lot of time and money. From there on, it took no time to change my plan and turn *Getting Used to Success* into my flagship project in 2014. Naturally, the scope of the project required outline changes, and some of the goals I had originally set for 2014 were pushed to the following year. As I write these lines in early 2015, it turns out to have been a great decision I am very pleased with. In other words, **focusing on the *goals* and on the plan dramatically increases your ability to accomplish.** I often see it among my clients: the moment they write their plan and they begin openly announcing to the universe what they wish to achieve, *circumstances* begin to turn in their favor. This can be partially explained by the *focus principle*, since focusing on their *goals* highlights the ways to accomplish them. Still, I'm not convinced this is the only reason; there seems to be at least one more law of nature working in their favor which science has yet to discover.

To conclude, these are the planning stages: *vision, goals, strategy, milestones*, and finally, the *execution*, which is the road to fulfillment and realization. If you stick to the planning method in this chapter, you will have an excellent tool that will help you in *Doing*. After presenting you with *Being* tools in the first part of the book in order to create the mental basis crucial for fulfillment with a *positive EYE*, the significance of this chapter is in providing you with a pure *Doing* tool. However, make no mistake— **without this book's teachings and the mental changes you made in your *TTT*, the *Doing* you learned here will have very limited effect on your ability to reach your *goals*, thrive, and succeed.** You need a lot more than rational thinking, excellent planning, and diligent performance to succeed; that is what Dr.

Braunstein-Bercovitz meant in the "profound inner reasons" statement I mentioned at the opening of this chapter. Only by creating an optimal basis by being *above the line*, controlling your thoughts and emotions, and using the other *tools* you've learned in previous chapters wisely can you create the ideal conditions for achieving your *goals* using the *breakthrough* method.

The significance of this book is in paving a complete, consistent route for you from *Being*, through *Doing*, and onward to realization and accomplishment. **Connecting *Being* and *Doing* is the ultimate solution for excellence and optimal results.**

After touching on the *Doing* and understanding where this book leads, we are now set up for the next chapter, which is the highlight of this book: it is dedicated to the connection between the mental and the realistic, between the *Being* and the *Doing*.

I shall conclude this chapter with another of my sayings:"*Say The Word, Then See The World*."

CHAPTER TWELVE:
The Ultimate Tool for Creating the Reality You Want

"To be or not to be; that is the question"
—Shakespeare

After dedicating the previous chapter to *Doing*, this chapter brings us back to *Being*, big time. I have previously posed the question, "Why am I rational, practical, even hardworking and diligent, yet my business, career or management isn't successful enough?" I have also reviewed a number of models and examples that offer partial answers and solutions. **In this chapter, I shall dive into the heart of this question, bringing you the full answer by using the ultimate *tool* for creating the reality you want.** You will better understand the solution to one of the greatest mysteries in human's ability to experience fulfillment and success.

"To be or not to be?" Shakespeare's Hamlet asks. "To be," I answer, "to be for sure!" The more relevant question is **how** to be? How to **be**come everything you ever dreamt of **be**coming? In this chapter, I shall present the opposite viewpoint to what you were taught all your life. I will introduce the **Being Model** which offers an important *tool* for performing a sustainable, transformation of being.

Human Being
In chapter two, I emphasized that we are a human *being*, not a human *doing*, as may be misconstrued by our upbringing and culture. However, no one has ever taught us how to "be," or what this *Being* is.

From early childhood, our teachers and parents have told us, "Work, study, think, perform, make an effort," so you can become a successful individual. All these actions belong to the *Doing* aspect, and are indeed important to one's success in life; nevertheless, most people work hard all their lives without achieving the results they wish for. Why? Because *Doing* alone isn't enough to garner success. Here's an example of a very common thought pattern in our society: "I'll **work** hard, **have** a lot of money, and then I'll **be** rich." But while many act according to this approach, only few manage to become rich from it. On the other hand, plenty of others who don't work hard at all become rich anyway; **this shows that hard work isn't necessarily the optimal way to achieve goals, succeed, and become wealthy.**

The Erroneous Formula

It's easy to see that the formula underlying the above example, which is how we were brought up and how we pursue almost anything in our life, is: Do → Have → Be; if I **do**, I will **have** (attain) so that I can **be**. For example, if I eat less and exercise more (= Do), I will lose X lbs (= Have, though it means *having* **less** in this case), I can be thin (= Be). Although many people try to lose weight using this strategy, only a few really do, because it's not the right formula for achieving results. Another classic example is our tendency to find happiness in material possessions—shopping, for instance. The basic approach is as follows: I will **buy** a pretty outfit, so I will **have** a rich wardrobe and will **get** compliments for my appearance, which will make me **feel** wonderful and I will **be** happy. The thing is that happiness attained through this approach is limited. It wears off very quickly, sending us back to buy the next new piece of clothing to experience more pleasure. I know a person who buys a new car every year or two so as to experience the euphoria of having a new vehicle. The same goes for the excitement of a fun vacation fading quickly once we're back in our routine. You probably know the saying, "I need a vacation from my vacation." If so, **the standard way in which we operate—according to the Do → Have → Be structure—is not the right approach to achieving what we want in life.**

What is a better way? **The right formula for achieving results is** *the Being Formula*: **Be → Do → Have**, which is the opposite of what we just saw. The first thing we need in order to achieve results (= to **have**) is not to **do**, but to **be**. Sound strange? Indeed, how can we **first** be who we **want** to be? Here's how it goes: First we need to **decide who we are**, and only then **act** to fulfill that, so that eventually we can **achieve** what our heart desires. Let's look at a few examples before we go any deeper, so we can better understand the *Being Formula*.

Examples for Applying the Being Formula

Weight loss—most people who try to lose weight start with a mindset of "I'm fat." This is a state of being that doesn't support weight loss, because it implies scarcity. Anything done with this mindset will then immediately run into the natural resistances of a "fat person." For example, resistance to sports and healthy, low-calorie eating that requires giving up fatty, sweet foods. The result is effort, frustration, suffering, and usually failure. On the other hand, when you approach a weight loss process with a "thin person's" **attitude**, the diet is usually successful. Don't get me wrong: physically, this person has a few extra pounds to lose, but **in his head** (his consciousness and awareness), he's decided he's a "thin person," and so begins to **act** like one. It's easier for a person with this state of mind to control his calorie consumption, follow a healthy, balanced diet, exercise, and so on.

The *Being Formula* is supported by research. In one study, one group of hotel maids were told that their physical housekeeping job contributed to weight loss, while a second group wasn't told that. Findings showed that the maids in the first group lost weight, while the second group didn't, even though no difference was detected in the scope of their work. This proves that it was enough that the maids in the first group thought their job was slimming them for them to lose weight. They believed it was slimming, perceived themselves as losing weight while working, and that was enough for them to lose weight for real.

If so, **the general conclusion is this**: the right way to achieve any objective is a **conscious decision** which determines your state of being. Then, the *Doing* entailed in fulfilling the decision becomes a lot easier and more fruitful, which results in *having*.

Smoking—another example is cigarettes. I know this firsthand, since I stopped smoking twice[66]. Most smokers try to **do** a lot of things to quit smoking: going to one healer or another, gradually reducing the quantity they smoke, taking smoking meds or using an electronic cigarette, or a variety of similar methods that usually fail. I stopped smoking on a moment's **decision**.

Without knowing the *Being Formula* back then, I made a firm decision: "I'm a nonsmoker." From that moment on, **quitting**

---

66   In case you ask yourself, "Why twice," here's why: the first time I stopped smoking was in 1994. A few years later, I began working for a startup company and most of its employees smoked. In those days it was permissible to smoke in the workplace, so I was experiencing massive passive smoking every day, until I finally started smoking again in 1998. In 2003, I stopped smoking again and have kept away from it to this day.

smoking became possible and simple for me to execute. Indeed, I didn't run into any major difficulty fulfilling that decision.

If so, the method to quit smoking while using the *Being Formula* is as follows:

Be—deciding "I'm a nonsmoker."
Do—quitting cigarettes all at once.
Have—a reduced amount of nicotine in my blood and no more addiction.

The Being Formula in Business

Aside from these common day-to-day examples, there are many other examples for applying the formula in business as well. It is first and foremost our mindset as business owners and managers that determines our ability to reap success in business. For example, our **approach to money**[67]. Business owners whose state of being regarding money is negative will find it hard to accumulate funds. Here are some of the more common limiting beliefs regarding money: money doesn't grow on trees; you have to work hard for your money; art doesn't make you rich[68]; I'll never get out of debt; rich people are corrupt; and so on. This negative approach to money is a state of being that prevents us from accumulating funds. On the other hand, an abundant state of being characterizes rich people. Are you familiar with the saying, "Money begets money?" **This is the "abundance consciousness" that attracts money.** This is also why, when

---

67   More about how to develop an "abundance consciousness" in this series of blog posts: https://www.hagaishalev.com/en/blog/abundance-a.

68   See the post "Art Doesn't Make You Rich:" https://www.hagaishalev.com/en/blog/art.

rich people declare bankruptcy—even multiple times, such as with Donald Trump—it's easy for them to quickly regain capital due to the abundance consciousness built into them.

◆

As emotional humans, our actions are influenced by our state of being. When we're affected by limiting beliefs, we are *below the line*. In this state, we lack the power, energy, and proper communication skills to succeed in *Doing*. Think about what you're willing to do for your beloved when you're in love, and how hard it is to make the same loving gestures when you're not. This can also be tied to the *positive attitude* and *focus* tool you're already familiar with; what you focus on expands, so if you focus on scarcity as an automatic conscious state, then scarcity fills up your world and serves as your basic state of being. The pool of automatic, limiting paradigms most people possess is a negative *TTT* that creates a negative reality. Everything has a reason, **and the mother of all reasons is your state of being, because it determines, more than anything, your ability to act with a *positive EYE*.**

You may rightfully ask, "How can I possess an abundance consciousness when the sword of debt is hanging over my head?" As a proper Jew, I will answer with another question: "How could the few outdo the many throughout our nation's history, leading us to victory and survival despite the blade of extinction hanging over their heads?" The answer is that is due to their fighting spirit and faith in the face of existential threat. Just like a fat person can think like a thin one, so can a poor man think like a rich man. You must practice that, letting go of the *autopilot* that holds onto the scarcity approach; you have to know how to control your thoughts and manage your emotions using the *E.T.F.B* model in order to reach that point. It's not simple, but it's certainly possible.

The numerous *tools* you are collecting throughout this book will prepare you for it; more about how to apply the *Being Formula* as this chapter unfolds.

The Naive Aaron Learns How to Market

A charming 24-year-old man by the name of Aaron (alias name) attended one of my workshops. He had decided to own an SEO[69] company, and not just any company—he wanted it to be one of the top ones! Back then, his business had been running for about six months, and he only had two clients. He wasn't well-off, as you can imagine. Aaron expressed his dream in the *vision* he wrote. Here is a key sentence from it: "I'm bringing the present into the future by developing initiatives and technologies that make people's lives easier and more interesting. The ideas I'm developing change humanity and bring people happiness." This amazing *vision* fit in wonderfully with Aaron's great ambition and high technological skills. However, Aaron was an introvert, somewhat naive, and lacking assertiveness and effective communication skills; he didn't have a strong enough belief in his power to fulfill his dream. Furthermore, **he disliked sales and marketing, thus limiting his ability to grow and thrive.** His state of being was too weak to support *Doing* with a *positive EYE*. I knew that only if Aaron changed his mindset would he be able to perform the necessary actions required to reap success in his business. And so it was; through the process brought to you in this book, Aaron changed his attitude towards business and sales. He sums up the change he underwent in the workshop as follows: "*I improved my sales ability in the workshop. Before the workshop, I was held captive by a paradigm of thinking 'I am not good enough of a salesman.' The workshop made me*

---

69 Search Engine Optimization.

realize that was limiting me, so I changed it. *I also improved in my communication skills, both speaking before an audience and to people in general. From being an introvert, I'm more outgoing today, and my self-confidence has improved as well.*"

Indeed, Aaron's state of being had sabotaged him and his business. Thus, the actions he took as an introvert who disliked sales didn't yield results. **Only when Aaron changed his *Being* did his *Doing* gain power and effectiveness.** Aaron talks further about what helped him make that inner mental transformation: *"I took a lot from the workshop. The CO-OP Formula helped me make positive, enhancing changes in myself and in my business, which I hadn't been able to do before. What's great about the formula is that it helps you persist in implementing the change until it becomes a new habit. It's one of the key elements I took away from the workshop.*" A few months later, Aaron joined a partner, they opened a company together, hired employees, and their business began to thrive.

The Business-Owner's Perception of Sales and Marketing Determines its Success

I know many business owners like Aaron who are outstanding professionals but hate marketing themselves. Their *Being* is one of "I'm not a salesperson," so when they try to market themselves with such a perception (because you can't avoid marketing), their *Doing* doesn't work. No matter how many marketing tools and techniques they learn, when their *Being* is anti-marketing, they don't attract enough clients. They always have more important things to do than market, so they usually postpone their marketing assignments, which results in an uneasy conscience and self-judgment. All of these are *below the line* characteristics. Just imagine what a business owner sounds like on the other side of the line when he finally makes that telemarketing phone call, reluctant and dispirited, only because "he has to." As I've said, when we're *below the line*, we cannot act with a *positive EYE*, and our results suffer. According to the *Being Formula*, my recommendation to business owners who dislike marketing is to act according to the following order—Be → Do → Have:

Be—Decide that marketing is part of your business and **see yourselves as the sales and marketing managers of your business**, just like you are its professionals. Give up waiting for a "messiah" who will market for you; that messiah won't arrive, because he is in each and every one of you, and all you have to do is connect to him. By using the *tools* in this book, **remove the limiting paradigms regarding marketing and change the beliefs that are blocking you**—those beliefs that are embedded deep down in your *operating system*. It's a relentless, unyielding decision. To make it easier for you to tap into the proper state of being, remember a time when "failure wasn't an option" for you; when you did extraordinary things you didn't believe you were capable of. Those of you who are parents, remember what you were willing to do for your child when he needed your help. This is the level of commitment needed for transforming your state of being, and you all have that capability.

Do—Learn about marketing and perform marketing activities to promote your business.

Have—It's only a matter of time before your marketing activities will begin to succeed and you will accumulate more clientele and greater income.

Aaron did that, I did that[70], and so did many more of my clients. "How do you do it?" You might ask; "You already know," I'll answer, "By using the *CO-OP Formula*."

Yes, It's All in Your Head, and It's All Your Decision

These examples show how starting with the proper state of *Being* in different life situations allows for achievements to come pouring in. **It's a mental decision:** "I'm going to do it" is a solid unyielding decision that makes it much easier to cope with challenges. The decision is first and foremost "who I am," not "what I will do." And it goes even deeper: "What is my essence? How do I perceive myself? What kind of a person am I?" **First decide, commit, and undertake, and only then act.**

Tools that help with that are values, *vision*, *goals*, and possessing as much acceptance, pleasure, and enthusiasm as possible—in other words, doing what we love and what gives our life meaning. It's easy to see that business owners, career changers, and managers who act out of a clear, powerful *vision*, staying true to their values with joy and enthusiasm, are more effective and productive. These are the "profound inner reasons" I discussed in chapter eleven.

---

70 As a CFO who one day became self-employed, I had no clue about marketing. In chapter one, I mentioned that after taking my coaching courses, I worked rationally, diligently, and perseveringly, but my business didn't take off and I couldn't understand why until I finally realized I had to change my approach to marketing and sales. I did that using the process described in this book, and the results soon arrived. Moreover, I learned to enjoy marketing and sales, which enabled me to identify more and more opportunities to increase my income and act effectively to achieve them.

In the language of this book, it all boils down to being **above the line**.

The band The Black Eyed Peas aimed for the *Being Formula* in their song, "I got a feeling that tonight's gonna be a good night…" Similarly, when I decide it's going to be a good day, it's a state of *Being*, and the *Doing* that stems from it causes that day to be good. Thus, it provides all the fun we wish for—*Having*. It's a proactive choice, which allows for an *internal locus of control* and free choice to determine your reality and fulfill the life you want. Use the *tools* in this book to allow yourself to make such powerful, effective choices.

"If you want to build a ship, don't drum up people to collect wood and don't assign them tasks and work, but rather teach them to long for the endless immensity of the sea."—Antoine de Saint-Exupery

I chose this quote as the theme for the entire book, since it symbolizes the ultimate road to fulfillment from *Being* to *Doing*, which is the main message of this book. The *Being Formula* beautifully sums up this basic principle, illustrated by the author of the *Little Prince*: if we have a passion (which is a state of being) for the vast and endless sea, all the *Doing* involved in building the ship will be easily executed, e.g., gathering wood and delegating tasks. The same goes for any area of life, as we've seen in the examples presented earlier. As we also mentioned earlier, most people act oppositely: **they don't look for the proper *Being*, but rush into *Doing*, and then wonder why their results—based on the wrong *Being*—aren't good enough.**

How to Enter the Desired State of Being

If you haven't noticed yet, **you've been given** *tools* **throughout the book to create your desired** *Being*. These *tools* come together to help you maintain such *Being*: *positive attitude and focus* on what's working and improving in your life; the *E.T.F.B* model to control your thoughts; giving up resistance and judgment; letting go of the need to control and know everything; increasing your commitment and reducing the effect of *circumstances* by using *internal locus of control*; changing limiting *paradigms*; building a *vision* you're emotionally connected to; and more. **Each** *tool* **in itself, and all of them together, will support a positive state of being—being** *above the line***, controlling the** *TTT***, and acting with a** *positive EYE***.**

You can always create these for yourself by using the outline of the *CO-OP*: *awareness* of the desired state of being, which determines your *Doing* and the results you want; *observing* your state of being in real time; identifying the mental glitches that require your intervention in order to step out of the *automatic program*; and finally, *choosing* the *tools* that will help you undergo a small change using *baby steps*. This change will grow into a bigger, sustainable transformation over time.

The Ultimate Tool for Entering Your Desired State of Being

Alongside the many *tools* to help you enter the desired state of being, as this chapter heading suggests, I also promised to give you the ultimate *tool* for creating your desired reality. I shall keep that promise now. The *tool* is called the **Being Question**, or the Be → Do → Have Question. It's a question you can ask yourself at any time when you wish to enter a more positive mindset that's more effective than the *autopilot mode* you're currently in.

Here is the question: "When I'm _____ (fill in your desired state of being—owning a successful business, successful in marketing and sales, feeling wealthy, excited about my business, etc.), what do I think about? What is the ideal picture I see in my imagination? What do I tell myself and others? What do I hear? What do I experience? **How do I feel?** What do I do?" The idea is simple: **by using this question, you activate your *TTT*, your imagination, and all your senses in order to enter your desired state of being.** Instead of expecting that your desired *circumstances* will appear, you bring them to you by imagining your desired state of mind and being, experiencing them with your senses and thus creating the "Be" required for fulfillment with a *positive EYE.* You needn't always ask all the questions; 3-4 key questions will suffice. I especially like the "how do I feel" question, because entering the right positive emotion puts me *above the line* and causes all other secondary questions to quickly and smoothly put me in the desired mental state of Be. After reading chapter six, you should also understand the importance of activating the imagination here in order to harness your super-computer—the unconscious mind—to help you achieve your goals.

Here are a few examples:

Before an important meeting, we're usually anxious, or even afraid. The *being question* to ask is, "When I have a successful meeting and achieve its goals, how do I feel? What do I experience? What do I think about?" Thirty seconds of focusing on answering these questions a few minutes before your meeting, preferably with your eyes closed, is enough to improve your feelings and create a positive mindset. This will support the *Doing* with a *positive EYE* during the meeting itself. As I mentioned in chapter six, imagination affects the body physically; if you've ever woken up sweating from a nightmare, you know what I mean.

Another example is athletes' moments of intense concentration before an important competition, such as an Olympic final. I always notice the intense focus of the high jumpers before a crucial jump. These athletes use their imagination to enter a state of victory. Have you ever heard the expression, "He's a winner!" outside a sports context? It means that a person has the mindset of a winner, and so he usually wins! Once again, our ability to act with a *positive EYE* is first and foremost an expression of our mental state while performing an action. The winner's attitude creates the desired state of mind. I experienced this firsthand after I left my job as a CFO, when my mindset for building my business was "Failure in not an option." This attitude helped me persist with determination until I reaped success. A negative example is a tightrope acrobat walking on the rope and fearing his fall. His chances or falling truly increase that way...

My favorite, final example involves marketing and sales. In order to enter an optimal state of being, you should ask yourself here: "When I market and sell my products well, how does my business function? What level of income do I bring home? How do I feel? What actions do I take?".

"Commitment is what transforms a promise into reality. It is the words that speak boldly of your intentions. And the actions which speak louder than the words."—Abraham Lincoln

Another way to enter the ideal state of being is a **promise** to perform something. A promise to whom? First of all, promise yourself; if possible, share it with another close person—your spouse, a coach, a friend, etc. Moreover, promise **him/her** something, too. Unfortunately, most people procrastinate when making important decisions; life's *circumstances* overpower them and encourage ongoing procrastination. It's important to understand that **indecisiveness is worse than making the wrong decision.** If you've made a wrong decision, you can usually fix it; **this is how successful people operate: they dare, try, fail, fix, and repeat.** It's a guaranteed recipe for success. Choosing not to decide maintains a status quo of blockage in most cases. Where there's no decision there's no change, and what doesn't change withers and expires. Some of our indecision stems from a weaker sense of commitment—a failure of **will and intent.** How many times have you said, "I **want to** get out of debt, or make a change, or do what I truly love," only for it to never really happen? We often say, "I wanted to, but it didn't work out." This shows you that **will alone isn't enough to elicit change**; neither is **intent.** If I tell a friend, "I'm **planning** to come by one of these evenings," what are the chances that it will happen? Very slim, indeed. Perhaps they're stronger than just "wanting to," but most likely I will not fulfill my intention. Even when we're **committed** to something and announce it, we often don't fulfill the obligation due to *circumstance.* If so, what is the highest level of commitment? A **promise** is a solid and indisputable decision, which you insist on despite *circumstances.* This is where the *Being Formula* comes in: **each time you make a fundamental decision, by promising, you change your mindset so that it supports manifestation.** For instance, during the first months of my business, when I wasn't generating any income, I was under the oath I made to my wife Osnat and my children Daniel and Shelly that I would provide for them no matter what. Such constituent decisions and promises are important because they create a new state of being, generate action, and inspire determination in fulfilling them; this is when results come in, too.

How to Apply the Being Question in Daily Life

You already know the answer: yes, by applying the *CO-OP Formula*. *Awareness* of the importance of your state of mind before any action; *observing* your state of being ahead of an important task; and *choosing* the *being question* in order to enter the right *state of being*—this is the way to implement the *being question tool* with a *positive EYE*. You can also apply the *being question* to practice a new state of mind in general, regardless of your specific situation. Say you want to increase your self-confidence: if you set twelve *observation* points throughout the day and use an *implementation structure* to remind you to observe[71], you can choose to ask the *being question* regarding self-confidence at each point (when I'm confident, how do I feel...), and so you get yourself into a self-confident state of mind. When you apply this for thirty days straight, the momentary self-confidence you created in all those points of *observation* and *choice* will slowly trickle into your unconscious mind and reinforce your self-confidence in general. This is the power of *baby steps* when implemented consistently!

"Think before you act"—Proverbs 13:16-25

The quickest and easiest way to learn how to succeed in business is by analyzing a successful case study. I believe that, for the most part, success doesn't require a special talent, and certainly not luck. Therefore, one can always learn from others' success. I chose IBM's success story as a case study that involves a few

---

71 As has been mentioned, after a consistent application of the structured *observations* using the *implementation structure*, you acquire the *self-observation habit*, and from there on you no longer need reminders; you've embedded a structured *self-observation* trait in your *operating system*.

tools I've discussed so you can learn how a consistent application of the *tools* yields excellent results in practice. I found the following example in *The E-Myth*, a book by Michael E. Gerber:

Tom Watson, the founder and CEO of IBM (1914-1956), was asked to what he attributed IBM's great success. Here is what he said [I bolded the text]: "**I had a very clear picture of what the company would look like when it was finally done**... once I had that picture, **I then asked myself how a company which looked like that would have to act.** *I realized that, unless we began to* **act that way** *from the very beginning, we would never get there.* *I realized that* **to become a great company it would have to act like a great company each and every day.** *At the end of each day, we asked ourselves how well we did, discovered the disparity between where we were and where we had committed ourselves to be, and, at the start of the following day,* **set out to make up** *for the difference.*"

Let's analyze the success principles embedded in this quote. Notice the third principle in particular:

PRINCIPLE #1—EVERYTHING BEGINS WITH THE MENTAL IMAGE

"I had a very clear picture," Watson said. The first stage in entrepreneurship is to see the final picture clearly in your imagination. In other words, ask yourself **what you want to create.** Notice that it's not just creating a *vision* and planning the future as you've learned in chapter eleven, but it's seeing things clearly in your imagination. I discussed that in detail in chapter six.

PRINCIPLE #2—FIRST DEFINE WHAT YOU WANT, AND ONLY THEN PLAN HOW TO GET IT

Thomas Watson teaches us that only after we see the future picture can we ask how this company will act. This is the proper planning method I discussed in chapter eleven. As has been said, this is contrary to how most people act: first they ask themselves, "How can I move from my current position and where?" and only later (maybe) do they choose a goal. This approach sabotages nearly any initiative, because uncertainty limits and suffocates action. Thomas Watson reminds us that the right way to plan is to first define "what" I want (not what is "attainable") and only then plan "how" to get there. Then we can focus on one step at a time in order to reach our goal.

PRINCIPLE #3—FIRST *BEING*, THEN *DOING*

This is the principle I reviewed in this chapter. Thomas Watson said that, **"to become a great company it would have to act like a great company each and every day." He talks about here and now, not in twelve years! This principle claims that in order to succeed, we have to decide who we want to be and live that state of being right now, as if we've already attained it.**

PRINCIPLE #4—ADVANCE IN *BABY STEPS*

We are usually impatient and want everything now, or even yesterday. We're constantly looking for that miracle solution, the "Rabbi's blessing," winning the lottery or God-given luck, but that **isn't** the success formula either. Thomas Watson attests that success is a daily task of **consistent, ongoing improvement** in business parameters: "*At the end of each day, we asked* *ourselves how well we did, discovered the disparity between where we were and where we had committed ourselves to be, and, at the start of the following day,* **set out to make up** *for the difference." That is, begin from where we are and work steadily and determinedly in baby steps to advance and improve.*

Want more proof for the right way to achieve ambitious *goals*? Think about the wonders of the world for a moment. The great pyramid of Giza was built about 4,500 years ago over dozens of years: 2.3 million stones, each weighing about 2.5 tons on average, and all this with the limited means of the ancient world; and it survives to this day! Someone placed the first stone there, followed by another, and another…this is what I call *vision*!

Indeed, you must think before you act; before we run to **do** something, let's apply a few thoughts. See the future picture; define the *what* and then the *how;* decide who we want **to be** and act accordingly today, using *baby steps* while consistently improving, with determination and persistence. In doing so, the *Being Formula* — Be → Do → Have — *provides us with the concise formula for success.*

The following proverb, attributed to Jesus Christ, applies here: "If you don't go within, you will go without."

We are nearing the end of the book. At this point, the jigsaw puzzle of "getting used to success" is almost completed. The picture combining the mental with the tangible is becoming clearer. In the following chapter, you will be given three more *tools*, all of which are practical applications for mental changes that critically affect your *Being* as well as your performance.

CHAPTER THIRTEEN:
Become the Person You Wish to Be

"The past is remote, the present is now to note, the future is yet to evoke, why, then, should one the worry provoke?"

—The Scriptures

In this chapter, we shall expand and deepen the ways to apply the *CO-OP Formula*, using three more *tools* that will help you become the person who achieves the results you want. By the time you finish reading this chapter, you will have a rich toolbox to draw the proper *tool* from in order to create change in many situations in your personal and professional life—situations where you run on an *auto mode* that no longer serves you.

Tool #1— Making Changes with New Paradigms
We all have life experiences and concrete opinions on everything around us. These experiences and opinions define our life's routine and worldview, which I have generally called *habits* in this book. Have you ever stopped to examine these *habits*? Have you ever asked yourself if these *habits* serve you and propel you towards your goals? Most people don't do that; they live in *auto mode*, which includes quite a few *habits* which seem to have a life of their own, thus affecting their owners' ability to succeed and achieve their goals. One of the *program's* main components is the **paradigms**. I shall present them here and guide you through how to use them as a *tool* for making changes and yielding results. After you learn and apply the *paradigm tool* to change your *TTT*, you will be able to get out of the box and transform yourself with a *positive EYE*, sometimes instantly.

What Is a Paradigm?

Your daily life in the 21st Century is no doubt complex. Imagine if, within this elaborate reality, you had to ignore your entire life's experiences every time you wanted to perform a task—even the simplest one—performing it as if you were doing it for the first time? For instance, driving a car as if it were your first driving lesson; dreadful, right? After all, you've gained the necessary driving experience to drive skillfully today. Your driving today is a *paradigm*—a *habit* you've acquired and which has become part of your *automatic program*. **A *paradigm* is a pattern of behavior, thoughts, or beliefs. It's a subjective view or perception of reality, based on our personal interpretation.** A *paradigm* isn't a proven fact, though we tend to believe it to be an absolute truth. It's something we're used to and live by day-to-day automatically. A paradigm usually helps us to simplify life, because it enables us to categorize different life situations that happen to us into familiar, memorable molds. *Paradigms* instill order, certainty, and control. When we need a certain thought or behavioral pattern, we know exactly how to enact it by referencing our experiences and habits. *Paradigms* make our lives easier because they allow us to clear our mind, make fast decisions, and act easily, based on the life experiences we've already acquired, and the thoughts or behavioral habits already embedded in us. It's easy to see that *paradigms* dwell in our unconscious mind.

If we compare our mind to a giant wall with thousands of drawers, we search for and find the right drawer that matches our current dilemma in life, and pull out the "instruction manual" that tells us how to act in this case. These instructions are the relevant *paradigm* that matches the situation.

If the Paradigm is So Helpful, What's the Problem?

Paradigms that contribute to our quality of life and success (like driving) are excellent and should be preserved. But, **the ease with which we adopt paradigms and automatically apply them is also dangerous, since they can be negative and limiting as well, and therefore fail to serve us.** Such a *paradigm* wouldn't contribute to our success, but by the power of *circumstances* and *habits* we are led to believe in it, adopt it, and implement it religiously as if it were written in stone. When we're held captive by such a *paradigm* and it becomes an automatic part of us, we have a problem.

Why? Because we usually treat *paradigms* as facts, though they are completely subjective perceptions and attitudes. For instance, we don't say, "it's 80 degrees outside with 80% humidity," but rather "it's very hot outside." We don't say, "he weighs 250 lbs," but rather, "he's fat." If I'm hot, I'm convinced that everyone around me is hot too, and it's hard for me to accept it if someone claims he's not hot at all. This means that **if I perceive a certain *paradigm* that doesn't serve me as a fact, it seems to be unchangeable, and I'm stuck with it.**

Let's illustrate that by using a metaphor: let's pretend the room you're in right now is your entire scope of possibility, and you wish to reach its upper corners, which signify the *goals* you wish to achieve. Let's also assume that the room is big, offering different ways to move in order to reach the upper corners. In this case, any negative *paradigm* you think of is a wall that blocks your access. How? If you say to yourself "I'm too young (or old) to do these things,"—bam!—you just put a "wall" up and blocked yourself from the possibility of doing them. This "wall" is now preventing you from reaching the desired corners, i.e., your *goals*. It may well be that "these things" are exactly what you need to be doing now to break through to a new, rewarding path. Because we spend most of our time on programmed *autopilot*, we don't notice these walls, which are really made of glass. **When we build many walls like this, using *paradigms* that no longer serve us, we quickly find ourselves trapped inside a glass box, yearning to be free of it but without a practical way of breaking out.**

If you look at different situations you experience daily, you can now surely identify a bunch of limiting *paradigms* in your life, which you mistakenly take for solid facts. Here are some of them:

I don't believe it's possible!
I'm not good enough to do this well!
I don't trust other people!Money doesn't grow on trees!
You have to work hard for your money!
I give to others before I give to myself!
You don't open a new business during a recession!
Taking risks is too dangerous! I need certainty before I can begin!
It's hard to be self-employed!
I'm discriminated against as a woman/minority!

Notice that what characterizes these sentences is that **they end with an exclamation mark.** It's a clear sign of a *paradigm*. Isn't it better to have question marks instead? Without getting into the relevance or details of these statements, I can assure you that these are blocking *paradigms* and not facts, because many others who are no better than you have already overcome these "walls" and obstacles—and if they did, why can't you?

The danger of holding onto these *paradigms* that don't serve us lies in our blind faith in them and how we treat them as absolute facts when they are not. All they are highly subjective reflections of our opinion. **This is how many *paradigms* block us from reaching our destination.**

Imagine we each get up in the morning wearing different colored glasses. One person has a red pair, while the other has a green pair. They will each view the world differently and be convinced that their color is the "right" color of the world. Now go convince the other person that it's only his worldview that determines the color he sees. The glasses through which we see the world represent the *three filters* I discussed in chapter three, which are made up of our own personal *paradigms*.

Finally, since people establish and run business organizations, similar *paradigms* naturally exist in these organizations as well, greatly influencing their ability to succeed. I have reviewed a few such business blocking *paradigms* in chapter 11.

The Paradigm That Blocked Me

Most people tend to remain in their comfort zone and justify it by surrounding themselves with a bunch of limiting *paradigms* that don't serve them. These *paradigms* prevent them from making changes in their life, career, or business. I recall the *paradigm* my father, of blessed memory, had, whereby he'd go out to the main street of his city a couple of times a week to do the "bank rounds," mostly consisting of printing bank statements and performing different transactions. Later on, he got sick and was very limited physically, so I suggested I'd teach him how to log onto his bank accounts online and save himself the pain of physically visiting the banks. His *paradigm*-based answer was, "No thanks, I prefer to continue my bank rounds I've been used to all my life." This attitude clearly reflected a *paradigm* that no longer served my father, and his unwillingness to change it hurt him. Furthermore, despite the physical pain, the traditional bank rounds were his comfort zone, a *paradigm* that was the glass wall blocking any change.

Sometimes, when we're stuck in a *paradigm* that no longer serves us, we behave just like a fly that's trying to get out of a room through the windowpane, ignoring the wide open window next to it.

Here's an example of a key negative *paradigm* in my life that held me back for at least two years prior to making the career change I finally made in 2005: around 2003, I adopted an important, positive paradigm—"I want to be self-employed and work in a different area that isn't financial management." However, at the same time, I added a blocking negative *paradigm*: "Any future occupation must pay me at least what I'm being paid today right from the start." My line of thought was very rational: because I'm the main breadwinner in my family and we live off my salary, it's only natural I'd want to maintain the lifestyle we were used to. But since, at that time, as the CFO of a high tech company, I was making over $100,000 USD a year with all the fringe benefits, this *paradigm* meant that **any career change was blocked.** After all, establishing an independent business in a new field can very often be accompanied by financial instability at the onset, and income, if any, is initially low. How would I be able to make a change if "someone" had to provide me with the same kind of income I was used to?

The turning point occurred when I took a pen and paper and calculated my savings. That's when I found out I had enough savings to tie us over during that transition period. **At that moment, the limiting *paradigm* was removed and many options for changing careers opened up for me**; first and foremost, quitting my job and dedicating my time to searching for and engaging in my next occupation.

How to Shift Paradigms That Don't Serve Us

Let's see what kind of process I unconsciously underwent back then, on my way to changing the blocking *paradigm*. As I've mentioned throughout the book regarding the *tools*, our biggest challenge as humans is first and foremost to be **aware** of the fact that our lives are full of *paradigms* and that we should **recognize them**[72], because without recognizing your main *paradigms*, you can't change those that don't serve you. The moment you recognize your *paradigms* and define them as such, **you acknowledge that they're not hard facts and have recognized them as subjective.** You have, in essence, told them, "You're changeable." Thus, your *paradigms* are no longer a solid, axiomatic fact—an external, independent predestination which you're a victim of; a glass wall you cannot see—but a personal, subjective perception of reality, which is only the outcome of your own interpretation. By the way, although according to my method it's not crucial for recognizing and changing *paradigms*, one should know that some of these *paradigms* will have been embedded in us since childhood, set by the very limited worldview of a small child; we could have also adapted them in certain *circumstances* in adulthood which are no longer relevant today (as with my father's *paradigm*).

Now that **you've identified the key *paradigms* in your life, you're ready to examine which of them don't serve you.** This will also open up a way for you to remove them and replace them. After identifying the *paradigms* and sorting them into positive (helpful) and negative (limiting) categories, you can replace any negative *paradigm* with a positive, empowering, better

---

72 In my blog, you will find a paradigm mapping questionnaire that will enable you to identify the key *paradigms* in your life that don't serve you. See https://www.hagaishalev.com/en/blog/paradigms-questionnaire.

paradigm—one that will move you closer to your *goals*. When you do that, you will have removed the glass wall that blocked you all at once. Additionally, you can always restore a *paradigm* you have removed if you eventually decide that the new *paradigm* you chose doesn't serve you, so the process of changing *paradigms* is reversible and entirely flexible.

Exchanging Old Paradigms for New Ones

After identifying the *paradigms* that don't serve you, choose five to seven of the *paradigms* that limit you the most and which you most want to change. Write them on the left side of a piece of paper. Against them, on the right side of the page, write the alternative *paradigms* you wish to adopt. These *paradigms* will be positive, of course.

Examples:

Negative *paradigms*	Alternative positive *paradigms*
I don't know how to sell.	I'm open and willing to learning how to sell.
I'm a chronic procrastinator.	More and more each day, I make sure to perform my tasks consistently and adhere to the plan I set for myself.
I'm very untidy and unorganized.	I'm learning to be more organized every day.
I'm anxious and very afraid of the future.	I focus on what works and adopt a positive, optimistic attitude towards my surroundings.
I must not make mistakes.	Mistakes are part of any learning and development process. If I don't dare, I don't try, and if I don't try, I don't make mistakes—and if I don't make mistakes, I won't succeed!
I do things for everyone else, so I have no time left for myself.	I take care of myself first so I can do for others as well.

What will they say about me?	I gradually learn to trust myself, my values, and my skills, and thus I get stronger from day to day in order to act independently.
I'm not good/professional enough.	I gradually focus on what I'm good at and it shows more and more in my work.

Note that for the *paradigms* that block you, **it's best not to write their total opposite *paradigms* right at the start.** For example, don't choose, "I'm very good," instead of, "I'm not good enough," because your *automatic program* will initially find it hard to accept a new *paradigm* that's so different from the one you were used to for years. Such a contrary approach will immediately awaken your ego's resistance and all your automatic mechanisms that resist change will kick in and instill doubt and fear in you. The *autopilot* will whisper to you in a teasing voice about the new *paradigm*: "It's not true, it's not true..." Hence, changing *paradigms* must be evolutionary and gradual. You must "trick" the resisting mechanisms; invisible, you sneak into your unconscious mind, trickling another drop of change into it, bypassing its built-in roadblocks; you do it carefully, one drop at a time, lest you wake up the guard that blocks the gate to the unconscious. This is what happened every time you think or say a new *paradigm* which isn't the far extreme of an existing one.

Therefore, I recommend first choosing new *paradigms* that **only change the direction of your *TTT*** and open you up to change. The idea is to first break out of the old, automatic *paradigms* that hold you back by using moderate new *paradigms*. **Only after the change gains momentum will you be able to move on to stronger, more positive *paradigms* that totally oppose the existing ones, thus reinforcing the positive change that *paradigms* allow for.**

What About Implementation?

Great question. Theory aside, how do we assimilate these new *paradigms* in place of the old ones? You already know the answer—as with any *tool* in this book, we apply it using the *CO-OP Formula*. When you're **aware** of the blocking *paradigms* and how to change them, you can **observe** and identify them during your 12 daily *observation points*; when the old *paradigms* automatically surface, you can **choose** the new ones each time. The *choice* is made on all *TTT* levels: repeat the new *paradigms* a few times in your **thoughts**, or **out loud** if possible, and finally, **do** something small that reinforces them. For example, if the new paradigm is, "I take care of myself first so I can help others as well," it's best if you also do something that expresses this self-care, something you haven't done yet because you were subject to the old *paradigm*. This way, you elicit a tiny change, which, over time, with persistence, determination and a *positive EYE*, becomes a big one. Initially, until you become proficient at implementing the *CO-OP Formula*, I suggest you work with one *paradigm* at a time. After **practicing** four to five weeks with each *paradigm*, you will create a **new habit** in accordance with the new *paradigm*. Then you will be able to move on to the next stage: choosing a set of stronger *paradigms* that reflect a bigger change from the old *paradigms*. Implementing each **new habit** over time will necessarily yield **improved results**.

Summary of the Paradigm Shifting Process

Here is the complete action list for changing limiting *paradigms* that don't serve you in your business or career:

1. Understand what a *paradigm* is, and acknowledge that *paradigms* can help you or limit you in life.

2. Identify your main *paradigms* in life, using the "paradigm mapping questionnaire" on my blog.

3. Sort them into positive *paradigms* that help you in life and negative *paradigms* that limit you and prevent you from achieving your desired results.

4. Define positive alternative *paradigms* and swap every limiting *paradigm* for a positive *paradigm* that serves you.

5. Apply and assimilate the process of change persistently and consistently 12 times each day, using the *CO-OP Formula*: *awareness* of your limiting *paradigms* and your ability to shift them; *self-observation* when the old *paradigms* automatically appear; *choosing* the new *paradigms*; repeating them again and again in thought and out loud; and doing something small during every *observation point* to reinforce and support the assimilation of the new *paradigms*.

If, for example, you tend to postpone marketing activities that are crucial to your business, and you've chosen a new *paradigm* of, "I'm gradually promoting my business through sales and marketing every day," engage in one small marketing and promotion activity for your business at every *observation point* during the day. By "one small activity," I mean even **one** phone call to a potential client you've put off, or a limited practice of the *being question* you've learned in chapter twelve. Then, gradually engage in more significant activities.

When changing my career, the new *paradigm* I adopted was, "I have enough savings to last me through the transition period while finding my new career." This new *paradigm* opened a huge opportunity for me to dramatically transform nearly every parameter of my life, and achieve a better, happier, and more rewarding life.

It was the most important *paradigm* shift in my life.

Tool #2 —The Ego and the Higher Self Model

The most prominent phenomenon I see with my clients, mainly through their process of engagement, is their built-in resistance to change. Therapists know exactly what I'm referring to—those fears and doubts that thwart and block any attempt to change. Expressions and *paradigms* frequently heard are: "It doesn't feel right to me," "I don't believe I can change," "I don't know if it's the right thing for me right now," and "I have to think about it." This is usually accompanied by a myriad of excuses, procrastination, and finally **choosing not to decide**. Sometimes, in our introductory phone conversation, they sound so frustrated and desperate, ready for a change here and now—but on the morning of the session, they cancel their appointment for one reason or another. This despite the clear fact that we both know our engagement will help and benefit them. I call it being circumstantial. This is only one example of a pattern that repeats itself among people at every crossroad in their lives where change is imminent. We discussed the built-in resistance in us to change at length in the first part of the book.

These are precisely the types of situations where I recommend adopting a simple *tool* that shows us what we're going through when we face change, and how to truly make the right decision for us: the *Ego and Higher Self* model.

Who Am I Anyway?

When I ask people, "Who are you?" they raise an eyebrow and blurt, "What do you mean? I am myself!"

That is to say, **we're used to addressing ourselves as singular entities—but the fact is, we're not!** Here is an interesting observation model that illuminates who we are as humans: in a very simplistic yet practical way, we can say that every human has two parts. The one part I call the **"ego,"** and the second part I call the **"higher self."** Some may call the *higher self* the human spirit, the human soul, the human psyche, or awareness; in my method they are all synonymous. The *ego* is the being we inhabit most of the time in our daily life. We spend at least 90% of the time in our *ego*; it is our reality interface, our connection to the physical world.

The Role of the Ego

Before lay out the model for you, I ask that you put aside everything you know about the *ego*, its alias names, adjectives, etc., from the various theories and methodologies you may know. I don't intend to give you a comprehensive review of *ego* in our culture here, and certainly not in the world of psychology, with its various scholars and writings, mainly by Freud. I'm simply presenting my narrow yet very focused perspective in order to give you a practical *tool* to generate change. It's only my personal opinion, of course, but **the ego has one role in our life: to protect us.** It represents the survival instinct in us, and so it prefers the status quo and rejects change. Any change that occurs in our lives is seen by the *ego* as uncertainty which may become a threat to our survival. Accordingly, **the ego's main job is to keep us inside our box.** Even if we're not that happy with the results we're producing inside the "box," or if we are suffering there, the *ego* doesn't care—its job is to keep us in place, in our limited, inferior comfort zone, because as long as we're alive, it's good enough, preferable to encouraging changes that may create uncertainty and undermine our existence.

How does it do this? **By using negative emotions.** Every time we try to get out of the box, to change, transform, grow, and develop, the *ego* shouts and kicks, eliciting doubt, fears, concerns, and other negative emotions. It creates skepticism: "What do I need this for?" "What's it good for?" "I've heard that already," and so on. Furthermore, the *ego*, as the "leader" against change within us, **produces negative chemistry inside our body that can be physically felt.** You're surely familiar with expressions like, "I have butterflies in my stomach," or "this doesn't feel right." The *ego* is our immature part that expresses negativity, doubt, and judgment, and reflects the *automatic program* and going *below the line*.

By using all the systems under its charge—emotions, senses and thoughts—**the *ego* wages an all-out war against any change.** That's how the tricky mechanism of the *ego* works, and most people aren't aware of it, listening to their *ego* as if it were their true essence.

Well, it's not!

The Human's Built-in Conflict

Beyond the *ego*, **there is a higher, more mature, more responsible, braver part within us.** That part yearns for fulfillment; it holds our *vision*, our life's purpose, the goodness, love, benevolence, and values—the **higher self.** For the *higher self*, anything is possible; its attitude is positive and its emotions are *above the line*. The *higher self* is eternal and brave, seeking to develop, grow, evolve, and give to others. The *higher self* is the one that brings people seeking change into my office, whose attitude and thinking is, "I'm not willing to compromise my life, I want to achieve what's important for me, I know I can do better, I'm not willing to settle for mediocrity and I want a better life." However, this is when the *autopilot* usually rears its head and takes over. The *ego* yells and kicks, taking center stage. It pulls all its tricks, dropping us *below the line*, silencing the *higher self*, so the *awareness* of the *higher self* and its wishes generally dissipates. Most people are tuned to their *ego* consciousness the majority of the time—some even say nearly 100% of it.

So the *higher self*, which was seeking change, falls silent and surrenders to the *ego*. It retreats and raises a white flag. All this happens because we're so strongly identified with our *ego* and **unaware** of our *higher self* and its abilities.

Being *unaware*, we only know the *ego* and see ourselves as *ego* alone, which takes charge and determines our future—a future we don't really want. And so the *ego*—the *autopilot*— blocks any possibility of choice, leaving "man hath no pre-eminence above beast" as a toothless aphorism.

The Responsible Parent in Our House

To further clarify and refine the conflict between the *ego* and the *higher self*, and in order to find the road to solve it, I offer a simple **metaphor**:

Imagine you're a house, and there's a little kid living in that house who is called the *ego*. Your "kid" is smart, talented, and adored, yet he's still a little kid, and is immature. As with all kids, if you let them run their own lives, chaos will reign: the kid will eat chocolate and watch TV all day, go in his pants, mess up the house, and so on. Education? Development? Growth? He couldn't care less—he care only for hedonism. Naturally, you can't complain to him about it, as he's still young and undeveloped, incapable of understanding what you mean or knowing how to behave or run his life independently.

On the other hand, **there's a responsible parent in the "house" that is you: the** *higher self*. This responsible parent's job is to educate and discipline the kid, to care for him and set his boundaries. In other words, the *higher self*'s role is to take charge of the house, and to run both the house that is you and the kid. The problem is that in our *autopilot,* the parent is hardly at home, and if he is, he's closed up in his room, shying away and letting the kid do as he pleases. Therefore, the kid grows up to be wild, undisciplined and immature. He lives without boundaries, framework, or knowledge. So are we when we go about our lives unaware: our *ego* reigns over our "house," dictating what we should do out of its immaturity and narrow-mindedness. The *higher self*'s voice isn't heard strongly enough, and **many of the changes that the** *higher self* **initiates are sabotaged, halted, and put away.**

Choosing, Not Refusing, Will Prevent You from Losing

So what do we do? As with all the solutions I propose in this book, we use the *CO-OP Formula* to leave the default, the *autopilot* and generate change. When you're **aware** of your *higher self* and its ability to become the "home owner" in charge of your house, every time the "kid" does as he pleases, you can **observe** the situation and **choose** to connect to your *higher self* and let only it, not the *ego*, **decide what to do** in the situation. For example, when you feel an automatic resistance to a decision that's been forced on you in the workplace, or by another person, e.g., a boss, a relative, or a friend, this resistance causes you to entrench yourself in the *ego's* position and drop *below the line.* In this situation, use *awareness* and *self-observation* to identify that the *ego* is running the show for you, and then *choose* to see things from your *higher self*'s perspective. By using the *higher self*, you will connect to your higher ability to see the full picture beyond your current *paradigm*, and new *choices* will open up to you.

Applying *choice* through the *higher self* with *baby steps* and a *positive EYE*—steadily and willfully over time—will empower the "responsible parent." His voice will be better heard, and he will become the main authority in the house for the benefit of the "kid," its education and its maturation. Yes, the "kid" will yell, cry, throw a tantrum, lie down on the floor, and resist the parental authority with all his might, but time will do its work and eventually the "kid" will accept the "parent's" authority, as usually happens in families where the parent is assertive enough.

Darel Rutherford[73], from whom I learnt the basis of this model, defines this **conflict resolution** as follows:

"As spirit, our mission is to grow in consciousness. As ego our mission is to maintain status quo. The two missions appear to be in conflict. They are really not. Spirit in us chooses who we will be; ego provides us with that experience. The conflict comes when we choose a goal and ego resists that change, temporarily. What you need to know is that once ego buys the newly chosen point of view, it will arrange for you to experience that point of view as your reality."

Choosing the Higher Self

So, each time you're in a dilemma, listen to the voices inside you. The first voice you will usually hear is probably the *ego*. Identify its voice, which constantly has *below the line* traits. This voice will always be skeptical, fearful, resistant, bitter, and averse to change. Now, **search for and listen to the voice of your Higher Self.** Ask yourself what's really important for you in life; connect to your *vision* and purpose, to benevolence, development, growth, and

---

73 See his website: http://richbits.com

fulfillment. Then, give your *higher self* more weight and authority to decide in your "house." We've seen that one can achieve much more when using his ability to *choose*. Indeed, **you have the ability to *choose*; use it, and *choose* to give your "responsible parent" authority and *choice*, for the sake of your "kid's" growth and development. Move from ego to essence!**

Your *higher self* is the voice of your intuition. It knows what's best for you. It's connected to your unconscious mind, and therefore has a significant effect on your ability to achieve *goals*. **It's the true voice you should listen to.** In order to hear it, you must silence the ruckus of the *ego* that is entrenched in routine. Again, the little kid metaphor helps you to do so. As a parent, you want to show your kid warmth and love, but you're also **responsible for his future.** Therefore, you must navigate between empathy, sensitivity, and compassion; and assertiveness and the setting of boundaries. It's best not to punish the "kid," to lock him up in his room or treat him in an aggressive, hurtful way. Still, despite the thin line between them, parental wisdom requires a delicate balance between satisfying a child's needs and ensuring his proper development so that he shall grow up to be an independent, mature, and successful person. This requires teaching him the ways of the world and how to navigate the vicissitudes of life, **mentoring him and helping him develop optimally, while still setting boundaries.**

You should know that without the *ego*, your daily reality will be devoid of life's little pleasures—good food, entertainment, travel, etc.—because the *higher self*, as an abstract entity, cannot experience them. When it grows and develops, the *ego* become a mature *ego*, still self-centered and hedonistic, but knowing how to give to others and gain pleasure from doing so.

To sum up *the ego and higher self tool*, in any dilemma, listen to the voices inside you and identify them. *Choose* wisely to connect to your *higher self* and not the *ego*, which is the automatic default. By practicing this *tool* over and over, you'll find it easier to distinguish between the two, making the *higher self* the natural, inevitable choice and a fixed *new habit*, which will help you to achieve *improved res*ults in your life. Move back from your *ego* to your genuine essence!

Tool #3—Self-judgment

Self-judgment is one of the biggest blockages on the road to transformation. I noticed that among many of my clients, there's a major bug in how they treat themselves: they constantly engage in self-judgment, hoping that it will help them succeed, but it doesn't. Actually, it's more like "hara kiri[74]." It must be stressed: there's a major difference between self-criticism, which is constructive and works *above the line*, and *self-judgment*, which is destructive and works *below the line*. In this chapter, I shall address the eradication of *self-judgment* as a *tool* for success, but before I dive into the depths of this very important *tool*, I must mention its cousin: **resistance.**

I've already discussed *resistance* in this book, emphasizing that it's a disastrous automatic habit of ours to resist nearly anything that comes our way. Whether it be people around us—spouses, parents, children, bosses, partners, etc.—or unpleasant events we run into daily—which I've called *circumstances*—we naturally resist everything under the sun. When the *resistance* relates to things you cannot change, it always causes suffering, dropping

---

74 A form of Japanese ritual suicide by disembowelment originally reserved for samurai.

below the line and becoming stuck. I will begin by sharing my own personal experience with facing my automatic *resistance*.

Sarah's Coaching Didn't Work

I don't always succeed at facilitating change in my clients. There are so many factors involved, it's sometimes hard to know the reasons. Although I'm aware of quite a lot of possible reasons and usually know how to prevent them, I won't further analyze this case here; I'll just say that there is a 70% success rate among my clients in achieving their goals through their coaching plans. The main reasons for lack of success in the plan are the **absence of sufficient openness and commitment** on the client's part in the transformation process, as I've mentioned numerous times throughout the book.

Sarah's (alias) business coaching plan didn't work out. I won't go into the reasons why, because they're not relevant to us; I'll only say that I did everything in my power to help Sarah succeed, including dedicating time to her beyond the call of duty, giving her priority, special personal attention, and more.

I was working partly through the Center for Entrepreneurship at the time, a branch of the Ministry of Industry in Israel that subsidizes and supports new businesses. This was in order to enable some clients who couldn't afford my rates to be able to work with me, as was the case with Sarah. Despite my best efforts, Sarah didn't achieve the anticipated results.

A few weeks after the coaching plan was completed, I received a surprising phone call from the Center's director: "Sarah complained about you. You're under suspicion of improper business conduct and the complaint is currently being submitted for examination by the Ministry of Industry." I was shocked! An unpleasant sensation of failure took over me, my stomach contracted and filled with "butterflies..."

In all fairness, there was some basis for Sarah's complaint, but my true intentions were distorted, and my sincere efforts to help Sarah in any way I could were overlooked. I won't go into more detail here either, since it's irrelevant, but I'll only mention that the nature of the complaint was strictly professional. Sarah must have been terribly hurt by me, when it was hardly of my intention to do so. A clarification conversation I held with Sarah didn't shed any more light on the subject and it reached a dead end.

A Letter from the Center's Director

The issue continued. I gave my version, stressing my positive reputation at the Center up until then, having worked with dozens of clients and being recommended by the Center to clients seeking a mentor. The case was simultaneously being examined by the Ministry of Industry, and to my surprise, I received the following letter from the Center's CEO:

To: Mr. Hagai Shalev

Re: In-depth examination July 2012 – financial deduction by the Ministry of Industry owing to mentorship

I hereby notify you that the appeal made by the Center for Entrepreneurship was not accepted, and that the Ministry of Industry has deducted a total of $1,200 from a mentorship you performed as follows:

1. Mentorship hours given to the entrepreneur XXX - $1,000

2. The center's overhead - $200

The above amount will be deducted from the current payment.

Sincerely,
XXX
CEO

I was dumbfounded! I felt a strong sense of grievance all at once: "Not only is the complaint unfounded, they dared to reach a one-sided decision and take away $1,200 which I justly deserve?!" I thought, "Even if my attempts to help Sarah didn't bear fruit, I still did the best I could and rightfully earned my fees!"

My automatic *resistance* kicked in and I thought, "I'm going to take it to the supreme court if I have to in order to clear my name and get a fair trial!"

And yet, **after thinking it over again, I accepted the decree**. Once my initial automatic reaction of anger and frustration subsided, I started thinking about the whole thing logically and applying the *E.T.F.B* model I discussed in chapter ten.

These were the thoughts running through my head:

"Observe your automatic reaction and think logically; justice and financial loss aside, what's the point in waging war? Is it only to satisfy the *ego*'s hunger for acknowledgement and victory? How much time and negative energy will be wasted here, and will it affect you negatively in the coming months? And if the matter leaks into the media, or at least on the internet, go figure how things will be interpreted and try to prove you were innocent. After all, it's only money, which comes and goes, and won't really make me any richer..."

You catch my drift. A course in karmic management I participated in at that time helped me make a final decision: **"Let go, accept, flow..."**

What I Learned and What You Can Learn From This Incident

This is where the *letting go and accepting tool* I've mentioned throughout the book, especially in chapter two, comes into play as the main motif in my personal development. I finally internalized the main lesson I had learned since my transformation began in 2005. In that case, I decided to focus on the half full cup. I gave up the *ego*, the control, and the automatic *resistance* to a situation I was, to say the least, not happy with.

Having a few years' perspective today, I have no doubt I chose correctly. Waging war wouldn't have been worth the suffering and loss it would have entailed. The relevant question was: What's right for me in the long run? *Resisting* and insisting on justice that may not be done, while risking a lot of suffering—**or** giving up, accepting, letting go of the past and focusing on the present and the better future I want to create for myself? **I chose to be wise rather than correct.** I made do with my own inner justice, where I was fully at peace with my actions.

Another thing that resulted from the incident:

I stopped working with the Center for Entrepreneurship. The writing was on the wall. It was time to take a leap of faith in my professional and personal self-image; to trust my ability to succeed and make a good living without the center's warm and cozy framework. The results soon came: not only did my income not decrease, it grew significantly. I recouped the $1,200 many times over. Yes, only good came out of it!

And now, my main message to you is:

I've mentioned numerous times throughout the book that as humans, we automatically *resist* anything that isn't to our liking. In chapter three, I showed the results of the experiment I run with my clients, which proves that automatic *resistance* occurs 99% of the time. This *resistance* drops us *below the line*, making us reactive, so that we operate from emotional rather than rational motives. This is the state we usually regret in retrospect, since automatic *resistance* brings out extremely destructive negativity and spite. **Each mishap we face is a sign of opportunity. Instead of being stuck in the negative circumstances, let's discover the growth possibilities they open for us.**

"God, grant me the serenity to accept the things I cannot Change, the courage to change the things I can, and the wisdom to know the difference."—"The Serenity Prayer," by Reinhold Niebuhr

I've already mentioned that "what you resist persists;" instead of giving in to a negative, automatic *resistance* impulse, I invite you to do the following:

First, accept the facts. It doesn't mean you must agree with them, but accepting them is vital, because:

1. They've already happened and there's nothing you can do to change them.

2. Only from a place of acceptance will you be able to think rationally and make the best decision for yourself in the long run. In other words, **only acceptance permits change.**

Additionally, be *aware* of your automatic tendency to resist, to drop *below the line*, and its negative consequences. *Observe* yourself in real time when *resistance* comes up, and then *choose* to think, to talk, and to do (*TTT*) what's ultimately good and right for you in the long run in order to create The Reality you want by letting go and accepting.

Also, **give up** your *ego*; give up the need to control and know all the details. Let go of your attachment to the issue and connect to your highest capacities—your *higher self*—that can make anything happen.

Finally, always **focus on the lesson** that any *circumstance*, hardship, or challenge is here to teach you, instead of focusing on the hardship itself. Learn the lesson from an *ego*-free place, since your main goal is to grow and develop as a person. Indeed, most times you can take that lemon and make lemonade!

Hence, the *resistance*—or, more accurately, the ability to accept, let go of the need to control, and give up the desire to know everything—is a *tool* in itself. Applying it through the *CO-OP Formula* will help you let go of the *automatic program* and make *choices* with a *positive EYE* and *baby steps*.

To sum up the subject of *resistance*, here is my expression once more: "What doesn't work by force of mind, works when resigned. Let go, give it up, and it will all line up…"

Self-Judgment—Spokes in the Wheels of Success

You surely want drive your "vehicle" far into the land of success. In chapter five, I presented the vehicle metaphor and all the malfunctions that can prevent your vehicle from taking you there. Now I shall focus on one of the worst malfunctions, one that throws major spokes in your wheels and renders your vehicle inoperable. Let's make it clear once and for all: **there is nothing enlightened or intellectual about judgment in general and self-judgment in particular!** In fact, it's one of the worst plagues that impedes our success. In the next few paragraphs, I will explain why and how to eradicate it.

Self-*judgment* doesn't indicate strong self-responsibility. It's a common mistake to think this. Many of us are responsible people, so we take on the burden of our every mistake and blunder, and while this indicates an *Internal locus of control* and assumption of responsibility—which are positive traits—self-*judgment* goes far beyond this, leading to disempowerment and confinement. This is because *judgment* in general and self-*judgment* in particular *focus* on what doesn't work in life, thus blocking a *positive attitude*, which is vital for success. And, since what you focus on expands, the experience becomes increasingly negative, pulling you *below the line* so you can't find solutions or seize opportunities. After all, when you're *below the line*, your energy is low, there is no initiative or action, and so there is no success.

Simply put, self-*judgment* blocks you!

Instead of *judgment*, try to focus on learning lessons and planning a better future. In general, the standard approach that making mistakes is a bad thing and is wrong. There is no success without error, and hardly anyone knows how to do everything right on the first try. I once read about a research study that showed how American millionaires failed (a problematic word in itself—I prefer "didn't succeed") an average of 16 times before they made it! My following saying is so true here: "He who doesn't risk doesn't dare; he who doesn't dare doesn't try; he who doesn't try doesn't err; and he who doesn't err doesn't succeed."

All mistakes are crucial for learning and succeeding; in fact, "the worst mistake of all is not learning from your mistakes," and that mistake is led to by self-*judgment*.

How Strong Responsibility and Self-Judgment Are Related

The word "responsible" is important in this context, so I will refer back to my words in chapter four: responsibility doesn't mean taking the blame, as we may sometimes think; a question like, "Who's **responsible** for the power outage?" indicates that there's someone to **blame** for it. One of Oxford dictionary's definitions of the word "responsibility" is "a moral obligation to behave correctly towards or in respect of." Meaning, responsibility is a moral or social principle. The word "responsibility" is a compound made up of the words "response" and "ability;" that is, the **ability to choose a response.** None of these words speak of blame; **there's nothing linking a strong sense of responsibility to blame and *judgment*.** On the contrary, responsibility fits in well with our ability to *choose* a response with a *positive EYE*. So from now on, remember that **a person with a strong sense of responsibility mustn't blame or judge himself for mistakes.**

Don't Do to Your Friends What You Don't Want Your Friends to Do to You

As kids, we learn the following proverb: "Don't do unto others what you don't want others to do unto you." This is the most basic moral and social value. Now let's see who our friends are. One of them is us, no doubt, for we spend all day with ourselves, helping ourselves, so we had better be good company! Simply put, **we are our own best friends!**

If so, why do we hurt ourselves in ways we wouldn't hurt our best friend? If we *judge* and criticize our best friend all the time, he will be hurt and cut ties with us, but we cannot abandon ourselves! Therefore, adhere to the directive, "Don't do unto yourself what you don't do unto others." Stop *judging* and criticizing yourself, just like you wouldn't judge and criticize your best friend.

"No man is rich enough to buy back his past."—Oscar Wilde
Self-*judgment* is *resistance* to what we cannot change. This is another reason why it blocks us: we make ourselves and what we've done "wrong," and in doing so, we refuse to accept the past. The absurdity of this is that the past is unchangeable, and so *judgment* only fixates on and perpetuates it. There is no point to it, as it only causes limitation and stagnation.

Self-*judgment* is a limiting *paradigm*, especially around the issue of success. It may be a "scratch[75]" such as "I'm not good enough," etc., or—as we've seen—taking on too much responsibility under the *paradigm* of "if it didn't work then I'm to blame." Either way, it's best to choose a new *paradigm* that opens up opportunities for enhancement. For example: "I learn from my mistakes and fix them," or, "I accept the past, exist in the present, and promote my

---

75 The term "scratches" appears in my friend Rachi Wertheimer's excellent book *Relationsheep*. It refers to the automatic limiting beliefs that arise in various situations in life, spiraling us *below the line*. These beliefs appear in the interpretation portion of the *E.T.F.B model*.

future," or, "I forgive myself, learn the lessons from my mistakes, and work persistently to fix them."

Many times, *judgment* stems from perfectionism, a "plague" of its own that should be eliminated[76]. Like any limiting *habit*, *resistance* and *judgment* can also be changed using the *CO-OP Formula*: the ability to become *aware* of them, *observe* them as they come up, and *choose* to accept them, then let go and give them up, is the way to get rid of their negative influence.

The Solution to Self-judgment Lies in the Following Insights and Actions:

1. Accept the past and yourself, and acknowledge our imperfection as human beings.

2. Forgive others and yourself. Harboring resentment harms us, and so forgiveness is meant first for us, and only then for the subject of our resentment. Saying something like "he doesn't deserve being forgiven" is wrong because it misses the true purpose of forgiveness: helping the harmed part of us rise *above the line* and restore damaged relationships.

3. Give up perfectionism and the need to do everything flawlessly (this doesn't go against being meticulous, which is a great quality; only against perfectionism).

4. Recognize your mistakes as part of the risk-taking involved in the process of fulfillment while learning from them, constantly

---

76 Space is too limited here to present perfectionism as another important *tool* in making *choices* with a *positive EYE*, but you can read my blog post on the topic: https://www.hagaishalev.com/en/blog/perfectionism. If you're a perfectionist, read how to get rid of this bad *habit*.

improving your performance, and focusing on opportunities and possibilities instead of mistakes.

5. Give up a judgmental manifestation in your *TTT*.

6. Identify the limiting judgmental *paradigm* and replace it with a new empowering and enhancing one.

As always, the practical application of these points is accomplished by **implementing** the *CO-OP Formula: awareness* of the automatic *resistance, self-judgment*, and their defects, **observing** the *judgment* and *resistance* and their derivatives as they automatically surface, and **choosing** one of the six activities above with a *positive EYE* and *baby steps*. Consistent, long-term **practice** of the *CO-OP Formula* at least 12 times a day, using *reminders* to stop momentarily at the *observation points*, will create a lasting change over time. This *practice* will enable you to eradicate self-*judgment* and automatic *resistance* while acquiring improved **new habits** for the sake of **improved results.**

I shall close this chapter with a powerful statement by Eckhart Tolle from his book, A New Earth: Awakening to Your Life's Purpose: *"Non-resistance, non-judgment and non-attachment are the three aspects of true freedom and enlightened living."* And if I may paraphrase it: accepting reality as it is, every person for who they are (including yourself), and the ability to give up the need to know all the details and have things always happen your way are the three aspects of true freedom and enlightened living.

CHAPTER FOURTEEN:
Epilogue

"You have to try the impossible to achieve the possible."

—Hermann Hesse

Congratulations! Our journey together through this book is coming to an end. Thank you for coming this far—it's no small feat! In this chapter, I shall sum up the entire book for you and emphasize the key points I suggest you remember so you can apply them and get used to success in practice. We will climb to an altitude of 30,000 feet in order to see the entire "forest," not just the "trees" I have "planted" for you along our journey together. I call this book a "journey," because this is what a real process of transformation is. Throughout the book, I've stressed more than once that the process of transformation is mostly evolutionary and not revolutionary. Yes, we live in fascinating and challenging times, everything happens so quickly and an instant-gratification culture has become the norm, but as long as our *operating system* doesn't change its core, transformation will continue to be a lengthy, drawn-out process for the most part. However, what are a few months working on change versus a whole lifetime? As you've witnessed through the book, **your best investment is investing in yourself—in changing your *TTT* so you can acquire better *new habits*, thrive and succeed.** As the Chinese proverb goes: "If you want one year of prosperity, grow seeds. If you want ten years of prosperity, grow trees. If you want a lifetime of prosperity, **grow your self-worth.**" Indeed, sometimes the short way is the long way, but it's still the most rewarding one!

And so, until a major evolutionary transformation happens in our *operating system*, we will mostly have to cope with changes the long evolutionary way, while facing all the inhibiting mechanisms I've reviewed in this book, first and foremost, the *ego*—the *autopilot* that resists any type of change.

In spite of all the difficulty involved, I've shown throughout this book that change is indeed possible. I've demonstrated a myriad of *tools*, all relying on the *CO-OP Formula*, and primarily on the formula's framework of *awareness, self-observation, and choice*, so you can make a change of being in your beliefs, thoughts, and habits—in your *TTT*—to enable you to achieve *improved results*.

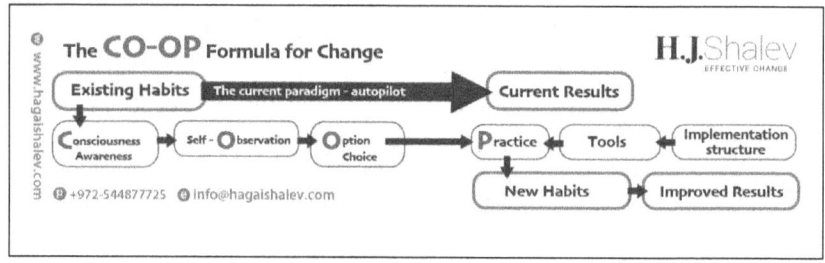

Diagram 14-1—Tools Bookmark

Here is the list of tools, most of which I reviewed in this book:

1. Openness and commitment to change.

2. The focus principle: focusing on what is working and enhancing those elements of your life.

3. Positive attitude.

4. Asking questions of opportunity and possibility: How and What, instead of Why.

5. Emotion as an indicator—choose to be above the line.

6. E.T.F.B Model as a tool for controlling thoughts and emotions.

7. Changing paradigms that don't serve you.

8. Choosing an internal locus of control and proactivity, "no to circumstances."

9. Don't resist automatically; accept what you cannot change.

10. Let go of the need to control and know everything.

11. Choose to want instead of need.

12. Accept the past, be in the present, and don't fear the future.

13. Give up self-judgment, be proactive and responsible, and don't focus on blame.

14. Forgive yourself and others.

15. Give up perfectionism.

16. The Fulfillment Pyramid—act according to the be-do-have principle.

17. The being question: When I'm in [state of being], how do I feel, think and act?

18. Choose the higher self consciousness instead of the ego.

19. Give up grumbling and complaining.

20. Choose gratitude.

21. Use business planning as a tool for fulfillment and success.

22. Use the imagination and program the unconscious mind for success.

23. Meditation—a tool to access the unconscious mind to create change in it.

24. Unconditional love of self and others.

All these *tools* appear in the *tools bookmark* attached to this book[77], which you can use as an *implementation structure* to support you in the process of acquiring *new habits* so you can achieve the *improved results* you desire.

Remember that "the difference between failure and success is not just talent." Even if you weren't born with God-given talents or great genius, assimilating these *tools* and implementing them consistently will pave the road to your success and prosperity.

"Communicating Vessels"

I call these *tools* "communicating vessels" due to the strong bond between them. No matter what *tool* you start off with, as soon as you apply it, other *tools* pop up, because they are inherently connected; all of them are meant to help you rise *above the line* and allow you to act with a *positive EYE* to promote your goals. If, for instance, you *choose* a *positive attitude* and *focus* on what's moving you forward, it becomes easier to combine *gratitude* for all the good in your life, more *acceptance* of reality and less automatic *resistance*, and giving up on *self-judgment, complaints, and grumbling.* In addition, it's only natural to ask *questions of opportunity and possibility* when you're focused on the positive. All of these are additional helpful *tools* for implementing the general principle of a *positive attitude.* When you're *aware* of them all and know how to *observe yourself* in real time, it's rather easy to retrieve this set of *tools*, combine them, and *choose* to apply them here and now to create changes in your *habits* using *baby*

---

77 If you haven't received the *tools bookmark* with your copy of this book, please send a message to office@hagaishalev.com and write on the subject line: "Please send me the English version of the Tools Bookmark", and I'll send it to you.

steps. You'll always have a few favorite *tools* which resonate with you and are relatively easy for you to implement, so choose them first!

I also suggest you keep the **tools bookmark folded and handy in your purse or wallet**, so that you can retrieve the right *tool* to make a change when you're *below the line.* Moreover, trust the knowledge you've gained and your intuition, and add other supporting *tools* to bolster the *tool* you've chosen. I'm not encouraging perfectionism by insisting you always connect the best *tool* to any *below the line* situation; as a great believer in simplicity, and based on my experiences, any *tool* you choose for any situation will do the job if you apply it consistently and let your intuition combine it with other *tools.* Nonetheless, I encourage you to use the **mega-tools** more frequently, as I've given them more weight in the book. They are:

The focus principle, positive attitude, E.T.F.B for controlling thoughts, changing paradigms, internal locus of control, giving up the automatic *resistance,* giving up *self-judgment, the Being Question,* choosing a *higher self* consciousness, and *using the imagination.*

What is Most Important to Remember and Apply

"To turn misery, disease and failure into joy, health, success and prosperity, I must think, speak, and act in ways which are the **exact reverse** of how most people think, speak, and act,"—James Arthur Ray

This quote works as a brief summary of the book. It sounds simple—just act exactly the opposite of how most people act! If most people watch the news consistently, don't do that; if most people take *circumstances* to heart and drop *below the line*, learn to cope with *circumstances* and overcome them; and if most people don't believe they can change, adhere to change as a way of life.

Nevertheless, this book isn't simple; it isn't simple to digest, let alone to implement, because your *autopilot* will use any means possible to sabotage your attempts at changing. Therefore, to make easier the integration and application of the abundant information you received, **here are a few key points to remember and apply:**

1. Openness and commitment

There is no mental *breakthrough* and no breaking of records without openness and commitment. In order to achieve the results you want and are capable of, you must be open and flexible to changes, as well as unyieldingly sworn to your path of accomplishment. It's not enough to want; it's not enough to intend; it's even not enough to commit. When you've **sworn** your *vision*, your life's purpose, your *goals* and the results you wish to achieve to yourself, wonderful things happen and dreams come true. Your ability to persistently and determinedly advance towards your *goals*, even if it means going slowly and using *baby steps* while constantly improving, is the basis for success. If you do that, if you have the grit, even with initial skepticism regarding your ability to succeed, positive results will come as your faith slowly grows through the journey with every *milestone* you achieve. The *tools* that will help you reinforce your commitment are mainly your *vision,* your connection to the *higher self*, and choosing an *internal locus of control* as a way of life.

2. Your senses are not fully credible

Most people give full credibility to their senses; expressions such as, "I've seen it with my own eyes," or, "I heard it with my own ears," illustrate that. In chapter three, I introduced the *three filters* that show how we view the world completely subjectively through our *paradigms*. Every person has a different set of *paradigms* that affects his perception of reality and his experiences. Thus, I've undermined the credibility of your senses. This key principle supports and encourages your openness and commitment to change. Simply put, don't automatically believe everything you hear and see; use your *awareness* and *self-observation* to notice if you're automatically reacting through your *paradigms*. If so, use your power to *choose* with a *positive EYE* more and more and be consistent with it over time by using *baby steps*.

3. The basis for any fulfillment is your Being

As an individual in general, and as a business owner or manager in particular, it is important that you create the *habits* vital to your success through the process described in this book—and that means thinking *habits* as well as doing *habits*. Express them through your *TTT* with uncompromising grit, and you're on the right path to success. Only when your *Doing* relies on a steady *Being* will it move you forward with a *positive EYE* towards your goals.

4. You can make any change in being in your unconscious mind using the CO-OP Formula

Most of all, adhere to the trio at the basis of the formula: open and expand your *awareness* using this book and other personal development guides; constantly *observe yourself*; notice the *autopilot* that doesn't serve you; make small *choices* with a *positive EYE* to eradicate the *automatic program* while using the toolbox (mainly the *mega-tools*); and apply these choices with consistent *baby steps*. This will allow you gain *new habits* that will yield *improved results* over time. If you haven't yet mastered the basic *habit* of *self-observation*, put *reminders* in your smartphone[78] that will serve as an *implementation structure* to encourage *observation*. Use the enclosed *tools bookmark* to help you practice; keep it in your wallet or purse and pull it out any time you feel *below the line* because something isn't working in your life. The bookmark has everything you need to create a change: pick a relevant *tool*, and use it according to the instruction on the bookmark to make *choices* with a *positive EYE* and *baby steps*.

5. Plan your Doing while defining the "what" before the "how"
I called this the *breakthrough* method and reviewed it at length in chapter eleven. Plan your actions regularly in writing: first define your *vision*, then your *goals,* and only then the execution plan. A strong *Being* foundation supported by a solid *vision* is critical to accomplishment in business planning as well. Then, act while adhering to the plan as you follow up on its execution while remaining open to change, thus creating a strong backbone for your fulfillment path. Remember to combine *Doing* with *Being* side by side throughout, while keeping a firm *Being* at the core. Neglecting either one of them will hinder your fulfillment ability. Remember: **"If you don't know what you desire, you'll never fly higher."**

---

78   Here again are the Hourly Chimes apps I mentioned in chapter 9: for iPhone users, HourMate or Soft Chines Orchimf. For Android users: Caynax Hourly Chime or BellMan or Time Signal. Note that these apps were available when the book was written, but that may change by the time you read this due to the dynamic nature of the app market.

6. Remember that there will always be circumstances

Your ability to reach your *goals* depends on your ability to say *no to circumstances* and keep a completely *internal locus of control*. Don't let obstacles on the way stop you. Cope with the *circumstances* you encounter while adhering to your *vision* with grit, persistence, and determination, and keep yourself *above the line* using the *tools* you've learned in this book. Remember: "A person moves from circumstance to circumstance, without it always making any sense." In addition, if you face a breakdown, use it as an opportunity to create a breakthrough.

7. Real change only occurs in your unconscious mind

As you've learned in this book, the road to changing your unconscious mind lies in consistent repetition of *small choices* with a *positive EYE* for a minimum of thirty days. The good news is that when you adhere to that, you'll create a permanent change in your unconscious mind, just like any other *habit* you've acquired in life, such as driving.

I shall end this subchapter with a wonderful quote from Paolo Coelho's book, *The Alchemist*: "Before a dream is realized, the Soul of the World tests everything that was learned along the way. It does this not because it is evil, but so that we can, in addition to realizing our dream, master the lessons we've learned as we've moved toward that dream. That's the point at which most people give up. It's the point at which, as we say in the language of the desert, one 'dies of thirst just when the palm trees have appeared on the horizon.' Every search begins with beginner's luck. And every search ends with the victor's being severely tested... the darkest hour *of the night came just* before the dawn."

The Vehicle that Will Take You to Your Destination

In chapter five I introduced the vehicle metaphor, comparing a person to a vehicle seeking its destination. When the vehicle is in good shape, all four wheels are attached, there are no flat tires and they are filled with air; when the engine is calibrated and working, the tank is full, and the driver is responsible and skilled, the vehicle will usually reach its destination. Of course, there could be hurdles along the way (which I've called *circumstances*) that may delay or even prevent the vehicle form reaching its destination. Only then is the driver tested—for his *awareness,* his ability to handle *circumstances*, find solutions, and still keep on the road until he reaches his destination. Now, as you reach the end of the book, it's easier for you to see, understand, and implement the principles of proper maintenance for "your vehicle."

The question is, what needs to be changed in the vehicle and the driver to increase their chances of reaching their destination? My personal challenge was to acknowledge that my vehicle was only using two wheels—rationality and practicality, i.e., *Doing*—and add the two right wheels of *Being*. I needed an accident, both physically and mentally, to make me realize I could add another two wheels to my vehicle. Thus, I gave up my Vespa and profession, both in the same year and both after 22 years. Everything that's happened to me ever since those accidents in 2005, despite the sometimes difficult *circumstances*, was for the best. These events have enabled my vehicle to move forward towards its destination and allowed me to truly succeed and fulfill my vision. This book is a good example of that accomplishment. Nonetheless, I'm not perfect and I, too, still experience "malfunctions" in the vehicle and the driver, as all humans do. The challenge is to learn how to cope with them by remaining *above the line* as much as possible, while still continuing the ongoing personal development.

Every client who approaches me is facing a similar challenge. We're all human; every vehicle has its malfunctions and every *operating system* has its bugs. Some clients lack a wheel or two; others have flat tires; some have sticks in their wheels—sometimes even full-blown stumps. If you're committed to your success, and after reading this book you still feel that something is delaying your vehicle from reaching its destination and allowing you to get used to success and wealth, **I invite you to approach me** through the contact information listed at the end of the book. I promise to help you in any way I can to enable your vehicle, and you, to reach your destination.

Just 6—24 Minutes a Day Will Upgrade Your Life

"Luck in business starts with having the humility to be **self-aware**, followed by the intellectual **curiosity** to ask the right **questions**, and concluding with the **belief** and courage that **something better** is always possible."—Anthony Tjan, CEO, Managing Partner, and Founder of the venture capital firm Cue Ball, as quoted in the Harvard Business Review, July 6th 2011.

By now you realize that success doesn't depend on luck, and that even if there is such thing as "luck," it's best not to count on it to show up on its own. Rather, choose a consistent, determined, proactive, and responsible *TTT* in order to attract luck. They say that "luck joins the best" and that "God helps those who help themselves;" both proverbs support this concept. Tjan's quote above also illustrates this principle nicely and sums up the book for you. Let's go over it, mainly referring to the words in bold:

So that the goddess of luck joins you, you must first be **humble and aware**. This means not being led astray by your *ego* and *autopilot program*, but being *aware* of them and of your *higher* *self's* ability to overcome them in order to serve your true objectives. Then you must be **curious** about everything you're going through—that is, actively *observe* what's going on with you, both inwardly and outwardly (the *circumstances*) with a **curious**, positive attitude that enables and enhances (staying *above the line*). This is contrary to the *below the line* attitude, which keeps you in a negative emotional state that blocks you from coping and changing. Generally, instead of the worry pattern so prevalent in our culture, let's maintain curiosity about what the future has in store for us. When you maintain a *positive attitude,* stay *above the line*, and are *accepting and let go* of the need for control, it's rather easy to **replace worry with curiosity.** While launching this book, for example, amidst the uncertainty of whether it would sell well, I repeated the following mantra and paradigm: "I trust the universe[79], I'm certain everything is working in my favor and in support of my success, and I'm curious to see how it unfolds."

---

79 I haven't used the term "universe" much in the book, but it's time to clarify it: by saying "universe," I more mean all the scientific and natural laws, not necessarily any spiritual entity. Though I certainly define myself as a spiritual person, I believe that the world we live in is founded on laws. Regrettably, despite scientific and technological progress, we've yet to discover many of these laws. This is where unexplained phenomena that often happen seem mystical and the people that instigate them seem odd; just like Galileo, who was regarded as crazy in his time, or the Wright Brothers, who seemed eccentric. I believe that as science develops we will discover more and more laws of nature we didn't know about, and so suddenly understand the reasons for such mystical phenomena. Perhaps the most spiritual dimension in me believes that these universal laws are inherently good and meant to help honest, decent people. This is based on the unexplained phenomenon I constantly see in my own life and among my clients; when people define a vision and a purpose and begin acting towards their fulfillment, good things happen to them, sometimes appearing as "coincidences."

Of course, I didn't stand idle, waiting for all this good to land in my lap, but I also acted in line with this approach of letting go of the need to know exactly how it will happen. Indeed, the book launch proved successful. I very much wanted my project to succeed, but I didn't need it to. I believe this to be one of the secrets of how the universe works, though science has yet to explain it, and it can be tapped into by wanting without needing.

Going back to the quote above: the way to apply your curiosity is by **asking questions**, which I called *questions of possibility and opportunity*. Then, when you're *above the line, aware and observing,* your ability to *choose* comes into full play and you strive to consistently improve, using *baby steps* and a *positive EYE* to accomplish and prosper. This is how your **belief** in your ability to succeed slowly builds as you constantly **improve**.

In order for that to happen, you must regularly apply the directives in this book. **The foundation is to dedicate 6 to 24 minutes a day to this.** "That's it?" You might ask. "Yes," I reply. Here's why: I've already mentioned that the weak link in your ability to change is the lack of *self-observation* skill. Without *self-observation*, there's no *choice*, and without *choice*, there's no change. To teach you how to *observe* yourself, I've defined the *implementation structures*, which are the 12 *self-observation* points throughout the day, according to your smartphone's reminders. In the moment of *observation*, when you identify the *autopilot* that no longer serves you, the *self-observation* points open up an opportunity for you to *choose* in real time. This is the entire theory in a nutshell. Use diagram 14-1 and the *tools bookmark* attached to the book to make it easier for you to implement *self-observation*.

This is the bottom line: in every *self-observation* point, **dedicate from 30 seconds to two minutes** to *observation* followed by *choice*, and no more! If you multiply that by the 12 observation points per day, you'll get those 6 to 24 minutes required to implement the *CO-OP Formula* every day.

Once *self-observation* becomes your new *habit*—natural and constant—you will no longer need reminders to *self-observe*. Meaning, for any *habit* you wish to change, you must first acquire the new *habit* of *self-observation*. The moment this new *habit* is assimilated through the reminders, you've opened up the door to *choosing* **for good**, without needing further reminding!

Apply this consistently with determination and persistence and you can change any part of your personality!

Earl Nightingale definition of success is the perfect way to close this subchapter: "Success is progressive realization of a worthy goal or ideal."

How to Continue Evolving

"It's what you learn after you know it all that counts,"
—John Wooden,
UCLA Basketball coach in the 1960s and 1970s; led his university to victories in 10 out of 12 NCAA championships, of which 7 were consecutive.

No matter where this book met you on your journey of personal development, what's important is what you got out of it, how you apply its directives, and how much you'll continue to develop and learn. After 10 years of endless learning and constant occupation with helping people grow, I can tell you it's a long, perhaps endless journey. Don't let that discourage you. On the contrary, the journey is fascinating and highly rewarding. Life changes for the better, and with that come results and achievements.

If you've been working on increasing your *awareness* for many years, I believe you will have gained a **different perspective on how to implement** *awareness* **towards results.** Apply the *CO-OP Formula* and you will be able to translate your high *awareness* into results. I'm entirely convinced of this, because I've worked with many moderately conscious to highly conscious people, some even more than myself, and have helped them get used to success and abundance too. I like working with conscious people the most, since they're usually very open and committed to their personal development process, and so they achieve results.

If this is your first introduction to the world of *awareness*— congratulations! Having come this far in the book means you've learned a major lesson in *awareness*. Nonetheless, as I've reiterated throughout the book, *awareness* **is only a portal to reaching results;** it's a mandatory prerequisite for a result-yielding transformation, but is not sufficient alone for that. Therefore, you must **make sure to apply the rest of the** *CO-OP Formula* **components,** especially *self-observation* as a way to reclaim *choice* in your life. Apply the formula consistently and you will achieve results. This holds true even if you already possess high self-*awareness*.

Here are a few recommendations for **how to preserve the achievements** you've reached by implementing this book, and how to continue your personal development in order to reap more achievements:

1. Continue on your path of personal development, read more

books, go to lectures, join workshops and seminars, read online[80] articles and posts, participate in webinars, and watch online videos.

2. Use down time (driving, waiting in line, etc.) or physical exercise (running, walking, biking) to learn via audiobooks. I believe 80% of my knowledge comes from my thousands of hours of listening to MP3 files I downloaded and bought online.

3. Make sure you continue to apply the implementation structures you learned in this book in order to obtain and assimilate the *self-observation* habit.

4. Continue to acquire habits that promote success[81].

5. Apply self-responsibility[82], self-discipline, free *choice*, and *internal locus of control,* without any expectations from others and with a positive expectation from yourself while remaining free of self-*judgment*.

6. Say *no to circumstances*. Move from change by chance to change by *choice*.

7. Hang around inspiring, empowering people. Don't listen to the worried voices around you that keep you from fulfilling your dreams.

---

80 Please visit my blog, which includes plenty personal development and business coaching articles and content constantly updated: https://www.hagaishalev.com/en/blog/perfectionism. Sign up to receive new blog posts at https://www.hagaishalev.com/en/gift.

81 I recommend you watch the following TED video: https://www.hagaishalev.com/en/blog/small-steps.

82 Remember the proper meaning of the word responsibility as defined in chapter 4: the ability to choose how to respond to circumstances.

8. Define a *vision* and adhere to it, set *goals*, plan the path to achieving them, and implement it[83]. Successful people make fast decisions and rarely change them.

9. Love yourself and those around you. Love is a tremendous emotional power that will help you overcome obstacles and break through.

As I used to say, "all beginnings are challenging and all endings are exciting, particularly when they include succeeding!" Apply this book and its directives, and you can achieve the excitement of success.

Last But Not Least...and yet it moves...

This is it for the book *Getting Used to Success.*

Thank you for joining me on this journey. I enjoyed myself thoroughly; how about you?

I would be happy to hear your feedback about the book and what you've gained from it in the book's page on Amazon.

I'll be happy and grateful if you referred your friends and acquaintances to this page, so they can purchase the book and reap its benefits, or if you choose to purchase additional copies as gifts for your loved ones. Complementary updates on articles and new posts can be found on my blog, https://www.hagaishalev. com/en/blog/business-plan-a, including contents that will help you continue to get used to your success.

---

83 Use the following form on my blog to plan: https://www.hagaishalev. com/en/blog/breakthrogh-form.

If you have questions about the book, suggestions, requests, or any other matters pertaining to your business, management, career, or personal life, I invite you to approach me directly via my contact details below.

If you want me to guide you toward fulfilling your goals—great and challenging as they may be—as a one-on-one consultation or in a group setting, don't hesitate to contact me for a complimentary introduction and evaluation session.

Further details about my coaching plans may be found on my website.

I selected this final quote for the book very carefully:

"Young souls learn to take responsibility for their **actions**
Mature souls learn to take responsibility for their **thoughts**
And old souls learn to take responsibility for their **happiness***"*

—The Universe[84]

As children, we learn to take responsibility for our actions; however, most people who are stuck on *autopilot* remain in this developmental stage. While reading the book, you have learned how to also take responsibility for your thoughts as the basis of any *Doing* with a *positive EYE*. Now, as you continue to practice and implement the book's principles, another opportunity presents itself to you for assuming responsibility over **your happiness**.

---

84 A fascinating service that sends daily emails with an inspirational message from "the universe." I've been a subscriber for at least 5 years, and have enjoyed its excellent content. You can sign up for the service through this link: www.tut.com.

Yes, this means saying *no to circumstances* and remaining way *above the line*. This is perhaps the key principle in the book that will open up your path to fulfillment and prosperity.

If can you take just one thing from this book, let it be the *above the line* principle. Use everything you've learned in the book to keep you way *above the line*. With that alone, you can find positive and enhancing energy, and find yourself drawn toward what you wish to achieve, focused on possibilities, taking advantage of all opportunities, and in better communication with yourself and your surroundings, thus experiencing fulfillment and success in all your endeavors—not to mention just being happier!

I believe in that with all my heart! If I could do it, so can you! See you later!

Ways to reach me:

Tel: +972-54-4877725
Email: info@hagaishalev.com
Website: https://www.hagaishalev.com/en

Sincerely yours in getting used to success,
H.J.

P.S. — if you found any grammatical or other errors in this book, please notify me of it at the above email address.

REFERENCES TO TERMS AND DEFINITIONS APPEARING IN THE BOOK:

(The **bold** page number includes the definition of the term)

90, 108, 109, 118, 119, 122, 124, 128, 130, 134, 137, 138, 139, 141, 142, 146, 147, 160, 161, 162, 163, 164, 165, 166, 167, 168, 169, 174, 175, 177, 178, 186, 187, 191, 194, 195, 196, 197, 198, 199, 204, 206, 209, 211, 213, 214, 215, 241, 257, 303, 304, 305, 332, 333, 334, 336, 339, 340, 348 332

10. Implementation structure - 200, 202, **203**, 204, 205, 206, 207, 209, 210, 211, 212, 213, 223, 225, 228, 299, 336, 340, 345, 348

11. Internal/External locus of control - **84**, 160, 176, 193, 194, 206, 207, 208, 212, 224, 225, 226, 294, 295, 328, 335, 337, 338, 341, 348

12. No to circumstances - 207, **212**, 335, 341, 348, 351

13. Observation in retrospect - **179**, 185

14. Paradigm - **43**, 50, 57, 67, 87, 89, 105, 107, 109, 118, 128, 136, 155, 156, 216, 233, 242, 251, 261, 266, 267, 271, 279, 289, 290, 292, 295, 303, 304, 305, 306, 307, 308, 309, 310, 311, 312, 313, 314, 318, 330, 332, 335, 337, 339, 344

15. Positive EYE - **E**fficiency, **Y**ield, and **E**xpediency - **46**, 57, 60, 63, 91, 93, 94, 110, 114, 121, 123, 142, 164, 173, 177, 181, 185, 190, 196, 197, 198, 200, 205, 208, 210, 211, 212, 213, 219, 224, 225, 227, 241, 242, 249, 254, 260, 261, 273, 276, 282, 289, 290, 292, 295, 296, 297, 299, 303, 312, 319, 327, 329, 331, 332, 336, 339, 340, 341, 345, 350.

16. Proactivity - **53**, 54, 335